CASH COW

CASH COW

How the Maternal Body
Became a Global Commodity –
and the Hidden Costs for Women

ALEV SCOTT

HarperCollins*Publishers*

Some names and identifying details have been changed
to protect the privacy of individuals.

HarperCollins*Publishers*
1 London Bridge Street
London SE1 9GF

www.harpercollins.co.uk

HarperCollins*Publishers*
Macken House, 39/40 Mayor Street Upper
Dublin 1, D01 C9W8, Ireland

First published by HarperCollins*Publishers* 2026

1 3 5 7 9 10 8 6 4 2

© Alev Scott 2026

Alev Scott asserts the moral right to be
identified as the author of this work

A catalogue record of this book is
available from the British Library

HB ISBN 978-0-00-872494-8
TPB ISBN 978-0-00-872495-5

Printed and bound in the UK using 100%
renewable electricity at CPI Group (UK) Ltd

All rights reserved. No part of this publication may be
reproduced, stored in a retrieval system, or transmitted,
in any form or by any means, electronic, mechanical,
photocopying, recording or otherwise, without the
prior written permission of the publishers.

Without limiting the exclusive rights of any author, contributor
or the publisher of this publication, any unauthorised use of
this publication to train generative artificial intelligence (AI)
technologies is expressly prohibited. HarperCollins also exercise
their rights under Article 4(3) of the Digital Single Market
Directive 2019/790 and expressly reserve this publication
from the text and data mining exception.

CONTENTS

PROLOGUE: FRESH OR FROZEN   1

INTRODUCTION   3

MILK   9

EGGS   73

PLACENTA   177

EPILOGUE: BABY   283

ACKNOWLEDGEMENTS   287

NOTES   289

PROLOGUE: FRESH OR FROZEN

Eleven p.m. Slumped at the kitchen table in a baggy T-shirt, plastic funnel attached to one breast, pumping. Over the rhythmic chug-chug of the vacuum, I can hear drops falling slowly into the bottle. The other breast is empty. I need some food.

Next to the pump is my laptop: I reply to emails from men who want to buy my milk – to grow their muscles, to arouse them, to cure them of their bowel disorders. Fresh or frozen; cash or PayPal; 'at least 40 ounces or as much as you can give'. Some ask politely if I will breastfeed them. Others want me to send them a video of this very scene: the pump, the tubes and the slowly filling bottle. They want to see where the magic happens. 'Face does not have to be in shot.'

Even as a faceless pair of breasts, I use a pseudonym while advertising my wares on a website called, aptly, Only The Breast. I think of Gogol's *The Nose* and realise that my breasts are leading a life of their own, attracting strangers and surpassing my current earning potential as I struggle through month four postpartum. Maybe this is how it feels to be a hand model, or a bottom double – eclipsed and enriched by your own body part.

CASH COW

Since I gave birth, my breasts have become desexualised, summoned to a higher cause – they are no longer mine. Exposed to family and friends, to strangers on airplanes, answering my baby's call 24/7. I have lost any shyness I once had, any sense of privacy.

So here we are, me and the milk-hungry men, exchanging emails late into the night.

INTRODUCTION

CASH COW is a book told from the perspective of a breastfeeding mother and journalist interested in how money is made from the desire – or ability – to have a baby in the twenty-first century. It is about how the promise of fertility is bought and sold, along with the byproducts of the maternal body. It has elements of both memoir and journalism, but my primary purpose has been to use my own experiences and those of other women to shine a light on an industry that has quietly become a major force in the modern world, with terrifyingly little public debate.

The conception of the book was unplanned: I stumbled across the commercial breast-milk market while researching how to donate my surplus milk to a hospital after the birth of my first child. Trawling through online marketplaces in the UK and the US, I posed as a seller, placing adverts, talking to other sellers and to customers.

I talked to milk-bank technicians, fetish experts, wet nurses and profit-making companies reliant on lactating donors. I went down a bizarre warren of rabbit holes, discovering a world of health zealotry, financial desperation and unexpected kink. Customers ranged from babies to bodybuilders to private hospital chains. While much of what I was uncovering was a product of our hyper-connected times, some of it was as old as human life itself. People have bought and sold human milk for millennia, an essential but morally complicated trade.

The modern breast-milk market – which is technically legal in most countries, but unregulated – raised bigger questions for me about the empowerment and exploitation of mothers and would-be mothers in other markets. I started looking into the competitive global markets in egg freezing, IVF and surrogacy services, where laws and regulations struggle to keep up with increasing demand. I wondered what it feels like to donate or sell your eggs, to carry someone else's baby for money – or for free – or have a stranger carry yours.

One in six couples suffer infertility, globally, and both individuals and governments are spending more and more money on having babies. In 2025, the United Nations Population Fund declared that world fertility rates are in an 'unprecedented decline', and not just because of rising infertility. Hundreds of millions of people say they cannot have the number of children they want because they cannot afford to, or because they cannot find a partner. Others, of course, simply do not want (more) children. By 2100, the population of South Korea, the most expensive country in the world to raise a child, is set to halve.[1] Its government, alongside others, has spent hundreds of billions of dollars on financial incentives to married couples to procreate – to little effect.

Meanwhile, many of my friends in their thirties, both single and partnered, are among those spending their personal

INTRODUCTION

savings on navigating the uncharted waters of the global fertility industry, which is estimated to be worth $70.27 billion by 2030.[2] (The surrogacy industry, meanwhile, is set to explode from $27.9 billion in 2025 to $201.8 billion by 2034 at the current rate of growth.[3]) The ethical arguments over these markets' winners and losers will only intensify as governments are forced to make decisions about who can profit from creating and brokering a new life, which parents can rely on state-funded fertility care, and what role altruism should play in an industry that relies on the kindness, desperation and gametes of strangers.

The fertility industry is the only legal industry where one person's biological bad luck can be another person's gain. A woman who can carry a pregnancy to term can choose to earn money doing exactly that for someone else; a woman who has plenty of breast milk can sell it; a woman with a healthy ovarian reserve can sell her eggs. This is a more direct, quantifiable form of biological luck than that of a professional athlete or model. The trade is as basic as it gets, and despite its ethical complexities it is largely legal, as opposed to its nearest comparable, large-scale trade: human organ trafficking.

From clinics charging tens of thousands of dollars for the most highly prized human eggs to private sales of a life-giving bodily fluid via complex surrogacy contracts, the maternal body has never been as comprehensively commodified, nose to tail, as it is today. While planning the structure of this book (Milk/Eggs/Placenta), I came across *PIG 05049* by Dutch artist Christien Meindertsma, a book which details the various uses of the body parts of a commercially raised pig.

(Meindertsma counts a total of 185 products derived from this single pig, including bullets, cigarettes and paint.) *PIG 05049* made my financial breakdown of the maternal body seem more grim than I had originally intended. I also realised that if the comparison is uncomfortable, that is – perhaps – the point.

I was drawn to the topics of this book not only by my personal foray into the breast-milk market, but by witnessing the fertility struggles of close friends, and what they have been prepared to put themselves through – physically, emotionally, financially – to create a family. In the countries I visited across Europe, and the interviews I conducted with people in the US, I came across some very different cultural attitudes to what kinds of laws should govern people's access to assisted reproduction, and how women's bodies should or should not be monetised. But there was also an important commonality.

'Baby lust' is a term first introduced to me by a surrogacy consultant. He meant the blindness or recklessness that people desperate to become parents can experience, wherever they live, and however wealthy they are. It is a very human, universal desperation that is easily monetised – and often exploited – and is a core reason why the global fertility and surrogacy industries function in the ways that they do.

The moral questions and dilemmas that I encountered while interviewing parents, surrogates and doctors often felt too big and too strange for me to grapple with alone. I found myself asking friends and acquaintances, as well as total strangers, questions like:

INTRODUCTION

How long would you pay to store your frozen embryos?
Should there be an age limit on becoming a parent?
Should we pay women for their breast milk?
Would you rather a close friend or a stranger carry your baby?
Would you pay to ensure your child could meet her egg donor?

And the billion-dollar question behind falling adoption rates and rising IVF and surrogacy rates worldwide:

If there is a universal right to biological parenthood, who should pay for it?

Many of my preconceptions about parenthood and fertility have been overturned or at least challenged during the course of my research, as I hope my readers' will be too. I am indebted to the many people who have contributed to this book, some of whom I have not been able to name.

It is dedicated to mothers everywhere, in particular my own, and to my babies, whose voracious appetites led me down the first rabbit hole.

MILK

Contains approximately 68 calories per 100ml. Melatonin, cortisol and fat content varies morning to night.

Stimulated by the hormone prolactin, released after childbirth. Requires an intake of approximately 500 extra calories per day for exclusive breastfeeding of a newborn.

Cost to customer: from $0 (altruistic donation); $50–60 per litre (private online market); $189 per litre (pharmaceutical provider).

Cost to producer: unquantifiable labour time; pumping costs.

FIRST DROPS

I gave birth to my first child mid-pandemic, in a snowy Amsterdam in January 2021. A strict lockdown was in place: the midwife who rushed to our apartment carried a document excusing her from the nightly curfew. Borders had closed; travel from the UK was banned. Cut off from my family and friends, I was daunted by motherhood and in particular breastfeeding. Irrationally convinced that my milk supply would dry up, I bought a hospital-grade electric breast pump, which looked and sounded like an instrument of torture.

Gingerly experimenting with the 'suction' and 'speed' dials, I overcame my initial fear and learned to self-milk, treading the line between pain and mere discomfort. Soon, I was pumping in the middle of the night and twice a day, between breastfeeding my hungry daughter. The more I pumped, the more my breasts produced, just as the midwife had told me. Before long, I had an oversupply of milk and a freezer full of earnestly marked little sachets ('150ml, 15 February, 6 p.m.'), which my baby would never consume – a physicalised diary of maternal anxiety.

Early-morning pumping sessions would elicit fountains of thin, blue-tinged milk. In the evenings, depleted, I would wait for slow, creamy-yellow drops to fall. I began to feel like Prometheus; his liver chewed away during the day and magically replenished overnight. Woken by my daughter's cries in the darkness, I learned to estimate the time by feeling my breasts. The fuller they were, the closer to dawn, when the cycle would repeat once more.

In this timeless space, I became obsessed by my baby's weight as a reflection of my ability to feed her. Every day, with my husband's help, I dangled her in luggage scales, wrapped like a tiny burrito. If she gained 30g, I was ecstatic. Any loss would reduce me to tears. Raging hormones were largely to blame, but in hindsight I was grappling with a novel problem: how to measure my performance as a mother.

Slowly, I adjusted to the responsibility of keeping my new baby alive with enormous yet desexualised breasts. She grew. I relaxed. But I continued to pump.

Months later, after the lockdown eased, I found myself back in the UK with another full freezer, more than my baby would ever need. I started researching how to donate my stores to premature babies and stumbled across the commercial breast-milk market, discovering that it is far easier to sell one's milk to strangers online than to go through the rigorous screenings required by a hospital milk bank. Whether those strangers were other parents buying for their babies or not was unclear; I would soon find out.

I realised the market could be viewed in very different ways. The positive view was as an opportunity for nursing mothers – largely excluded from the labour force – to earn money while helping other parents and carers in need, and perhaps other kinds of customers too. The less positive view was as an ethically troubling, even dangerous industry where both buyers and sellers were vulnerable to exploitation, and sellers' babies open to neglect. Should breast milk be treated as a commodity?

Stuck at home and excluded from the labour force myself, I scrolled on my phone as I breastfed my child, browsing online marketplaces and reading academic articles about the historic practices of wet-nursing and (unpaid) cross-feeding. I tried to imagine how it would feel to breastfeed a stranger's child, or to give my own to be fed by – and to bond with – another woman. With or without money changing hands, it seemed unthinkable. Yet I knew women have done it for millennia.

I was struggling to adapt to my new physical reality as I considered these ethical questions. When I first started to breastfeed, it felt like I was suddenly in possession of a pair of huge, lactating penises, entirely powered by hormones. The rush of the let-down of milk, particularly in the morning, was almost orgasmic – a huge concentration of the 'love hormone', oxytocin. When too much time had passed since the last feed and my breasts were hard and engorged, I felt desperate to relieve them. If I heard a baby crying – any baby, not necessarily my own – they would start leaking of their own accord.

Conversely, when I tried to pump at the end of the day, exhausted and depleted after my baby had gone to sleep, I would have the opposite problem – to get myself to lactate, I had to watch videos of my baby being cute. As I watched, my hormones responded to what I saw and the milk started to flow. A tell-tale tingle would be followed by drops, falling slowly, almost painfully, at first, then faster – like salivating in response to a delicious meal.

Friends of mine had similar experiences, and we would joke about them, but only among ourselves – the penis comparison is, obviously, weird and uncomfortable to voice. When I put the comparison in the context of lactation porn, I had a dizzying and sickening realisation – that sex and hormones, milk and babies, comfort and pleasure, were connected in ways I had never anticipated, not just in the minds and appetites of men, but in myself.

BREAST MILK FOR STRANGERS

Shortly after I gave birth, I shared my worries about maintaining my milk supply on a local WhatsApp group for new mothers in Amsterdam. Most of us were ex-pats and had never met in real life. Soon, a message from another mother pinged up on my phone – would I like some of her milk, frozen not long ago?

I was shocked and mildly disgusted. Was this just squeamishness at a stranger's bodily fluid? Pride? Perhaps I wanted to continue the idea of a connection between my own body and my baby's – a sense of breast milk as an extension of the umbilical cord. Whatever the reason, sentimental or otherwise, I wanted to feed my baby my own milk. I declined, politely.

Ana, a first-time mother and entrepreneur from Spain, gave birth around the same time as me in Amsterdam and did not produce any milk for ten days because she had gestational diabetes. She told me over the phone, more than a year later, that she had experienced the same kind of over-anxiety I had during the early postpartum days, recoiling at the idea of infant formula.

'At the beginning, I was super-frustrated because I couldn't produce milk. I was crying, feeling like I wasn't a mother. For me, formula was kind of a poison. It was not natural.'

Ana's self-flagellation has deep societal roots. Women who have either struggled or chosen not to breastfeed have long been vilified, viewed as 'not a mother', as 'not natural' – by other women, as well as by men. As a child, a fifteen-year-old schoolgirl with no interest in babies or motherhood, I remember sitting in class, horrified, as we read Lady Macbeth's prayer to unseen spirits to 'unsex me here . . . Come to my woman's breasts,/And take my milk for gall'. It is perhaps the most famously violent rejection of breastfeeding in Western literature and probably left a disproportionate impression on me.

Lady Macbeth's later soliloquy conjures up an image far more disturbing than any murder Macbeth commits, because it violates our expectations of maternal instinct – I found it almost unbearable to read again as a new mother.

> I have given suck, and know
> How tender 'tis to love the babe that milks me:
> I would, while it was smiling in my face,
> Have plucked my nipple from his boneless gums
> And dashed the brains out, had I so sworn
> As you have done to this
>
> *Macbeth*, Act I, Scene 7

Ana's story had a happier ending: she found another mother willing to give her enough frozen milk for two weeks, until her own milk came in. At first, Ana and her husband were nervous about accepting the offer – 'In Amsterdam a lot of people smoke weed, so you never know!' – but ultimately, they accepted it gratefully.

Ana didn't feel bad about giving her baby another mother's milk.

'I felt relieved.'

As I listened to Ana, these words almost felt like a rebuke to me. Was she a better mother than I was, gratefully accepting breast milk that would benefit her child, rather than letting squeamishness get in the way? And why was I so fixated on breastfeeding my child anyway, knowing (in my rational mind) that modern infant formula is far from 'poison'?

Why is maternal guilt so intense, so soon?

I soon recovered from my initial disgust at the idea of sharing milk – but I wanted to be the donor, not the recipient.

One sunny morning in Somerset, about six months after I gave birth, the doorbell rang. I opened the door to a smiling woman and handed over a large freezer bag containing 4 litres of my breast milk in little rock-hard plastic sachets, ranging in colour from white to creamy-yellow. I remember feeling lighter, unburdened.

To get to this point, I'd made several trips to my GP for medical screenings. I'd had my blood tested for STDs, filled out hygiene protocol forms, promised to forgo ibuprofen (as well as harder drugs) and to produce at least 2 litres of milk by this date. My clinical odyssey would soon be over – the sachets unfrozen, screened for pathogens, pasteurised, screened again and stored in the milk bank at Bristol's Southmead Hospital. Within a few months, it would be fed to premature babies in their neonatal intensive care unit (NICU), or passed on to hospitals further afield.

When I read the email confirming that my milk was legit and would soon be deployed, I had a surreal thought: I'd never done jury service, but my breasts had done their civic duty.

This had only been possible with the aid of the terrifying pump I had first encountered a few days after giving birth. It no longer terrified me, and as I dutifully cleaned its plastic funnels and silicon tubes, I wondered about its less efficient predecessors. Crude breast pumps in ancient times used water to create a weak vacuum, I discovered, while prototypes for commercial sale – reliant on hand-operated bellows – were patented in the mid-nineteenth century.

It was not until 1991, when the Swiss company Medela launched a hospital-grade electric pump for home use – significantly more effective than a manual pump – that women could efficiently collect their own milk (and store it, thanks to the gradual popularising of home freezers since the 1970s[1]).

Other companies followed Medela, changing the game for mothers worldwide by allowing them to continue producing and storing breast milk for their babies even after returning to work (although many workplaces still make it difficult, if not impossible, for women to express their milk). The breast-pump market, part of the 'femtech' space, is now worth over $3 billion,[2] and the humble pump has developed into something of a luxury accessory.

The UK-based company Elvie sells app-controlled double breast pumps for £499[3] – not an accessible price for the mothers who might most need to return to work after giving birth. The almost-silent and invisible products seem designed to appeal to women who might need to pump with maximum discretion, during a board meeting perhaps. Elvie had a rapid rise and fall from grace: the company attracted over $136 million of investment before falling into administration after it was sued for patent infringement by a rival, US-based company Willow (which subsequently acquired it). This, along with a decade-long lawsuit that has dominated two other companies in the US that sell breast-milk-derived products for profit,[4] paints a picture of fierce competition in the relatively small world of corporate milk.

It struck me while thinking about the commercial and social value of breast milk that 'milk bank' is a strangely apt term – both in the obvious sense of a hoarded commodity, and in the sense of a riverbank controlling the flow of a natural substance. The advent of the home breast pump changed not only the value of human milk but its final destination. Now, a mother could store her milk not just for her own baby, but for other recipients of her choosing, via non-profit milk banks, social media groups or online marketplaces.

When talking to Ana, I had asked her whether she would have been prepared to buy breast milk, if she had not found a donor. She said no.

'In 2021, I was without work at all. Financially, we couldn't afford this at that time – even formula was expensive.'

Ana was right – breast milk is expensive. It is the only bodily fluid legally classed as a food by the Food Standards Agency (FSA) in the UK and the Food and Drug Administration (FDA) in the US, so its sale is legal in both countries – though neither agency endorses it. The market is unregulated, and I was about to find out just how wild it can get.

MILK AND PORN

Much of my first few months postpartum is now a blur. I cannot remember exactly how I stumbled across the informal online marketplaces where breast milk is shared and sold, but I do remember spending a lot of time browsing the main one: Only The Breast, which serves the US market and, to a lesser extent, the UK.

Only The Breast is a bamboozling place, somewhere between Tinder and an à la carte human dairy farm. You can place an ad as a seller or buyer, and the going rate in the UK is around £30–£50 per litre for milk. Prices vary according to whether the buyer wants to buy in bulk, frozen or fresh, and what attributes they consider to be valuable. Milk is generally more expensive from sellers who advertise themselves as vegan, with an organic, gluten-/caffeine-/diary-free diet, or as having Covid antibodies, or as being vaccinated or unvaccinated, according to taste. Younger women also command higher prices.

Almost every seller claims to be an oversupplier, to have 'excess' – this assuages any guilt in the buyer that the seller's own baby is being deprived in order for the sale to happen.

The very real downside for the buyer, of course, is that the milk is unscreened. For parents who do not qualify for breast milk from a non-profit bank, the unknown quality of marketplace milk is the price they pay. The safety risks are considerable – potential drug or bacterial contamination, or the risk of STDs – which is why the FDA and FSA both advise against buying online. Plenty of people disregard that advice.

I discovered that the popularity of online breast milk sales is in some part due, ironically perhaps, to the wellness industry. The colostrum that women produce in the first days postpartum, as well the later milk itself, is often touted as 'liquid gold' – not just for babies, but for adults convinced that its elixir-like properties extend beyond infancy. Bodybuilders buy colostrum and breast milk, as do cancer survivors and those who suffer from digestive complaints like IBS – I was to meet one of the latter type: a man so desperate for breast milk he regularly drives across the UK to source it.

Majority scientific opinion has so far held that breast milk has no significant benefits for adults, but this is beginning to change, and isolated studies have suggested otherwise. Back in 1995, for example, scientists in Lund University in Sweden discovered 'by serendipity' that a component of breast milk – which they called 'HAMLET' – kills cancer cells.[5] In

MILK

September 2024, a small-scale study showed that HAMLET reduced the size of 88 per cent of tumours in bladder-cancer patients with no side effects.[6] Other recent studies have shown that bacteria in breast milk (which was previously assumed to be sterile) improves the gut microbiome.[7] I remembered this when I later discovered that Norwegian milk banks do not pasteurise breast milk, believing that it does more harm than good.

These studies are certainly interesting, but I do feel a certain level of alarm contemplating the consequences. If breast milk were proven to have significant benefits for adults, it is not unthinkable that some form of human dairy industry could result. Later in my research, I came across parts of the world where financially desperate mothers sell their milk, to the possible detriment of their own babies, because it is the highest income they can find.

What I did not expect to discover was that the largest cohort of customers for breast milk sold online are not the health conscious, but men with a fetish for both breast milk itself and for the bodies of breastfeeding mothers. They are part of a market for 'erotic lactation', a genre of porn I ended up encountering first-hand, having been completely and blissfully ignorant of its existence.

When I started my research on Only The Breast, one of the most popular categories of sellers' adverts was 'Willing to Sell to Men'. Meanwhile, among the buyers' adverts, 'Men Seeking Breast Milk' had the most traffic. When I contacted the website in 2022 asking whether the founders' original stated purpose of milk-sharing between mothers had been complicated by the obviously high number of male customers, I got no reply. Ditto to my follow-up email.

Soon afterwards, I noticed that both categories mentioning men had been removed. Now, sellers state in their ads whether they are willing to sell to men, and men post requests in the 'Seeking Milk' category. It has become less obvious without dedicated categories, but the male customer base still seems to be well represented.

Initially nervous about my plan to pose as a seller, I set up an account on Only The Breast under a pseudonym. I had no intention of actually making a sale. Scrolling through the existing ads, I noticed that photos of cleavage or faces got many more views than photos of neatly arranged milk bottles, as did ads posted by women who said they were in their twenties. I noticed other unsettling details on the site; in particular, men in the 'Seeking to Buy' section often found it necessary to describe themselves to their potential providers – as 'white, and clean cut', for example.

I decided to appear as clinical and non-sexual as possible. I posted an offer of fresh or frozen milk at a relatively low UK price (£1 per ounce) accompanied by a no-nonsense photo of a full bottle I had just pumped. Nothing about my age or appearance, only the facts that my baby and I were healthy, I had excess milk and had previously donated to a hospital. Of the many requests I received within hours of posting the ad, all but one were from men, and most were overtly sexual.

Chris from the US (central time zone) asked if I provided videos; he offered to pay $5 a minute, wanting 'hand expression, breast and face only, self-suck if possible'.

When I declined, he asked simply: 'What would make you do it?'

One twenty-five-year-old 'athletic' man from London initially said he was a gym-goer wanting fresh milk, before asking – almost in passing – if I would wet-nurse (breastfeed) him. With some trepidation, I asked what exactly he proposed. For moral support, I insisted my husband read the exchange over my shoulder: 'If you want I can host somewhere and we can go from there if you wish to?' he offered. As a surreal afterthought, he added: 'I understand your child comes first so please don't hesitate to tend to your child.'

I decided to probe a little further: 'Is it primarily for your health or a pleasure thing (I'm guessing the latter as freshly pumped is just as good)?'

His unconvincing response: 'It's just for my health really, there is some pleasure with it but strictly for my health.'

This echoed the words of Mark, who said he wanted it for bodybuilding, but admitted in a later email it was a 'turn-on'. Reading these emails, in particular those of men who denied getting any sexual pleasure from the idea of drinking breast milk, I wondered if they told the women in their lives about their purchases. It also occurred to me that I could ask them to enter a thought experiment: if it were biologically possible for the male body to produce milk (and in fact, it is, with hormone treatment that trans women can undergo), would they drink their own?

I suspect not.

One man, Paul, claimed he would pay me in advance on a regular basis if I sent him ten-minute videos of myself using my electric pump. This seemed far more bizarre than what Chris was after. Paul sent me videos of previous commissions 'for inspiration'. Some of the instructions related to audio – he wanted to 'listen perfectly [to] each drop that flows with the sound of the milk into the big bottle'. In a later email, he demanded proof that I was creating this video especially for him, requiring highly specific photos along with a written note – 'Paul, I am fully engorged for you' – a common feature of bespoke porn.

It was at this point that I felt out of my depth, so I talked to Karen Pollock, a psychotherapist and kink specialist, who happened to have worked as a breastfeeding counsellor at the National Childbirth Trust (NCT) twenty years ago.

When I expressed to Karen the strangeness of a man being turned on by a quintessentially maternal act, I was told that it is probably as instinctive as it gets to be attracted to someone who has proved their fertility. Men who are attracted to lactating women are related to those who are attracted to pregnant women, apparently – 'they're two sides of the same coin'.

I mentioned to Karen my uncomfortable brush with a stranger while seven months pregnant with my second child. I was buying some fruit at a market in France and the vendor – a big, middle-aged, sunburnt farmer wearing an apron – insistently stretched out his hands over the rows of peaches towards my bulging belly. To an onlooker, it must have looked like a Renaissance depiction of an ancient myth of fecundity, replete with ripe fruits and bellies. He leaned closer and closer. Instead of saying no, or knocking his hands away, I was paralysed by embarrassment.

MILK

Eventually he handed me my change and I left, only for him to catch me up and place a greedy hand on my belly before I pulled away. He may or may not have had a fetish. Perhaps he had personal reasons for being moved by the sight of a pregnant belly. Perhaps he was superstitious. In some cultures, rubbing a baby in utero is good luck; in others it is bad.

Working on the assumption, however, that perhaps there was some kink involved, Karen's response was surprisingly pragmatic: 'You see, if we did not make these things so taboo, this man would have a natural outlet for his desires and he would not feel compelled to express it in unhealthy ways, like trying to touch the body of a stranger.'

I was not sure what this 'natural outlet' would be, beyond porn, or employing a pregnant sex worker – or perhaps one of the OnlyFans accounts run by pregnant or lactating women – but I had to let it go. Karen was soon to tell me about another category of male milk customer, interested in wet-nursing.

'These are men with a mummy fetish, including "adult babies". There are sexualised adult babies, and non-sexualised. Some people really do just want to return to infancy – some of the men who contacted you will have just wanted that. They have no interest in children, they're not paedophiles – they want to *be* the child.'

We agreed that these were in the minority – most of my requests were sexual. On Pornhub, adult wet-nursing is a subcategory of the surprisingly popular 'pregnancy' search term. There are many more wet nurses advertising their services on Only The Breast in the US than in the UK, partly because of respective laws regarding sex work. In the US, where both the purchase and sale of sex is illegal in all states bar Nevada, women sometimes advertise as wet nurses when they are primarily sex workers, taking hormones to lactate.

What about the male customers – could buying breast milk under the guise of caring for one's health serve as a fig leaf for a more basic sexual impulse?

'A lot of people carry a lot of shame about it,' said Karen. 'But not all men are ashamed – some people are very open about it. Some of the men contacting you will just have got a thrill out of the exchange itself. Why do men send dick pics on the internet? They are saying, "Look at me, I'm a bad boy." They want to shock. That's the sole motivation for some men, to jump over the moral line.'

Strangely, that disturbed me more than the more explicit requests – the idea that I invited these responses by posting the ad in the first place.

Men purchasing breast milk online for their own consumption is a modern phenomenon, but its cultural roots are ancient. Openly acknowledged instances of adult breastfeeding are rare but have always received disproportionate attention. When I lived in Amsterdam, every time I visited the Rijksmuseum, I was struck by Rubens' painting of the Greek myth of Pero breastfeeding her imprisoned father, Cimon, to save him from starvation – beautiful, weird, wrong.

Rubens' painting is probably the most famous depiction of Pero breastfeeding Cimon, but a striking number of other artists (fifteen by my count – Greuze, van der Werff, Vouet, Peale, Loth, Janssens, Bloemaert, Zick, Cignani, Meyvogel, Cagnacci, van Baburen, Fabre, Sigrist and an anonymous follower of Caravaggio) all felt compelled to depict this obscure scene. For the writer Margie Orford, the scene conveys a sense of 'the countless women who have been feasted on and silenced by men, for whom women's bodies feed and sustain their sense of power, authority and invincibility'.[8]

In the final scene of John Steinbeck's *The Grapes of Wrath*, a newly bereaved mother in Depression-era America breastfeeds a starving man she meets in a barn. The shock factor for most readers, particularly the adolescent students for whom the book is often an exam text, is not so much the level of destitution and desperation the act suggests, but the visual image of a grown man sucking on a woman's breast for nourishment rather than sexual gratification.

I was soon to discover that there is not such a clear line between the two.

Steve was the only man I felt guilty about when I was advertising my milk with no intention of selling it. He was a sixty-year-old lorry driver who suffered from crippling IBS and seemed to be in distress. He claimed breast milk was the only thing that alleviated his symptoms (although 'not a silver bullet', he admitted). He bought it once or twice a month, as much as possible, paying anywhere between £1 and £2.50 per ounce. He collected it from across Somerset, Wiltshire and Wales, and emailed me sometimes several times a day asking if I could help him – he lived just an hour away.

Breastfeeding my second child, more than a year after Steve first contacted me, I checked my freezer stocks – about 500ml in total, more than three months old and thus useless to the milk bank, which requires at least 2–3 litres to be produced a strict maximum of three months previously. Ordinarily, I would throw it away. I considered the idea of selling it to Steve and donating the money to the milk bank, but selling still felt fundamentally wrong.

Feeling uneasy, I offered it to Steve for free, if we could meet and talk about his six-year history of buying milk online. I had mixed emotions when he agreed.

First, we spoke on the phone. Steve talked in a huge rush, as though it was a relief to talk openly to a stranger about a subject so dear to him. He complained that the British market on Only The Breast was less active than it had been pre-pandemic, presumably because buyers were concerned about imbibing Covid.

On the upside, he said, the average price had stayed more or less the same – 'the cost of making it hasn't changed', he joked, while conceding that the cost-of-living crisis might have made a difference.

Apparently, his suppliers ranged widely in age. 'I've met mothers who are seventeen, eighteen, others in their late thirties.'

I found the idea of a seventeen-year-old selling her milk to a sixty-year-old completely disgusting. I asked him how he had first discovered this unexpected 'cure'.

'I had stomach problems for years. When I met [my ex] a couple of months after she had a baby, she said, "Why don't you try my milk?" I said, "What are you on about?" [. . .] She said, "Don't be a baby, drink it," so I did.'

Transcribing his words and reading back what I'd written, my eyes fixed on the phrase 'don't be a baby'. Steve did not acknowledge the irony as he ploughed on, talking like a sommelier about what different women's milk tasted like. He claimed to be able to tell if his supplier had a high-dairy diet or ate a lot of fruit.

'Some milks are quite fatty, others taste a bit gravelly, more rougher, some a more bitter taste, others taste like cow's milk. You can notice the difference if it's pumped in the morning or in the evening, and you can tell the difference if it's been in the fridge before it goes in the freezer, versus if it's been straight into the freezer – when it thaws, you can tell [from] how it sits in the bag.'

He also spoke disapprovingly of having tasted nuts in one woman's milk – 'I told her, "You can send someone with an allergy into toxic shock!" She said she hadn't thought of that.'

Then a bombshell – or perhaps, in hindsight, it shouldn't have been: Steve revealed that he had also tried wet-nursing. My unease about having promised him my milk deepened. He claimed, repeatedly, that it was not a sexual experience – this woman had been supplying him with milk, trusted him and had wanted to try wet-nursing as another potential source of income. Her partner had left her a couple of months after the birth of their baby, who was now six months old.

'It was a comfort thing; it was quite nice. The warmth of a human body . . . it's always nice to cuddle someone . . . It was relaxing, she had some nice music on. It was about an hour or more.'

Later, he told me he had also paid £100 to a woman in Kent for ninety minutes of wet-nursing. He was obviously lonely, and his account of these experiences reminded me of Japan's 'cuddle cafés', where you can pay to cuddle and sleep (literally) with a stranger. I also thought of the comfort that adult baby fetishists derive from wearing nappies. I was becoming increasingly convinced that IBS was an excuse for a lonely man to get himself some emotional nourishment.

The morning I was due to meet Steve and hand over my milk, I felt physically sick; my instinct was to cancel, but I felt strangely beholden to my promise. So off I went, with my husband following at a safe distance just in case. (Steve had claimed that he always asks if his suppliers' partners are OK with the transaction: 'Last thing you want to do is drive a wedge between a woman and her partner.' Luckily, my husband did not feel proprietorial over my milk, but Steve hadn't asked.)

As I walked towards Steve, who was waiting by his lorry at the side of the road in a high-vis jacket, I held my zip-lock bag of yellowish frozen sachets and tried to imagine they contained another bodily fluid. I remembered the catheter and bag of urine dangling from my hospital bed after my second birth and epidural. The mind games didn't work. Normally unsentimental, I felt like crying. I was giving away my child's milk, my life force – strangely, my mind went to the Aztec warriors who ate the hearts of their enemies, believing it granted them superhuman powers. This, to my sleep-deprived mind, was a warped, sexual form of cannibalism, but for some reason I had decided it was too late to back out.

The meeting was brief, and in the end unexpectedly mundane. I handed over the bag like a mother handing over a lunchbox to her child, we chatted and Steve drove away. The next morning, he sent me an email thanking me again: 'Your milk was very creamy and very sweet[;] a bit almond to taste but very nice. When I got up this morning [my stomach] was good. No pain so your milk works.'

Again, a sensation of wanting to cry.

I wanted to know more about the women selling milk online. I contacted several; most confirmed they were almost exclusively contacted by men – 'freaks', one called them. Most of my contacts were defensive when asked why they chose to sell rather than donate, or ignored my question.

Sellers are aware that many people regard the breast-milk market as immoral, even disturbing. Some critics believe it is an abuse of the sacrosanct bond between mother and child, and many of these critics are other mothers – I've seen the most vicious condemnation on supposedly supportive forums like Netmums.com.

Some ads placed by women on Only The Breast hint at real desperation for money, such as this one sent from Placer County, California, by a woman who had only just given birth and was yet to start lactating properly:

Buy my first ounces!

I've just induced successfully and am only getting drops but my amount is increasing. As soon as I am able to pump a worthy amount I'd like to sell on a regular basis fresh or frozen.

Several women were surrogates. One, a 'healthy first time surrogate' from Los Angeles, was advertising her milk six months in advance, knowing that her baby's parents would take him or her away soon after birth and she would be left with a useless supply. (Some parents pay their surrogates in a separate arrangement for a few months' supply of pumped milk, as I was to find out during my interviews with surrogates.)

I asked 'Jessica', a breastfeeding mum from Kansas, why she sold her milk. She compared the process of pumping to work: 'I sell [rather than] donate because it's literally a second job – I wake up twice at night to pump, spend thirty minutes per pump, and pump every three to four hours throughout the day.

'It's time, money to keep the pumping material clean and updated every few months, sterilisation machine costs money, plus there's a handful of foods/fluids you need to eat to produce good milk.'

This I could certainly relate to. I had been warned by a midwife that I would need around 500 extra calories per day while breastfeeding, and had already noticed that I produced more milk when eating enormous quantities of food – I was the human equivalent of an expensively maintained Jersey cow.

Crucially, Jessica's moral argument was: 'If women are OK buying formula, why wouldn't they be OK buying fresh, healthy milk from women that spend a large amount of their personal time towards producing it?'

I saw her point. So why was I uncomfortable with selling my milk, even to other mothers rather than men – even as an experiment, to justify my presence on this marketplace? If I had needed the money badly enough, I might well have felt differently, and Jessica was right – producing milk is, in many senses, work. It is also very specific to one's baby, whose saliva interacts with its mother's milk to create 'biochemical synergism'[9] – in other words, the milk is tailored precisely to the baby's needs. It is a mysterious alchemy, and a strange substance to have a market value, determined – as with most products – by supply and demand.

Jessica's stance on lactating as labour was first expressed in earnest, and in the mainstream at least, in the feminist movement of the 1970s. In her 1975 pamphlet *Wages Against Housework*, the American feminist and teacher Silvia Federici wrote of housework: 'They say it is love. We say it is unwaged work.'[10] As part of a coalition of feminists, her demand for money in exchange for the work of a housewife (including birthing and rearing children) was intended primarily as a political statement,[11] considerably less effective than the sex strike carried out by angry Athenian women in Aristophanes' ancient comedy *Lysistrata*.

In 2019, the British artist Jessy Young, inspired in part by Federici's idea, kept a meticulous log of the first six months of breastfeeding her first child – a total of 720 hours, 7 minutes.

Out of this log, she created an artwork called *Milk Report*,[12] which sets out its mission in unemotional, almost officious language: 'Seeking full remuneration for the labour-intensive work undertaken, based on the 2019 National Living Wage of £8.21 per hour, an edition of 720 copies of *Milk Report* have been printed to be sold for £8.21 each. This will equate to a wage of £5,916.95 once all of the Milk Reports are sold.'

When my copy arrived in the post, I pored over the log sheet, remembering the early days with my first child, when I noted down every minute I spent breastfeeding to ensure I was giving her enough. My records have long since disappeared, deleted from my phone. Reading another woman's made me feel a strange mixture of sadness and pride.

I did not, I admit, feel anger or a sense of injustice that I had been cheated of thousands of pounds. But I did feel stunned in retrospect by the sheer effort, the labour of love – a seemingly unending stretch of time reduced, now, to the blink of an eye in the epic saga of parenting.

THE WORK OF WET-NURSING

In some contexts, breastfeeding is not necessarily a labour of love. It is just labour.

There is a small but active commercial wet-nursing section on Only The Breast. The women who advertise their services here all have intriguing backstories, but I was fascinated by one woman in particular.

Janet, 'the Golden Wet Nurse', based in Texas, gave her newly born daughter up for adoption on Mother's Day in June 2022, 'due to inflation', according to her advert. When I emailed her asking for more details, Janet explained that the baby's father had walked out on her, and that she was already struggling to look after her existing child. Suddenly this bizarre, sometimes grotesque world I'd infiltrated appeared desperately sad.

Janet told me she started wet-nursing when she had her first child at nineteen, and that some of her customers are men, whom she charges considerably more than she does babies. As I typed my questions to her, asking how much she charges and why, I could barely believe I'd get answers, but they arrived just a few hours later.

'If a mom is in critical condition and can't wet-nurse or take care of her child and wants me to do both, I charge around $2,000 monthly. [If] she just wants her kid to breastfeed every other day and buys milk I charge 75 cents per ounce and $50 [per day] to wet-nurse.' For men, however, 'it ranges from $150 to $400 [per day].'

I tried to ask her more about breastfeeding men without seeming judgemental or voyeuristic – does she feel safe?

'When I have men, I keep my gun in my pocket next to me. But I never have to use it because [before wet-nursing them] I meet them at a public place.'

She went on to describe the vetting process. 'First we chat, and I see if I'm interested, if I'm interested I then accept the offer, but the men have to pay before they get the address.'

She told me she doesn't think too closely about why men want to breastfeed, accepting the common line that they have 'something wrong with them [physically], and breast milk helps it'. While she seemed to think the money is relatively good, I got a sense that Janet is still uncomfortable with feeding men.

'I should've said "only babies" but I never knew men had such interest in this until I made the ad.'

The image of Janet breastfeeding male customers with a gun in her pocket stayed with me – the warped maternal act of nourishment, the lethal potential of the phallic gun. There is so much more I would like to ask her about, if we ever met in person. How reliant is she on the money? Does she prioritise men or baby-related requests? How many of the men request sex too? How does she explain, or hide, the wet-nursing from her child, or the child from her customers?

Janet's work straddles the worlds of prostitution and wet-nursing in time-honoured tradition, as I discovered while reading academic articles alongside my strange emailing sessions. If prostitution can lay claim to the title of humankind's oldest profession – or oldest form of exploitation, depending on your view – wet-nursing could be a close second. Both prostitutes and wet nurses have been simultaneously depended on and stigmatised for millennia.

Before the advent of formula, breastfeeding was essential for infant survival. If a mother could not feed her own baby, or died in childbirth, the task fell to another woman. In ancient times, this was often a female slave, or a family member (Tutankhamun's wet nurse is now thought to have been his sister[13]). Professional wet nurses, employed by choice rather than necessity, were in high demand until the late nineteenth century in wealthy families in Britain, France, North America and elsewhere.

As a new mother in a world (almost) devoid of wet nurses, it was difficult for me to imagine breastfeeding a stranger's child, and even more difficult to imagine paying or forcing another woman to feed my baby. Yet wet-nursing was, in the words of a British doctor in 1871, a service 'resorted to from one end of the country to the other',[14] not only among royalty and nobility but the 'gentry'. Queen Victoria was disgusted by the idea of breastfeeding her own children, warning her daughter Princess Vicky in a letter that 'a child can never be as well nursed by a lady of rank and nervous and refined temperament – for the less feeling and more like an animal the wet nurse is, the better for the child.'[15] She was horrified when both Vicky and Alice chose to breastfeed anyway, and allegedly named a cow in the royal dairy after Alice.

When I was browsing breast-milk ads, I was struck by how consistently sellers advertised their organic, vegan or gluten-free diets, knowing this could command a higher price. Historically, people have always believed that certain qualities of a lactating woman affect her milk, and therefore whoever imbibes it. Nineteenth-century wet nurses in the US were forbidden from eating pickles and drinking iced water, because that would 'spoil' their milk.[16] Sometimes, actual medical conditions gave cause for concern: in eighteenth-century

France, doctors noticed syphilis spreading among wet-nursed babies.[17]

More often, people worried about wet nurses' mental characteristics, and they were often assumed to be morally deficient. A wet nurse was 'one-quarter cow, three-quarters devil', in the view of one nineteenth-century American doctor.[18] A hysterical article published in the *Lancet* in 1858 warned of the dangers of employing 'fallen' or unmarried women as wet nurses, and allowing them to live in the households of the 'virtuous and the pure'.[19]

Occasionally, a wet nurse has been credited for passing on her virtuous characteristics. According to Michelangelo's biographer, Ascanio Condivi (1525–74), the artist believed his wet nurse, who was the wife and daughter of stonemasons, had blessed him with his skill.

'It is no wonder he delighted in the use of the chisel, for it is known that the milk of the wet nurse has the power to alter the temperature of the body and change one's natural disposition.'[20]

Sometimes a wet nurse's race was deemed to be a deciding factor in the quality of her milk production. In 1922, Julius Hess, the American 'father of neonatal medicine', wrote that: 'The phlegmatic temperaments as seen in women of Northern and Central Europe and of Teutonic and Slavic descent offer the ideal material,' while 'Italians and Southern negroes when removed from their home environment . . . secrete a milk poor in quality.'[21]

Unsurprisingly, we have little insight into the first-hand experiences of wet nurses, many of whom were regarded as belonging to the lowest social ranks, and were illiterate. Historians have relied on the accounts of the families who employed them, on paintings, newspaper advertisements, and on the paediatricians who acted as brokers matching wet nurses to families.

I was particularly interested in the women employed as 'in-house' hospital wet nurses in the early twentieth century (the precursors to today's milk banks). These were allowed to keep and nurse their own babies while they pumped milk throughout the day for the hospitalised newborns. This was not an act of charity on their employer's part: without a child to feed and skin-to-skin contact, it would have been much harder to maintain sufficient levels of oxytocin to keep reliably lactating – the babies were essential accessories to their mothers' work.

While some wet nurses – for example, those who nursed royal babies in medieval Japan[22] – could achieve great wealth and political power, most had difficult lives. 'The class of society from which wet-nurses are drawn is a very low one,' according to the nineteenth-century Chicago paediatrician Arthur Meigs. These women were often resented by the mothers who hired them and routinely dismissed, despite offering such a vital service – fired for being slovenly, unclean or disobeying orders about what to eat. As the academic Jacqueline Wolf puts it, 'Mothers felt simultaneously superior to and jealous of the wet nurses who suckled their babies and consequently hid their jealousy behind an impenetrable wall of moral judgment.'[23]

The crimes of wet nurses included not producing enough milk and pining after their own babies, who were usually left or 'placed out' at 'baby-farms' with high mortality rates (these 'farms' were generally the homes of rural people who accepted a lump sum or monthly fee to look after other people's babies). The sheer number of wet nurses' babies dying did not escape attention at the time. Not one but two articles published in the *British Medical Journal* in 1861 denounced the practice as 'child murder',[24] but it would take nearly another half-century for baby farms to be outlawed in the UK in the Children Act of 1908.

I came across one particularly horrible account of abuse from a late-nineteenth-century mother from Massachusetts: Fanny Workman, who hired and fired several wet nurses whom she found unsatisfactory. She wrote about the experience in the New York magazine *Babyhood*, complaining about the behaviour of her final wet nurse, whose own baby died two weeks after being 'placed out'. The wet nurse wanted to attend her baby's funeral, but Workman did not allow her. She became 'very unruly and obstinate', so Workman fired her.

I found reading these accounts incredibly distressing. I also found it unsurprising that the wet nurses struggled to settle or produce enough milk, knowing how stress and lack of sleep affected my milk supply. How would it feel to be far from one's own baby in a strange and often hostile environment? How easy would it be, physiologically, to lactate for another woman's baby? Would the all-important 'love hormone', oxytocin, flow as readily?

Two images came to mind: first, the twentieth-century hospital wet nurses allowed to nurse their own babies alongside their pumping duties, because it increased their output.

Second, a dystopian scene from the 2015 film *Mad Max: Fury Road*, set in a future world drained of water and oil. In a dark room, a row of enslaved, naked women are hooked up to machines, pumping milk for their overlords, metal-clad warriors. There is no sign of any babies. Instead, they hold woollen dolls to help them lactate.

I found myself thinking a lot about the Golden Wet Nurse and the baby she gave up; the surplus milk she decided to monetise. By comparison to other women advertising their wet-nursing services, she did not charge much – evidence, perhaps, of her desperation. I found myself corresponding with a woman based in Georgia who I'll call Bess. She has seven children of her own, eighteen years of experience, and was willing in 2022 to combine babysitting and wet-nursing for $2,000 a week, offering to eliminate 'anything from [her] diet that will upset the baby's tummy'.

Bess told me that while she didn't mind selling her milk to men, she only breastfed babies. She also claimed that 'what I am honestly looking for [is] to help with this formula shortage that we are currently dealing with in our society.' (In 2022, a major infant formula factory in Michigan closed down amid concerns over contaminated products. The closure caused supply issues and a months-long, nationwide shortage. Mothers facing empty shelves turned to the breast milk of strangers; milk banks across the US reported an increase in demand and, in response, a heartening increase in donations. But the crisis brought into focus the relative scarcity of American milk banks.)

Bess wanted to help – at a price. And why not? Here, again, was the thorny question – do mothers deserve to be paid for the labour of producing milk, or should mothers help each other for free? Should breast milk be treated as a commodity – to be sold to any customer of the maker's choosing – or does it exist on a different social and moral plane? If men could breastfeed, would this subject be as ethically confused? I found myself wondering whether we expect more altruism of women than we do of men – a question I have often asked myself since becoming a mother.

Although I already had my own instinctive answers to these questions, I felt that being a breastfeeding mother myself was making it difficult, or perhaps impossible, to analyse the subject with cold-eyed clarity. While I was scouring adverts for wet-nursing online, I realised that I was struggling to envisage feeding another woman's child as a natural thing to do – was this personal to me, or a reflection of the culture in which I lived?

MILK SIBLINGS

When I interviewed Ana, the mother in Amsterdam who received a breast-milk donation from a woman she did not know, she told me she had initially been hesitant to seek out a stranger's milk – and not just because of health concerns.

'At the beginning, I was kind of ashamed,' she said. 'But I shared [the news] with my mother and she was like, "Ah, your son is going to have a milk brother!" She told me it used to happen a lot, and that made me more confident, knowing that used to be a thing.'

Ana's mother was referring to a deep-rooted tradition of 'cross-feeding' that has long existed alongside a history of milking for profit: mothers informally feeding each other's babies in close-knit communities across the world. In doing so, they have balanced out over- and undersupply among individual women – friends, relatives and neighbours – and created the unique bonds of milk 'kinship'.

I first heard about cross-feeding in 2017, while carrying out some research in Haifa, northern Israel. I interviewed a woman called Lisa, from an old Jerusalemite family; her mother was a Moroccan Sephardic Jew, and her father an Ashkenazi Jew from Russia, killed before the outbreak of Israel's War of Independence in 1948. Lisa told me her grandmother had a 'milk brother' – a Muslim Arab boy who was breastfed by Lisa's great-grandmother in a neighbourhood in Jerusalem.

The Israeli political scientist Menachem Klein writes about Jewish and Arab families in the early twentieth century who would cross-feed when a new mother found she could not breastfeed and asked a friend to help.[25] It was also a common practice in the Jewish-majority city of Thessaloniki (Salonika) in Ottoman times, another ethnically diverse city like Jerusalem. Thinking about it in the context of Palestine and Israel today is almost too grotesquely tragic to bear.

My years living in Turkey had already made me aware of the principle of kinship in Islamic cultures, not in terms of the prohibition of anonymous donor milk (the creation of 'milk siblings' creates the possibility of incest in Islamic law), but the prohibition of adoption. The cousin of a Turkish friend of mine from Mersin, southern Turkey, found out in adulthood that he was not, in fact, the biological son of the people he thought were his parents. He was the second-born son of an aunt who gave him to her childless sister to raise as her own – an example of child 'sharing' within extended families. I see an overlap with cross-feeding, a collective attitude that children belong to the community rather than strictly to an individual parent or couple, and a belief that the resources (of fertile couples) should be shared – just like breast milk.

In light of how unusual cross-feeding is today, I was particularly intrigued by the small number of women on Only The Breast who offered their breastfeeding services for free. Several of them cited the 2022 US infant formula shortage as the reason they had offered their help; some of them just seemed genuinely passionate about breastfeeding.

I missed breastfeeding my daughter once she weaned, and not just on an emotional level. There is an oxytocin hit that comes with every breastfeeding session, and the hormonal comedown when you stop is widely recognised, sometimes leading to severe depression. Continuing to breastfeed a younger baby would alleviate that – which does not detract from the generosity of the act.

Gay and trans couples who are keen to give their babies breast milk but are unable to breastfeed sometimes rely on friends to help them out. In 2015, one incredible woman, Lara Olchanetzky Duke,[26] started relactating seven years after she finished breastfeeding her own children, in order to help her gay friends who had recently had a baby via a surrogate.

Lara re-established her milk supply six months before the birth by taking hormones and hand-expressing. Then, from London, she shipped a total of 35.06 frozen litres to her friends in Hong Kong so that their baby – Lara's godson – could be fed exclusively with breast milk for the first three months. It is an epic story of friendship, but also of the innovations (pumping, freezing, the synthetic stimulation of hormones) that have allowed such a feat to be performed. I contacted Lara a decade after her donation; in the intervening time, she had qualified as a midwife and was working as a lactation consultant.

Around the time I became pregnant, my friend Lizzy was also pregnant with twins but lost one baby in the womb. Lizzy's daughter, Sadie, survived against the odds. When she was born, she was in the bottom 9 per cent of newborn babies by weight.

More anxious than most mothers, perhaps, to ensure that Sadie was healthy, Lizzy was breastfeeding her a year later, despite finding it a huge struggle. As a stressed-out human rights barrister, she spent hours in court, escaping for a few minutes at a time to pump in the female robing room, producing small bottles of milk that she would take home to her daughter. During the same period, I was donating litres of breast milk to strangers' babies in a local hospital.

Conscious of how lucky I was to have an excess of milk, I wanted to help Lizzy but was uncertain how to broach it.

Would she be as shocked as I had been soon after giving birth, when another mother on a WhatsApp group offered me some of her milk? Six months on from that experience, I was both more relaxed as a mother and more attuned to the anxieties of other mothers, so I went ahead and asked. Lizzy said yes immediately.

Later, when I asked her how she felt about it, she sent me a voice note explaining that there had been a time when she'd even considered giving Sadie to someone else to breastfeed. I listened, surprised to hear what she had never expressed to me in person at the time, despite the closeness of our friendship.

'When my pregnancy wasn't going well,' Lizzy's disembodied voice explained, 'one of the fears that I had was that I would be unwell after having Sadie and my milk wouldn't come, or I would be too unwell to breastfeed . . . I think I so desperately wanted her to live and be OK that the whole pride thing disappeared.

'I did a lot of research and apparently the second-best thing [for your baby] after your own milk is another woman's milk, but even better is the child sucking on someone's boob and feeling safe and secure. I sort of decided in my mind that I would be OK with that, so when you mentioned giving your milk to me it wasn't a big deal – I was so happy about it.'

I was reminded of this sentiment when I later interviewed a woman in the US who was told by doctors that she would never carry any pregnancy to term. She and her husband chose a surrogate to carry twins for them. They discussed with their lawyer the contract they were due to sign, looking at a clause referring to the compensation the surrogate should receive for breastfeeding the babies.

'My lawyers said to me, "You won't want her to breastfeed them. It'll make you sad." And I said: "I'm already sad, I want what's going to make them healthy."'

When I'd handed over my milk to the Bristol milk bank, I felt relieved that I'd pumped enough, that I could relax. I never really thought about the experience again, until writing this. Donating was almost an abstract act. With Lizzy, I knew in concrete terms that I was helping someone I cared about.

Lizzy would send me photos of Sadie guzzling a half-empty bottle: 'Only a few bags left now!' I realised how much more personal this was, how much more satisfying – this was what the economist James Andreoni called 'impure altruism'. I was getting something out of it too.

My daughter and Lizzy's daughter will always have the somewhat anachronistic title of 'milk sisters'. We have no idea how they will feel about this, of course, but we hope they will embrace it – in our own way, Lizzy and I have become milk sisters too.

GLOBAL BANKING

Before I donated to a hospital bank, I knew very little about how and why it would be used. Instinctively, I just didn't want it to go to waste. Most people who have not had or known a child who has spent time in NICU have no idea why hospitals need breast milk so badly.

Three years after I made my donation, I find myself peering into an industrial freezer packed with bottles in Bristol's Southmead Hospital. These bottles contain milk destined for premature babies whose own mothers are ill, or who are yet to establish their milk supply; it is crucial for 'prems' as they struggle to digest infant formula. A digital thermometer on the freezer shows a reading of −24°C; next to it, another freezer warns 'DO NOT USE: Waiting for maternal blood results'. As I angle my phone to take a close-up of the bottles, Ali Roy, the milk-bank manager, intervenes.

'I'm afraid I can't let you do that; these are labelled – some of them are from bereaved mothers.'

I delete the photo as Ali carefully locks the freezer and finds another key to open its neighbour – later, I find out that these freezers will hold more than 1,050 litres of milk over the course of this year. All Ali's movements are methodical; she is a quiet, middle-aged woman who came to the NHS from the private sector because this particular job appealed to her. Although she spends much of her time checking freezers, she says that every time she glimpses a premature baby being wheeled along the corridor she feels a quiet satisfaction in her work.

Together, we examine the bottles arranged in batches from each mother, grouped by the month they were donated: some of the milk is yellow and creamy-looking; other batches thinner, nearly blue – I recognise the Promethean palette, evocative of exhaustion and replenishment. For a moment, I allow myself to wonder what it must feel like to express milk for strangers' babies while mourning the loss of your own.

The three freezers in this tiny room are full of 'stock', which makes me think of a warehouse. Some of it is to be discarded for failing the pathogen tests (this is usually around 9 per cent of the total donations). We walk back into the processing room, which constitutes the main milk bank. It is small, like a school kitchen, with bare, stainless-steel counters, two more freezers and a fridge, and a compact pasteurising machine that I mistake for a dishwasher. Inside, its metal filaments give off a familiar aroma: the musky sweetness of spilt breast milk.

Ali shows me the circular foils that the technicians use to seal the chilled bottles, exactly like the foils on supermarket milk (an image of a cornflakes packet appears in my mind's eye). I open cupboards at head height to find whisks and sieves stacked neatly in Tupperware tubs, intensifying the impression of a school kitchen. Ali notes my surprise.

'Yes, some of this is quite basic – we literally pour the raw milk into jugs, whisk it gently and pour it through sieves. The technicians wear gowns, masks, hair caps – like in an operating theatre. Sometimes they find a hair or a bogey, even after the milk has passed the microbiology tests.'

This is not encouraging, but there is still the pasteurising stage to come, which blasts the milk and any pathogens to 62.5°C and extends its frozen shelf life, though in practice stores are used up well within that time. Pasteurising is a stage that Norwegian banks have controversially done without for the past eighty years,[27] believing that breast milk au naturel (but post-screening) is much better for babies than heating and altering the milk's composition. A couple of German banks have followed suit.[28]

Ali and I ponder this – it makes sense. You would never pasteurise donated blood.

'It would cost a lot less and be a lot quicker not to,' says Ali wistfully. Then we remember the bogies.

I notice an iPad sitting, lonely as a cloud, on a steel countertop; Ali says it was recently installed after a two-year wait for digital monitoring of the freezers. Its sole purpose is to alert the hospital reception of any temperature abnormalities in the absence of staff in the room. The freezers, I am realising, are everything; if they stop functioning, the milk is worthless.

The term 'liquid gold' has never seemed so apt; I feel like I am in some kind of makeshift bank vault, housed in a spotlessly clean kitchen, deep in the bowels of a hospital so vast I needed a map to find my way here from one of the many car parks. It feels cobbled together and surprisingly professional at the same time.

A friendly nurse pops in for a chat; this is Cathy Budd, in charge of infant feeding on the neonatal ward. (I am wearing my woolly hat to ward against the chill that neither of the other women seem to feel in this room; I notice that Cathy is bare-armed). She tells me she initiated the creation of this bank with a few colleagues in 2011; they ran it as a charity called Precious Drops for five years. Soon, they were struggling to keep up with demand and NHS England stepped in with funding. Now, the bank supplies twelve neonatal wards across the south-west of England, on an annual budget of £163,813; the bank relies on a team of volunteers to collect the donations.

There has been no official cost-benefit analysis, Ali tells me, but the milk saves both lives and money by preventing cases of necrotising enterocolitis (a gastric disease that infant formula-fed babies are much more likely to develop – the fact that it is expensive to treat is, unfortunately, a relevant additional detail).

I am slightly blown away by the news that this tiny school kitchen feeds the entire south-west of the country – it is a huge endeavour for a bank that runs part-time, and depends on unpredictable donations, and the time and energy of volunteers.

'Donations fluctuate,' says Ali. 'This week we had to ask our existing donors to give us whatever stock they have because we were running low.'

The bank does not advertise for donations, the reasons for which I would discover later. At several points in the past, Cathy tells me, they have had to buy milk from the Chester Milk Bank, in the north-west of the country, which always seems to have plenty of stock. Once, they were pitched by a representative from the American company Prolacta Bioscience, which compensates donors to make breast milk 'fortifier' products to sell to hospitals, at a profit – a totally different model to this hospital's entirely altruistic model. The sales rep was told no, a team decision by the neonatal consultants. I underline my notes on this part of the conversation emphatically – this is something to return to.

As I'm leaving, the two women are curious as to why I've asked to tour the milk bank. I tell them about my forays into online milk sales, and their professional personas slip slightly as they wince at the details of the male customers who approached me. I judge that it's the right moment to ask about their donors: have they ever had a mother – unable to lactate herself, for whatever reason – refuse to accept donated milk?

Both of them ponder this. 'No,' says Cathy eventually. 'We did have a mother once who wanted to donate, but wanted to be told exactly who would receive her milk. We told her we couldn't do that, so she didn't donate.'

We agree this was probably about milk kinship – the principle of Islamic law that babies who drink milk from the same mother become siblings of a sort, prohibiting future marriages and making anonymous donations problematic.

'Sometimes, one of the matrons from NICU will ask us for custardy milk if a baby is struggling,' says Ali, meaning the creamy-yellow, high-calorie bottles we had seen in the freezer. 'So we give them a particular batch. But usually the batches are allocated at random. It's not all pooled together like the Americans do it.'

Americans, Norwegians, British – every country has a different style. French milk banks, Ali told me, accept a much higher volume of donations because they have lower standards for their microbiology tests. I wanted to know what drives countries in different directions, and most of all: what makes America, with its commercial banks, such an outlier in what is generally an altruistic endeavour?

* * *

MILK

Today in Europe, there are 282 active milk banks, with eighteen more in the pipeline, according to the European Milk Bank Association (EMBA).[29] This was not actually as many as I expected for a life-giving substance, but it is a lot more than a hundred years ago.

I discovered that the first human milk bank was established in Vienna in 1909 after wet-nursing fell out of fashion – there was no one to pay to lactate for your baby if you were unable or unwilling to do so yourself. The Vienna model was gradually copied by German-speaking countries and then further afield in Europe and beyond. Many banks closed in the 1960s as infant formula became more popular (and healthier)[30] than its earliest, basic incarnations of sugar and cow's milk (still an improvement on 'pap', an unappealing mixture of bread and water fed to babies in the nineteenth century[31]).

Milk banks also became less popular in the 1980s during the HIV crisis,[32] when fear of contamination was justified – unlike some of the fears that surrounded the disease at the time. Reading about this, I remembered the blood tests for STDs I'd had at my local doctor's surgery before I donated. At the time, I'd rationally understood their necessity but was also slightly annoyed by all the paperwork and delays. Now, the horrific possibility of transmitting HIV to a newborn baby from a well-meaning stranger's milk actually came home to me.

Scrutinising the EMBA's map of milk banks and the huge discrepancies between different countries' numbers, I found myself thinking about how local culture affects openness to donated milk – in sometimes unpredictable ways. Turkey, for example, where I used to live, has no milk banks at all, despite high rates of breastfeeding; 62 per cent of children under two in Turkey are still breastfed[33] – far longer than the UK's average of around 50 per cent of babies aged six to eight weeks[34] – so there is a potentially high supply of donors.

The country's lack of banks is almost certainly connected to the Islamic principle of milk kinship and wariness of anonymous donations, something that likely contributed to a 2025 ban on sales of breast milk (which was officially due to health concerns over anonymous sales).[35] The will to donate is there, however. In 2022, an academic study found that 57.9 per cent of both Turkish and refugee women living in a rural area of western Turkey would be willing to donate their milk, but only 27.7 per cent would be willing to give donor milk to their children.[36] In these statistics, I recognised myself, comfortable with giving my own milk but not receiving it.

Conversely, the UK, despite having one of the lowest breastfeeding rates in the world, has a relatively impressive sixteen milk banks, or one for every 4 million people. The US has far fewer: around one for every 10 million people – striking, given that its rates of breastfeeding are much higher than the UK's (55 per cent of babies are breastfed at six months of age).[37]

Japan, with its population of 125 million people, has only two banks. Italy – 58 million – has thirty-nine, the most in Europe, but fewer per capita than Norway (twelve banks for 5.5 million, and a claim to having the most generous donors). But arguably the world's biggest milk-banking success story – 227 banks and counting – is Brazil.

MILK

Brazil has undergone an ideological, legal and logistical transformation to get to where it is today. In the nineteenth century, it was common there, as it was in the American South, for enslaved black women to be forced to act as wet nurses for their slave owners' children, or to be rented out to other white families – black women's milk appropriated for white babies.[38] The legacy of exploitation continued long beyond the era of slavery. In the 1980s, desperately poor Brazilian women were still selling their breast milk until a pioneering chemist, João Aprígio Guerra de Almeida, set up a network of milk donation centres, which used radically economical measures like sterilised mayonnaise jars in place of expensive storage equipment to succeed at scale.[39] He also lobbied for a national ban on human milk sales, establishing a pro-breastfeeding culture that led to a 2006 ban on the marketing of infant formula products,[40] and a 2022 injunction against Swiss food and drink company Nestlé for promoting its 'toddler milk'.[41] The Brazilian government still lobbies against infant formula on the world stage today – a relatively controversial approach, when stigmatising women who do not breastfeed is a politically charged decision.

Brazil clearly offers a model in organising and promoting milk donation, whatever your feelings about the ethics of sales of human milk, or of infant formula. Twelve years after the first bank opened in 1985, and alongside the introduction of family health programmes, the infant mortality rate in Brazil dropped by around 40 per cent[42] – an overall good that has arguably come at the cost of cutting off a source of income for the poorest women in the country, as I discovered elsewhere.

* * *

I had never seen an advert to donate milk until I started looking online. Many people, including breastfeeding mothers I've spoken to, had never even heard of it. Actually visiting a processing unit in a hospital inevitably made me think about another kind of donation: a more essential bodily fluid for the wider public than breast milk, with many more available donors, and much more visibility.

Blood is ubiquitous, impersonal, unisex – efficiently siphoned off with minimal effort and zero sentimentality. The atmosphere of a blood donor centre – a relaxed, communal environment, full of biscuits, chats and goodwill – contrasts starkly with the isolated and thankless task of pumping milk alone at home, which is also more time-consuming and (literally) draining. I can't quite imagine a milk donation centre with rows of women with their boobs out – perhaps it would look like the scene from *Mad Max*, NHS edition.

I began to realise that blood donation is not as 'unisex' as I had first assumed. The journalist Hannah Partos, whose life was saved by a stem cell transplant from an anonymous 'chunky lad', has written an excellent analysis on the differences among female and male donors: women donate more blood than men,[43] even though they are usually allowed to donate less frequently, because they have lower iron stores (in the UK, for example, the maximum frequency is every sixteen weeks to men's twelve).[44] Women also donate more stem cells, are more likely to donate a kidney, and make up the majority of the organ donor register. Their bodies also contain more oxytocin – the 'feel-good' hormone I learned was crucial to producing breast milk. Oxytocin has been shown to have an effect on trust; studies have proved that there is a correlation between individuals with higher levels of oxytocin giving away money in economic trust-based games.[45] Men are more easily incentivised by gifts, like free coffee mugs.[46]

I was curious to know whether women are more generous donors of money to charitable causes than men. This is more difficult to ascertain; donating patterns are more complicated (how often, how much at a time), but it seems that, adjusting for the pay gap, women do give more.[47] Even setting that aside, it seems irrefutable that women are more generous donors of their physical selves, whether that can be explained by hormones or more complicated social factors – generations of collective experience of motherhood, perhaps.

I wondered, again, whether we expect more altruism – more selflessness – of women than we do of men. If we did not depend on this altruism, what would be the alternative? Should we pay women for their milk, as we pay some people for their plasma?

Governments are as confused as me, apparently. Laws that control the commercialisation of the human body are notoriously inconsistent from country to country, and fluctuate according to supply. Recently, there has been a shift in Europe. The Council of Europe's Oviedo Convention states that 'the human body and its parts shall not, as such, give rise to financial gain'.[48] In theory, any remuneration for blood, plasma, skin, corneas, eggs and sperm is not allowed (in 2022, there was also a push to include breast milk).[49] Compensation should be modest and capped, for reasonable 'expenses' or time off work.

Yet four outlying European countries – Austria, the Czech Republic, Germany and Hungary – have a tradition of paying donors for their plasma, as does the US. Since 2022, the European Parliament has been agonising over changing its rules due to a critical lack of plasma in Europe and reliance on paid imports from the US.[50] In 2023, the US earned $37 billion from exports of blood products[51] – more than from coal or gold.[52] In April 2024, changes were finally introduced in Europe that meant, now, countries can draw up their own rules – as Germany and others were already doing.

The issue is a divisive one, and the recent change in Europe was enthusiastically supported by prominent voices who argue for greater financial incentives for donors. In the US, an estimated 20 million people donate up to twice a week and can earn hundreds of dollars from their plasma, which is collected at more than a thousand centres.[53]

The journalist Kathleen McLaughlin, who depends on regular plasma injections herself, has written objectively and bravely about the ethical problems of the US industry from which she has benefited for twenty years – and the guilt she feels about that. Reading her descriptions of plasma centres clustered in impoverished areas of the country, and particularly in areas where non-white people live, like the Mexican border,[54] I could not help but compare this phenomenon to Brazil. I thought of the nameless non-white women selling their breast milk forty years before the country's mindset and infrastructure transformed so completely to its altruistic model today. It seems unlikely that the US plasma industry will undergo the same transformation.

MILK

BIG PHARMA

One element of the breast-milk market disturbed me more, in some ways, than fetishists buying it from women online. Commercial providers of breast milk in the UK and US like NeoKare, Medolac Laboratories and Prolacta Bioscience present themselves as pharmaceutical companies. They screen and pasteurise breast milk like hospital milk banks, and are part of the biotech industry that has grown at a dizzying rate in recent years. They sell frozen breast milk and its derivatives – powders, liquids and fortifiers – for prices that exceed those of high-end champagne.

In 2022, NeoKare charged its customers £45 for 300ml, or roughly £150 per litre. The UK-based company invited 'donations' from lactating mothers, whom it compensated with 50p per ounce, or £17 per litre. Their strapline, 'Become a Milk Provider, Save a Life', implied that donors' milk would always go to babies in the direst need, using the language of a charitable enterprise rather than a profit-making one. Arguably, their business leached milk that would otherwise be donated by mothers to hospital milk banks.

In 2023, the FSA announced it was working with Trading Standards to investigate how a small number of NeoKare's products, which were being fed to babies in hospital trials, contained elevated levels of lead.[55] All NeoKare's products were recalled, and the company has now removed its prices from its website. Unsurprisingly, they stopped responding to my emails.

CASH COW

NeoKare is a UK iteration of a US company founded decades ago. In 1999, a thirty-five-year-old mother called Elena Medo founded Prolacta Bioscience in Los Angeles, creating a controversial business model reliant on compensated 'donations' that has become wildly successful. Today, Prolacta sells exclusively to hospitals – over 400 currently – and has recently initiated commercial activities in Europe. The company is currently unlisted but has an estimated annual revenue of $101.6 million, and has received $83.6 million in investment.[56] (A company PR sent me lots of medical endorsements but no hard evidence that its products are safer or more effective than cow's-milk-based equivalents.)

In 2015, its male board sued Prolacta's founder Medo for stealing 'trade secrets' to use in the new company she founded in 2009, Medolac Laboratories (the lawsuit is ongoing).[57] The optics were not good – men turning on the woman who pioneered the use of products designed to save the lives of babies – and Medo has plenty of supporters and crowdsourcing campaigns for her legal fight. But it is not clear, to me at least, how defensible Medo's own decisions have been, potentially rerouting breast milk donations from the non-profit to the profit sector.

Would Medo have received more criticism if her company had benefited not from the milk of American mothers, but from mothers living in some of the poorest areas of the world?

In 2015, Bronzson Woods, a former Mormon missionary, founded Ambrosia Labs in Utah.[58] (The idea of a missionary setting up a breast-milk plant named after the food of pagan gods struck me as poetic.) He immediately set up operations in a poverty-stricken district of Cambodia, recruiting local women as milk donors. These women were compensated $0.50 per ounce for their milk, which was then processed and sold in the US for $20 per 5-ounce pack, or eight times the price. In 2017, Cambodia banned the export of breast milk after Ambrosia's operations attracted the criticism of groups such as UNICEF, who argued that local women were being exploited and were depriving their own babies of breast milk.[59]

The Cambodian government's decision was controversial; some women's rights groups argued that the company had been empowering local women to earn a relatively high wage, enabling them to better support their families while spending more time at home, actively caring for them. Local women agreed, mourning the departure of Ambrosia in media reports.[60]

Ambrosia Labs versus the Cambodian government is not an isolated case – India's food safety authority also banned the sale of breast milk in 2024 after firms operating under 'dairy' licences were shut down by the government.[61] These cases tap into the question of empowerment versus exploitation that is at the heart of the commodification of the maternal body as a whole; it was a theme I kept coming back to throughout my research.

CASH COW

THE CUP O'ERFLOWETH

How should we control what is, essentially, a very precious surplus bodily fluid? The value of breast milk ties into questions about bodily autonomy, women's rights and national health, but there is no national conversation about how to answer these questions.

Looking back at my own breastfeeding experiences, and talking to women who have received milk, sold their own milk and given it away, I realised that I am still conflicted about the ethics of selling breast milk. Financially, I have never had to consider selling my own. I cannot judge the women who do choose to sell theirs, and feel instinctively that women should be allowed to do what they want with their bodies. Yet I also feel that breast milk is so crucial for the babies who most need it that it cannot be treated as a normal commodity on the open market, especially in the context of profit-making companies. Putting ideological arguments aside, offering compensation to donors does not seem to solve the problem of supply and demand – even the American milk banks that compensate donors always need more milk.

So how can communities ensure that they have enough milk for their babies? It is hard not to be impressed by the example set by Brazil. Yet a national network may not suit every country – smaller, more informal systems also work.

My friends Lewis and Andre had a child by surrogate in December 2021 in Calgary. Here, a small community-based network called the NorthernStar Mothers Milk Bank –

non-profit and unfunded by government or hospitals – ensures that donated, screened milk is available to new parents via paid prescription from pharmacies.[62] The milk is intended for babies who would not qualify to receive it in a neonatal ward; the parents' only other options would be close friends or family, or anonymous sources online.

Lewis and Andre trudged through snow every day to a pharmacy in Calgary to pick up donated breast milk for their baby. They were entitled to ten bottles of 120ml, costing CAN $18 at the time (the price rose to $20 in 2024). The price is high, translating to 120 US dollars per litre, while (unscreened) milk on the private market costs roughly 50–60 US dollars per litre. With a special prescription, other parents are entitled to buy more – for example, if a doctor has diagnosed delayed lactation in a postpartum mother with gestational diabetes, as Ana had. The price of the milk covers operational costs like processing, testing, pasteurisation and distribution. Each year, NorthernStar raises between $65,000 and $100,000 to provide milk for babies who are ill or immunocompromised or discharged from hospital but still in need of help, and whose families cannot afford the cost.

Jannette Festival, the director of NorthernStar, was scathing – in the most professional language possible – about profit-making milk companies like Prolacta when I contacted her over email, pointing out that the cost of paying 'suppliers' is directly applied to the cost of the milk for the baby, and that some families might misuse the system for financial gain.

'They are not "donors" but suppliers of milk – a very important distinction.'

(This point confirmed for me the euphemistic fluidity of the word 'donor' when used by companies like Prolacta – something that I encountered again while researching egg donation in the US, which is often highly 'compensated', to use the legal term.)

Lindsay Groff, the executive director of the non-profit Human Milk Banking Association of North America (HMBANA), echoed Janette's sentiments when I asked her what her position was on for-profit breast-milk companies. Her answer was similarly diplomatic – she did not explicitly criticise the likes of Prolacta but said: 'We are thinking about the health outcome. We are motivated by mission, not by profit.'

While HMBANA donations have risen steadily in the last twenty years, Groff says the banks always need more milk. 'The need for donor milk is constant – just like the blood banking industry. Raising awareness and making it easy for donors to donate their milk is so important.'

NorthernStar struck me not only as an ethical model, but also as innovative in a practical sense, straddling the best of state and private healthcare. The small-scale community element probably appeals to new mothers who cannot muster the energy to donate to a hospital many miles away, or who just prefer to donate within their own community.

As the full proverb goes, 'Charity begins at home but should not end there.' Currently, NorthernStar is Canada's only community milk bank, but there is an obvious need for something similar in other countries, even countries served by a public healthcare system that funds local banks like the NHS in the UK.

MILK

The structural weaknesses of the NHS milk-banking system – ever stretched – were made clear to me by Marta Staff, a fellow mother who lives near me in Somerset. Marta is a former molecular biologist and a current PhD candidate in operations research who creates models of milk-banking systems, helping policymakers plan infrastructure to ensure adequate supplies. She looks at the birth weights and gestational ages of babies born in past years to model a system that could in future support not just babies with very low birth weight, but others that would still benefit from breast milk. She cites Singapore, a country with high breastfeeding rates, which has enough breast milk to provide to any parent who wants it – the dream scenario.

Ironically, Marta was turned down when she tried to donate her own milk. After she gave birth to twins, she struggled to feed them at first. Then, with her milk supply established, she contacted three NHS milk banks, offering them her frozen supplies. They all said no, two of them explaining that they did not have the capacity to process it. This, I realised, was why the Southmead Hospital milk bank does not advertise for donations.

'I got a bit upset, a bit emotional, as you can imagine – being a new mother and all that energy invested in pumping the milk.'

She told me she ended up pouring it all down the drain. We share a moment of silence, thinking about the waste.

Maybe it does make more sense to share directly from the breast. When I was donating my own milk, I remembered thinking how private that experience was, almost hermetically sealed – how different from the experiences of women in countries where not only sharing milk, but directly feeding someone else's baby is still normal. The practice is poorly documented, particularly online, but I did discover that in rural Mongolia in 2011, cross-feeding was still more common than feeding young babies infant formula.[63] In much of the world, and certainly in the UK, where I live, it is a taboo concept.

Once, it would have existed alongside paid wet-nursing. What has changed? Have we become more individualistic, and more proprietorial of our children, as communities become more disparate?

Why did I initially find it such a disgusting idea?

MONETISED ANXIETY

Experiencing my first pregnancy during the earliest lockdown of the 2020 pandemic was a sharp introduction to maternal anxiety: how it can be exacerbated by isolation, and how money can be made from it.

Every Wednesday during the last six months of my pregnancy, I would wobble slowly on my bicycle to a yoga studio in Amsterdam. There, my mat separated from the other big-bellied, mask-wearing women, I would contort myself into various uncomfortable positions to prepare myself for childbirth. We were told that we could learn to manage our contractions, or 'surges', as they are euphemistically referred to in the language of hypnobirthing, through breath and mental resilience alone. During one of our yoga poses, the teacher clutched my defenceless vulva with typical Dutch candour, and ordered me to relax it.

Was I in a cult? Perhaps, but it seemed prudent to remain enveloped in the soft glow of antenatal grace and candlelight with other believers – a rare instance of community.

At the time, I was convinced that these classes were essential – that without them I would be hopelessly underprepared, that my baby would suffer as I struggled, or maybe failed entirely, to push her out. I was vaguely aware that my maternal anxiety was being exploited, but it didn't matter: greedily, I bought the apps, the books, the courses, feeling grateful for every opportunity to purchase advice. The hypocrisy of commercial hypnobirthing only struck me later: trust yourself, is the message; follow your intuitions – you are a goddess, your body was designed to give birth, you are all-powerful. But you also need to purchase the means to understand and implement this eternal truth.

My anxiety about labour was exacerbated by the knowledge that in the Dutch health system, pain relief like the gas and air given as standard in NHS hospitals is not the cultural norm. According to my health insurance plan – which every resident of the Netherlands must have – if my birth was not 'medically indicated' and I asked for pain relief, I would have to pay extra. This made me think about pain in a new light. What did that even mean? Is palliative care medically necessary? To hedge against whatever might befall me, I hired the scary yoga instructor as my doula, to guide me through labour with a suitably relaxed vagina.

CASH COW

In retrospect, the classes and courses served as a kind of self-soothing therapy. They did not actually prepare me for childbirth; the techniques I had earnestly practised evaporated as soon as my contractions began. My baby got stuck, and I screamed for the forbidden pain relief as an ambulance whisked me to hospital. After I'd given birth, I continued to use the privilege that had meant I could purchase private classes during my pregnancy – in the absence of my own mother, I employed a postpartum doula for a week as a kind of professional alternative. She took the baby while I showered, made me food, told me everything would be all right in my darkest moments. I cried when she left.

If I could afford it, and had it been available, I might even have booked myself into a postpartum hotel or 'confinement centre', like the ones that are wildly popular in Asia (and growing in popularity in the US and UK). Sanctuary or prison, depending on who you ask, these centres look after new mothers and their babies for the month following childbirth, protecting them from well-meaning but tiring visitors (I had none of these, luckily). I became fascinated by the concept, imagining a protective womb holding the fragile, newborn maternal self. The hotels also made me think, surreally, of private rehab clinics – institutions that also combine medical and emotional nurturing in a time of personal upheaval, available only to the wealthy.

After I started writing about the commodification of the maternal body, I realised that mine and my friends' experiences of pre- and post-natal consumerism were part of the same picture. While I was undoubtedly very privileged to have the money to spend on products and services, I felt I was being wrung out, not just in the process of birthing a child, but as a customer. The vast business of selling things to new mothers means that, even back in 2013,[64] identifying a pregnant woman was 200 times more valuable to advertisers than knowing the age, gender and location of a non-pregnant person. It is likely even more valuable now, based on data in the US suggesting that parents now spend 31 per cent of their average household income on raising a baby in its first year of life.[65] We spend like crazy, even as we expend our own physical resources birthing, nourishing, 'producing' a new person, a future consumer. A fertile woman is a capitalist's wet dream – but then, so is an infertile woman, in more specific but no less lucrative ways.

The desire to become a mother is followed closely by the desire to mother correctly; both are lucrative to providers, particularly in a world where the 'village' traditionally required to raise a child is increasingly splintered and difficult to access, especially in hands-on wisdom and care. We look to others for guidance, often in the bowels of Mumsnet at 3 a.m., closely followed by the algorithms of Amazon, possibly via some targeted YouTube channels. Social influencers sharing videos of their children for advertising revenue and brand sponsorship deals is probably the peak manifestation of the monetisation of motherhood: the fascinating and somewhat gruesome world of mum vlogging.

I am as guilty as any of spending money on the dream of sleep, and peace of mind. One thing I thankfully realised would only exacerbate my maternal anxiety was the Owlet

Dream Sock, a gadget that monitors the heart rate and oxygen-saturation levels of a newborn baby, alerting parents to abnormal readings. Its previous model was condemned by the FDA in 2021 and taken off the market because of the high frequency of false alarms.[66] One of my friends, who had hoped its monitoring would allow her to relax enough to get some sleep, described it as 'extremely stressful'.

Years after I obsessively tracked my newborn daughter's consumption of my milk, weighing her on a daily basis and counting the ounces of milk I had pumped that day, I confessed all this to an old school friend, and she said she was currently doing the same with her second baby. We agreed that a desire to track our babies' growth was fundamentally a desire for control – a kind of reverse anorexia. My friend summed it up with grim clarity: 'The part of my brain that is still like a teenage girl counting calories is activated by the tracking.' But we were far from the only target customers for the Owlet Dream Sock.

In my peer group, I have experienced solidarity, support and a great deal of communal joy and humour as we have shared the ups and downs of parenting. But I have also noticed a peculiar kind of unspoken judgement, which can place us in informal and opposing tribes. Our choices to sleep-train, or not sleep-train, our children, or when to stop breastfeeding them, for example, create subtle divisions as we sign up to various schools of parenting. Many of them come with expensive products and expert advice attached, and all of them claim to make your child healthier and happier than the alternatives.

To me, parenting on a societal level often seems more competitive than collaborative – isolating, even. The proverbial village that raises the child is one you must choose, organise and finance yourself. Maybe nothing very fundamental has changed; people spend more time in their own homes, and less time in communal spaces actively parenting together. Either way, living in such a close-knit community that you could casually offer to breastfeed your neighbour's baby, or vice versa, seems unthinkable in my own community. We share our milk discreetly, privately, carefully cleaning the various components of our high-tech pumps and labelling our freezer bags, home alone.

While I was writing this section of the book, I was still breastfeeding my second child. The day I decided to stop pumping, I felt relief, certainly, but also a kind of guilt that I was not 'maximising output' for him. My pump still lies unused in a kitchen cupboard. The next step will be to donate it, but for now it serves as a kind of historical artefact – a reminder of happy servitude.

EGGS

Human oocyte – 100 microns in diameter (visible to the naked eye), approximately 1–2 million at birth, 100 at menopause.

Cost of freezing own eggs: from €1,700 (Ukraine) to > $20,000 (US).

Cost of donor eggs: from $1,500 per cycle (Iran) to POA (US).

Payment to egg donor: from €250 (Finland) to > $50,000 (US).

Sanitary products over a lifetime of roughly 450 periods: approximately US $9,000.

THE EGG FILES

A young woman kneels on a bed, wearing a black corset and arching her back. Her eyes are closed as she tilts her head, blonde hair cascading over one shoulder, hands gripping bare thighs. Her make-up is perfectly applied – pink lip gloss, soft peach eyeshadow, nails shiny black, matching the corset. She could be anywhere between eighteen and thirty.

I check her profile information to find out, swiping past the photos in her file.

Date of birth: 31/03/99
Height: 170cm
Weight: 53kg
Nationality: Ukrainian

It is an intimate scene, but the lighting and white drapery behind the bed suggest a professional photography studio; someone has invested in this shot. Other photos in her file show similar poses, standing in purple lingerie behind the same drapery, fingers pulling slightly at the edges of her knickers. I open another woman's file. These photos are more casual – a brunette gazing over her shoulder on a beach, then close-ups pouting at the camera. I check some details.

CASH COW

Menstrual cycle: Regular
Previous pregnancies: 1
Donated previously: Yes
Number of eggs collected: 25-30

Hers is the last file in a folder containing eighteen profiles of what appear to be mainly Ukrainian egg donors. I open the next folder on the Google Drive, a collection of Kazakh, Uzbek and Kyrgyz women, and Russian women of mixed ethnicity. Another folder appears to contain only white Russian women. The last contains Turkish women.

None of the folders explicitly categorises the women along ethnic or national grounds, but I pick up clues from the profiles themselves, which include some personal information – the names of these women's hometowns, the university or high school they have graduated from, or simply their nationality. In the photos there are also clues. In the first folder, several women express their love for their country by wearing blue and yellow or posing beneath a Ukrainian flag, while one woman is leaning extravagantly against the bonnet of an unremarkable car with a Ukrainian number plate.

The Turkish donors are the easiest for me to spot; I notice an undotted ı in some of the forms, characteristic of a Turkish keyboard, and recognise scenes of Istanbul, my former home, and popular seaside towns in the background of their photos. Later, I discover, with a vague sense of patriotic umbrage, that the eggs of these women are included for free in the price of the IVF package I am being offered. The others cost several thousand euros extra – an avenue to be explored.

These files have been sent to me by an Israeli agency that sources international egg donors and surrogates for their clients, working in partnership with local clinics in low-cost fertility hubs around the world. With some trepidation, I have decided that the best way to understand the global egg market is to apply to some of these agencies as a potential customer of advanced maternal age – someone who needs a younger woman's eggs.

I have been communicating with the agency representatives online and over the phone, knowing that they are skirting the already opaque laws of the countries in which they operate. A few months in to these conversations, I encounter some of their representatives in person at an international event in Dublin. I get to put a face to the names; I hope they don't recognise my voice.

THE FUTURE FERTILITY TRADE SHOW

I have been to trade shows before, but nothing like this. Under the cavernous arches of the Royal Dublin Society's exhibition hall, competing IVF clinics from all over the world have set up colourful stands, festooned with balloons and goody bags, for the Future Fertility Show. Well-groomed, smiling women in lab coats try to catch my eye, like sales reps in duty-free. Swerving aside, I almost collide with a plastic plant, its fronds shaped like sperm, decorating the stall of a bespoke embryo-transporting courier service. On a table next to it, a cryogenic container –

presumably devoid of frozen embryos – stands as a prop. It looks like an oversized Thermos flask.

The variety is dizzying. Some companies offer to analyse my blood, sell me sperm, freeze my eggs, or jump straight in and make an in vitro baby. Others advertise perinatal psychotherapy and counselling for donor-conceived children. Opposite the stand of the European Sperm Bank, I spot some Chinese acupuncturists at work. A heavily punctured member of the public is lying in a somewhat undignified fashion on a treatment bed, under a huge picture of a pregnant woman cradling her belly. As I walk past her, for some reason averting my eyes, I overhear a man in doctor's scrubs talking about the vaginal microbiome; his stall advertises his services as a 'shamanic nutritionist'. Like an undecided punter at Glastonbury, I wander between three stages, each with a packed schedule of talks and panel discussions featuring world-renowned embryologists, family lawyers and fertility-optimising therapists of varying levels of plausibility.

A few stands have brought babies as live props. Many of the exhibitors are wearing suits; it is unclear whether they are from the medical industry or not. Greek, Spanish and Canadian accents are dominant alongside Irish. There are several surrogacy agencies here, hailing from Northern Cyprus and Georgia. Some of them introduce themselves to me, unaware that we have spoken on the phone, and I feel a mixture of panic and guilt. I overhear one man who is, to my trained ear, a Turkish Cypriot from North London. I am sure he is from the world of surrogacy and make a mental note to speak to him later, hoping I can find my way back through the colourful, disorienting maze of slogans and cardboard screens.

It does not help my orientation that this industry show merges seamlessly with its 'sister event', the Future Beauty Show, through an interconnecting arch. Access to both shows, whether you want to attend both or not, cost me €19 for an early-bird single day ticket (the event makes most of its money from the companies who pay to exhibit, but its business model profits in two ways). To get to the Future Fertility Show, I have walked through a similar hall filled with stands advertising biohacking, microdermabrasion and LED treatments. The emphasis seems to be more on rejuvenation than beauty per se – an increasingly blurred line. Eager women are queueing to get their crow's feet and jowls analysed in front of well-lit mirrors; others are waiting to try out an IV drip to infuse their veins with vitamin B12 and selenium.

I watch several of the women wander from the beauty hall into the fertility hall, and vice versa. There is obviously a shared customer base and marketing crossover here: sell women hope, particularly the hope that the end of youth is not the end of hope. As a consumer, being offered the chance to make yourself look younger and more attractive is fundamentally a more upbeat experience than shopping for a cure for your infertility. There is a happy buzz in the beauty hall that is notably absent next door.

The exhibitors in the Future Fertility Show, in common with their neighbours, have paid thousands of euros for the opportunity to be here, and perhaps for a chance to speak on one of the stages (one Canadian rep tells me her company has paid a total of €7,000 for a larger-than-average stand and two panel-talk appearances). The investment shows – in the painstaking preparation of their pocket of territory, in their body language. The adrenaline is obvious – eyes dart around the hall, looking for networking opportunities, checking out competitors, appraising customers.

Most of the couples wandering through the hall are heterosexual, and have a quiet energy. They do not want to be here, and they don't know quite what they are looking for. In a talk about miscarriage and the effects of stress on fertility, I glance around the audience and notice couples sitting together but apart, not touching. They look drawn, anxious. One woman nods adamantly as the speaker mentions the mental exhaustion of trying to conceive, while her partner sits, hunched, impassive, beside her. In many ways, I realise, this is a kind of convention of grief.

I am struck by the extent to which women outnumber men. Many women seem to have come alone – either their partners have stayed at home, or, more likely, they are single. There is no mention of male infertility on the schedules of workshops and talks, despite the fact that half of infertility cases are related to sperm, and that global sperm counts have halved in the past forty years. It is women – for whom the biological clock infamously tolls – who are overwhelmingly targeted by adverts for fertility-related apps, supplements and procedures, and who attend events like this.

One single man stands out; he is tirelessly working the hall, raising his hand to ask questions after talks, approaching reps whenever I spot him. I am oddly touched by how earnestly he is approaching the whole thing, and notice I don't feel the same about the single women here – a double standard, because broody single men are unusual, 'special'. I talk to him and learn that he is looking for advice on the best place to have a baby by surrogate. He is thirty-seven, and says his recent relationships have failed because he is so anxious to have children that potential partners are put off – a familiar story among single women his age. He says he does not know any other single men in his position; I assure him I know of others. We swap email addresses, and I move on.

Scanning the hall, I spot one of the stands that has brought a baby as a prop and decide to investigate. NaPro Technology is the name of the organisation – presumably an IVF clinic – but as I get closer, I notice a stack of business cards on the table emblazoned with the Christian cross. An elderly woman engages me in conversation while her colleague bounces the cheerful baby. NaPro Technology, it turns out, stands for 'Natural Procreative Technology', and was developed by a Catholic doctor called Dr Hilgers, founder of the Saint Paul VI Institute in Canada, 'an environment consistent with Catholic moral principles'.[1]

I scan the leaflet the lady has given me: the pregnancy success rates of their natural cycle-tracking techniques are comparable, apparently, to IVF, and its listed benefits include a lower risk of divorce. (It does not seem to be a serious money-making venture – Dr Hilgers wrote a book that is available to order for CAN $210.[2]) I nod blankly as the lady talks, realising that this is a religious organisation masquerading as medicine.

CASH COW

Fifty metres away, an actual IVF clinic is doing the exact opposite. The Victory Reproductive Care stall has the usual stand, attached to what appears to be a confessional booth. I spot three pairs of feet and some stools under a long black curtain. Dr Rahi Victory, a renowned Canadian fertility doctor whom I met in Dublin the previous evening, is in there giving some discreet advice to a couple. His colleague Lisa, a nurse, tells me the booth has proved wildly popular.

'People love it,' she says. 'They don't like getting to the front of a busy queue, shouting about their miscarriages or infertility in front of strangers. They appreciate having the privacy.'

When Dr Victory emerges, I compliment him on the booth and note it is very appropriate to Catholic Ireland. He laughs, and we talk about the similarities between fertility care and religion; in both, people are seeking some kind of salvation. Often, they have nothing left but a kind of desperate hope, and medical practitioners take on the role of priest, or even saviour. Dr Victory, who describes himself as a deeply religious man, belongs to the Bahá'í sect that fled religious persecution in Iran centuries ago. He takes the priestly comparison with good humour; he long ago noticed that dynamic playing out. The previous evening, we'd had a prolonged debate about God complexes among fertility doctors and a lack of ethics in his industry – a topic I will later debate with an American surrogacy lawyer.

Like a repetitive dream, I traverse the exhibition hall, weaving back and forth between hazily familiar stands. I am drawn back to the sperm fronds of the embryo-courier stall, where its director of operations is gossiping with a surrogacy consultant. The fertility industry, although geographically and financially vast, seems to be a small world – everyone knows everyone, either by reputation or in direct dealings, and I have noticed the same faces cropping up in subsequent fertility shows I have attended. I insert myself into the conversation. They are talking about a couple of notorious couriers who extort parents-to-be by demanding extra money to take their embryos from one country to another, knowing the parents are in no position to argue and will pay almost anything to get their embryos to the target clinic within the tight parameters of IVF treatment schedules.

'It's like kidnapping,' I say. There is a silence; clearly this is an overstatement for these seasoned professionals, and I realise that, much like the Alabama Supreme Court, I have effectively decreed that an embryo is a child.[3] The courier director expresses her surprise that one particularly unethical operator ('K') is still working, despite his terrible reputation. Later, I look K up and discover one-star reviews all over the internet for his London-based services, which are nevertheless recommended by some Harley Street clinics – 'absolute scammer', 'criminal enterprise', 'DO NOT USE'. Three of his five almost identically named companies are listed as dissolved on Companies House; two are active. He has been around for decades, a known name that clinics probably prefer to newcomers. I also look up an apparently ruthless doctor in Mexico City who withholds embryo export permits from foreign parents using his clinic, so that he can control the export procedure – and price – himself. Nothing but glowing reviews, which makes me wonder about relative consumer power in Mexico versus London.

The courier director, who I'll call 'M', is a polished woman in her sixties who has worked in embryo shipping for nearly twenty years. She describes how she chooses and trains her team of sixteen hand couriers, who ironically have few family commitments to ensure they can fly long haul at short notice. M will not tell me what she pays them, or what she charges her clients, because her services are bespoke and 'every journey is different'.

As M talks, she sounds like some kind of spymaster, describing how her agents cross international borders, evading capture. The reality is not so different – armed with highly sensitive genetic material, these couriers must navigate the danger spots of every major airport as the clock ticks and the embryos risk deteriorating if their journey is delayed. Depending on the size of the cryogenic container, the time frame for frozen embryo stability is usually ten days, but this particular company is proud of its guaranteed 24–72-hour door-to-door service – freight can take much longer.

I learn that M's couriers avoid Dublin and Vienna altogether, because airport staff insist on X-raying hand luggage, which would be dangerous to the embryos; they travel by train or taxi to nearby airports instead. Some airline ground staff are convinced that the cylinders contain liquid, although in fact they contain dry ice; her couriers are trained to persuade them otherwise without opening the cylinder to prove it. Greece will only transport embryos to another EU country, so her team will fly from Athens to Slovakia to transfer to countries outside the EU. Spain can be tricky, she says, because even though it is a popular IVF destination, exit permits for embryos can take months to come through.

This was my introduction to the scale of complexity when it comes to international regulations on genetic material, and why an expensive 'bespoke' service is probably worth it. Later, I learned from a Colombian fertility lawyer that while it is legal to ship non-anonymous eggs to Colombia, it is in practice difficult to get them into the country because eggs are considered human tissue. Embryos, by contrast, are genetic material, so different laws apply. A skilled courier has to know all this, and act accordingly.

M speaks scathingly of rival companies that advertise themselves as a hand courier service when actually they send embryos as unaccompanied freight. When I checked out some of her rivals at another fertility show, I was shown a cryogenic container complete with a remotely monitored thermometer attached to the lid, an Apple AirTag enabling customers to track their embryos in transit, and 'a personal embryologist on call throughout the journey' – this made me worry about what might necessitate an emergency call.

When I ask M what the main international routes are, she says there are none – the industry is always in flux, with patients buying eggs or sperm, or freezing their own, in one country and undergoing IVF or pursuing surrogacy in another, while laws and prices change in the intervening weeks and months. Until mid-2024, Argentina was a popular IVF destination, but now the government has tightened export laws for embryos as well as surrogacy laws, so demand among foreign clients has collapsed.

'People are going wherever surrogacy is,' she tells me. 'Northern Cyprus is big, so are Georgia and Colombia. Brazil was big, but no longer.' She tells me which clinics operate 'by the book' in terms of export permits, and which do not. She refuses to work with some of them, including one in Northern Cyprus.

'Is that one still in business?' asks the surrogacy expert incredulously.

I make a note of its name.

ISLAND OF APHRODITE

A month later, I am in Northen Cyprus's capital city of Lefkoşa, in the infamous clinic. It seems as legitimate as all the others, busy, slick, bustling with professional-looking staff. I soon realise it is impossible from appearances to know one clinic from another; potential clients might as well stick a pin in a map bristling with rival names. Even my taxi driver, who was visibly delighted to be taking me to a fertility clinic, craning his head round to congratulate me on my quest to make babies, extolled the virtues of its founding doctor and managing director – 'a very good man!'

By now I had realised that one of the most popular low-cost countries to pursue fertility treatment is Northern Cyprus, which, appropriately enough, happens to be my motherland.

My mother was born and brought up in Lefkoşa, and I spent my childhood summers on the coast.

The numerous fertility clinics in the Turkish Republic of Northern Cyprus, which is recognised only by the Republic of Turkey, operate under much more relaxed laws than those in the south of the island, an EU member state. There is no central body that checks the IVF success results that the clinics publish, and it has no regulatory body, although it is not unique in this – neither does the US.

Laws are variously interpreted by local clinics and agencies, but even clinics that operate by the book offer patients options like gender selection of embryos, which is banned in most countries outside the US. Many of these clinics have a good word-of-mouth reputation, and, crucially, prices for egg freezing and IVF are ultra-competitive in a crowded market (I was quoted around €2,500 by various clinics to harvest and freeze my eggs in Northern Cyprus – about a third of the cost at a private London clinic – and around the same price for IVF treatment). On the flipside, some medical insurance plans – which might insure against medical malpractice – do not include Northern Cyprus in their cover.[4]

Donor egg prices here vary wildly, off the books at least. Women up to the age of fifty-five are allowed to undergo IVF, with their own frozen or donated eggs; in some cases, women over the age of fifty-five are also treated, if approved by the Ministry of Health.[5] Single women and men, as well as unmarried heterosexual and homosexual couples, are eligible to receive treatment and donor eggs or sperm, making Northern Cyprus an all-welcoming, gay-friendly outlier in the non-European market. Commercial surrogacy is a legal grey area – as local lawyers would later admit to me – but in practice it is easily accessible and very popular, at a third or quarter of the cost in the US.

Northern Cyprus has changed a lot since my childhood. Now, I visit every few years with mixed emotions. The familiar landmarks are still there – the Five Fingers mountains looming over the capital, the medieval monasteries, the wild beauty of the Karpaz peninsula; the distinctive dialect; the food. I revel in the familiar. But the island itself has been warped almost beyond recognition by overdevelopment in the last fifteen years. Whenever I drive from Lefkoşa to the coastal city of Kyrenia, I feel I am witnessing the expansion of a Mediterranean Vegas: sprawling casino-hotel complexes cover the crowded coastline, while new, gilt-covered mosques pop up along the highway alongside adverts for Johnnie Walker.

Nearly 2 million tourists come to the north of the island every year, and this includes people travelling for IVF procedures – as I was told in one clinic, 'IVF has seasons like tourism – summer is high season, so is December and then Easter. [Patients] come and make vacation.' Fertility clinics' websites devote paragraphs of marketing spiel to the golden sands of Cyprus, 'home of Aphrodite, the goddess of love and fertility'.

My first encounter with Aphrodite's medical services happened during a chance personal experience. When I was around five months pregnant with my second child, I flew to Cyprus and felt a strange, sharp movement in my belly on the plane. As soon as I arrived, I jumped in a taxi to a maternity hospital on the outskirts of Girne (Kyrenia), where I was ushered into a room with a chain-smoking, unshaven obstetrician whose eyes rarely left his phone. Nonchalantly, he waved a lubricated ultrasound wand over my bump, before stopping and looking intently at the image on the screen. I held my breath, fearing the worst. 'A boy! You're having a boy!' Beaming, he indicated that all was well; the appointment was over. I paid about €40 and left, not entirely reassured.

Three years later, I was back, interviewing doctors and lawyers as a journalist, posing as a customer in some clinics, and marvelling at the changes in some parts of the country. The old walled city of Lefkoşa itself remains much the same, but in its urbanised neighbourhoods the explosion of IVF clinics is striking – I counted seventeen in northern Lefkoşa alone, a city of roughly 100,000 people, and there are more in the coastal towns. Lefkoşa's population is a mix of locals, many of whom are from Turkey, students from Africa and the Middle East, and workers from Asia. In the latter group, I was to discover, are travelling surrogates from Central Asian countries like Uzbekistan, Kazakhstan, Turkmenistan and Kyrgyzstan.

Wealthy ex-pats gravitate to Kyrenia, the gambling capital of the island, which is brimming with foreign-exchange bureaus, casinos and adverts for obscure crypto-currencies. My hotel, on the outskirts of the city, was just a few hundred metres from both a casino and an IVF clinic – which was not, perhaps, a coincidence. The proliferation of both is the result of a local economy that plays to its strengths, offering what more regulated countries cannot. Both sell a form of risk, and business is booming.

Percentages of risk and return pepper all my conversations with patient coordinators and doctors in Northern Cypriot clinics. One doctor told me that if my embryos were deemed to have a 50 per cent chance of success, that would be a great outcome 'for your age', but embryos from an egg donor would have a significantly higher success rate, so would be a wiser investment. Paying a discounted rate upfront for at least two transfers would also be a sensible choice. My age (thirty-seven) was a known factor; the quality of my eggs was not. It seemed more like Russian roulette than poker to me.

Before my arrival, I had contacted several international agencies operating in Northern Cyprus, each of them boasting gloriously imaginative names that no Harley Street clinic would have the chutzpah to use. Most of these agencies are headquartered in Israel, Cyprus or Ukraine, and partner with clinics in low-cost fertility hotspots like Georgia, the Czech Republic and Mexico (Ukraine was the market leader in Europe before the Russian invasion). It was not clear to me how many of the staff at these agencies were actually stationed in Northern Cyprus – I communicated mainly with staff who used Ukrainian telephone codes, rarely Cypriot. A couple of the agencies have a physical office in Limassol on the south side of the island but work with clinics in the north. This is a truly international market, converging on half a Mediterranean island with a militarised border.

I decided to get the most out of my fabricated persona: I was making my enquiries in the capacity of an infertile woman who needed donor eggs to create an embryo with her husband's sperm, plus (potentially, if this didn't work) the services of a surrogate. Hyper-conscious of my existing biological children, this charade felt in equal parts blasphemous and bizarre – I felt like I was cheating on my children by pretending they didn't exist. I had realised, however, that these agencies, operating in a grey market, would be unlikely to respond openly to my questions as a journalist.

After various email exchanges and phone calls, 'Sofia', the patient coordinator of one of the Israeli agencies – a relatively expensive contender – started sending me egg donor files to browse over WhatsApp. The ethnic categorisation of these folders was not strict but seemed fairly consistent – I was curious to know how this affected price. Many photos in the profiles appeared to be borrowed from dating or possibly escort profiles, like that of the woman in the corset. These were sometimes juxtaposed with cute photos of the donor as a baby, to give some idea to the viewer of what her genetic offspring might look like. Some files included photos of the donor posing with her own children, which struck me as problematic but was probably an effective marketing tool – a tantalising glimpse of parenthood for the viewer.

No names at this stage – only details like hair colour, height and weight, and year of birth, though some donors offered more: their full date of birth, or a description of their personality. I would go on to realise that donors in most markets exist on a complex spectrum of knowability – from totally anonymous and without photos (the cheapest and only strictly legal option in some countries, including Northern Cyprus) to 'open ID' or ID release (named and contactable), via everything in between. Access to extra information, or contact with the donor, is priced accordingly.

At the first clinic I visited in Northern Cyprus, I sat in a busy waiting room filled with women and a few men (though many seemed to prefer to wait outside) – some of these couples seemed to be European, some Arab, and there were a couple of older African women, unaccompanied. Nurses in pink scrubs, pink plastic clogs and pink hairnets came and went; I noticed this Barbie-esque uniform crop up in other gynaecology wards and IVF clinics I visited later.

Soon I was summoned into an office for my consultation with a patient coordinator, a forceful Greek Cypriot woman who grilled me on my fertility history. She strongly advised me to get a blood test to have my hormone levels tested, particularly my anti-Müllerian hormone, or AMH – an indication of the number of eggs I have left. The result would be anywhere between around 3 and 50 pmol/l, a number that depends on individual fertility and age. The doctor needed to know my levels before starting treatment – would I come through to the phlebotomy room now?

Although I had no intention of starting treatment, the test cost very little – €30 – and would tell me something potentially interesting. I felt a strange resistance and realised I didn't want to know how many eggs I had left. I would much rather remain ignorant, undefined by a number that would be decreed good, average or poor for a woman of my age. Was this about ageing and mortality, or how I felt about myself as a woman? Was this a relic of my years spent comparing grades at an ultra-competitive all-girls school? Obviously, I did not share these thoughts with the insistent patient coordinator, who looked at me quizzically as I stalled, feeing panicked.

I was scared of knowing a number that did not affect my health in any material way – absurd. With the luxury of already having children, I did not, in reality, need to have my hormones scrutinised, and I told the patient coordinator I would think about getting the test back in the UK. But I felt strangely guilty, in that moment, that I was not emotionally robust enough to undergo even the least invasive of the processes that other women have to undergo for IVF.

Back on the hunt for egg donors, I soon realised that outside of the official setting of a clinic, and certainly on the private channels of a WhatsApp exchange, non-anonymous egg donors seem to be extremely available – when I told a local fertility lawyer that the clinic had only offered me anonymous donors in line with the law, he raised an eyebrow. 'They said that?' he asked incredulously.

At the next clinic I visited in Northern Cyprus, probably the one with the best reputation I'd encountered so far, I pushed a little harder, mentioning that in the UK, anonymous donation is illegal. (The law was changed in 2005, when previously donation had been anonymous, because the Human Fertilisation & Embryology Authority (HFEA) decided that a child's right to know their genetic origins trumped a donor's right to anonymity.[6])

'Well,' said the patient coordinator of the clinic, a middle-aged, non-nonsense Romanian woman, 'you can of course import frozen eggs from a donor of your choosing. That is not illegal.'

What the patient coordinator probably knew is that there is no law in the UK to stop anyone purchasing anonymous eggs or sperm abroad, and a baby born of such a donation is a fait accompli. In Ireland, however, recent changes in surrogacy law stipulate that egg donors, even those used overseas, must be identified with full contact details in pre-approved arrangements entered into by Irish citizens – potentially a problem for the Northern Cypriot market.[7]

Back in my hotel after the clinic visit, I flicked through the donor files on my phone sent to me by Sofia, feeling like a straight man on Tinder. I wondered how I was supposed to make my choice, and thought of the Madonna–whore complex: what kind of desire are potential parents meant to feel for these women? For their appearance, for their genes, for the freshness or the number of their eggs, or for the fact that some of them have proved themselves as mothers – reassurance that their eggs are a reliable investment?

I looked again at the Turkish egg donors in the package offered by the agency – I would pay nothing extra on top of the cost of the IVF package for their eggs, but I would save €10,000 if I used my own eggs, so they did have a market value after all. Then something else caught my eye – €88,000 for the deluxe, 'guaranteed' IVF-plus-surrogate service, i.e. as many attempts as it takes to produce a baby within two years, or your money back. The confidence of this promise took me aback – to what extent was this a plausible offer, or a sensible financial decision on the part of the client – or the agency?

The 'guaranteed' price plan cost only €9,000 more than the 'attempt by attempt' plan (a single cycle of IVF) – surely most clients would be tempted to pay the extra money? I noticed that sometimes Sofia referred to it as the 'unlimited IVF' programme, a daunting and ultimately unrealistic prospect.

Initially assuming this was the kind of offer made in an unregulated market, I later discovered a similar option in the UK from the financing platform Gaia Family, which exists solely to offer fertility patients the option to 'de-risk' their IVF attempts.[8] What they offer to fertility patients has been received as something of a revolution in the UK market although the company now seem to be switching their focus to the US. For an unrefundable protection fee of around £3,000, Gaia ensures that their customers are not charged the full amount for their IVF cycles if they are unsuccessful.[9] If they are unsuccessful after three cycles, they are refunded between 50–100 per cent of their treatment costs. In essence, this struck me as very similar to the 'guaranteed' plan in Northern Cyprus – both share the magic of the classic 'no win, no fee' model.

Sofia, the agency coordinator, who was authoritative but friendly both over the phone and over email, said I would have to pay between €4,000 and €8,000 extra – on top of the €88,000 for the guaranteed programme – for any egg donors from the other folders, meaning the Russian, Ukrainian and Kazakh women.

A back and forth ensues. Our emails have progressed to a WhatsApp text exchange involving superfluous heart emojis. This feels like a courtship, a two-way seduction, that is heading in the right direction. Sofia, who has started calling me 'dear', explains how the donor pricing system works – the women in each folder fall into set price brackets, but she has to double-check the price of each individual woman.

'If you can see one you would choose, I can ask,' she types.

I pick a Russian profile at random, claiming she looks like me, and ask how much her eggs would be.

Four thousand five hundred euros, comes the answer.

I ask if the price depends on the woman's nationality and wait, curious for her reply as she types.

'Yes it is by nationality as it depends on their tickets to come here for egg donation etc. so the prices range.'

I stare at the text sceptically. This makes sense, up to a point. I know that fertility clinics in Northern Cyprus often use student egg donors from the many local universities on the island, many of whom are not ethnically Turkish or Turkish Cypriot. These young women require no transport or accommodation costs, and are paid a few hundred euros per egg retrieval, though this is not a fixed payment, as I was to discover. They undergo the usual egg-retrieval process: starting on day two to three of their menstrual cycle, they inject themselves with hormones to stimulate their ovaries to produce many more eggs than usual; every couple of days, the clinic monitors their progress with ultrasound scans and blood tests.

Around ten days later, a trigger shot of egg-maturing hormone is injected. The following day, the eggs are harvested under sedation (or general anaesthetic, as I discovered was the norm here), and the women go home. Overall, it is a process of a few weeks, factoring in the wait for the individual donor's natural menstrual cycle to begin, and it is exactly the same process that women undergo to freeze their eggs for their own future use – the only difference is that the clinic pays the woman, rather than vice versa.

So why was I unconvinced by the rep's explanation for the Russian donor costing more? It made sense that harvesting fresh local eggs – especially on an island like Cyprus – is simpler for the clinics than buying and flying in frozen eggs from abroad, with all the complications of import and export permits, paperwork exchanges and extra commissions to other agencies involved. There is also a greater risk of damaging frozen eggs during the thawing process, for which the clinic bears the cost. Frozen eggs require a specially trained embryologist to perform a process called ICSI (intracytoplasmic sperm injection), directly injecting the sperm through the brittle shell of a thawed egg – it is around 25 per cent more expensive than standard IVF in the UK.[10] Not all clinics offer it.

Most clinics prefer fresh to frozen eggs, but if clients require particular physical or ethnic characteristics not provided by local donors, more expensive 'travelling donors' must be engaged. I was sceptical of the rep's explanation of the higher prices because I knew that travelling donors are often paid a lot more than just their air travel and accommodation – they are not recouping costs but making an income. While they usually operate in higher-cost fertility markets like the US, they also operate in Northern Cyprus – one clinic in the city of Famagusta, for example, is officially partnered with a South African company literally called Traveling Donors.[11] As another agent told me: 'Young girls, they are coming and going, let's say the donor is charging €5,000 plus transport and accommodation . . . It climbs to €10,000 easily.'

My suspicions that phenotypes are relevant to pricing were confirmed by a rival fertility agency in Northern Cyprus, cheaper than its competitors. Its customer liaison is noticeably less polished; the coordinator, 'Oksana', speaks poor English and juggles my call with others. She confirms that the clinic uses only fresh egg donors, and that they are usually local university students. More expensive options – from a folder she sends me entitled 'VIP Donors' – are flown in from Russia, and each profile comes with a password-protected video. Then the truth bomb from Oksana:

'Girls with blonde hair and blue eyes more expensive,' she tells me matter-of-factly. 'They have more model appearance. And these girls cost €600, the others are 450.'

I nod sagely, as though this is perfectly normal information to receive. Then I notice my voice recorder has stopped, so I restart it and ask her to repeat what she has just said. She complies, to my surprise. This is not controversial to her. What she has quoted me is in fact a suspiciously bargain price compared to the more expensive agency, but it confirms the same pricing pattern.

LAWS OF ATTRACTION

I find myself looking through the egg donor files almost obsessively, hunting for clues like a stalker. The Google Drive filled with categorised folders is regularly updated by the agency that first sent it to me, and after a few weeks I notice some folders appearing titled with the acronyms of rival agencies. I begin to recognise the same photos cropping up, and realise that the agencies share a pool of women, presumably receiving a cut when one of 'their' donors is chosen by a competitor's client. It is hard not to think of this as pimping.

Comparing the model poses interspliced with photos of their children, I think about the pressures on women to appear sexy while also maternal – in the sense of capable of producing life – until we become sufficiently old enough to drop out of the game. For egg donors, the cut-off stipulated by most clinics is around thirty, or at most thirty-five – a brutal acknowledgement of real-life biology. Clinics will not invest beyond that point.

Swiping through the photos, I wonder how I would feel if I were browsing these photos alongside my husband; how would I feel when he pointed out the woman he liked? I am of course aware of which women I find more beautiful than others, even if I am not sexually attracted to them. I realise that all of my superficial ideals of beauty have come bubbling to the fore.

Feeling troubled by the thought experiment, I force myself to answer the question: if I had to choose one of these women's eggs, whose would it be?

I instinctively start browsing for a woman who looks like me. None of these donors do, at least by my own estimation. Some of them at least have brown eyes and hair – so do I want a brunette Russian, Ukrainian, Kazakh or Turkish woman? I decide she should be Turkish, to match my ethnic background.

But the Turkish brunette I alight upon is not very physically attractive, though she looks friendly and un-vain in her pictures – beaming toothily rather than pouting. She has a normal, un-honed body, no make-up, no filter. Perhaps this is the kind of genetic personality type I should be aiming for? I fail to convince myself.

Most of the profiles come with comments from the donor about their personality and life goals, and a little message about why she has decided to donate her eggs. Some read as glib and insincere, while others sound surprisingly authentic, or matter-of-fact (one Turkish woman states that her reason for donating is 'saving money'). Some have chosen to share details like their religious values, or whether they are on birth control – others have not. I realise that I find the mysterious ones in some ways more compelling; it is easier to imagine them as the ideal fantasy donor, unsullied by mundane facts: a Pygmalion creation of the perfect woman, with perfect eggs to match.

One day, I spot a new folder in the Google Drive called 'VIP'. It contains a collection of profiles of different ethnicities including Kazakh, Croatian, Belarusian and, to my surprise, one Iranian woman. Noticeably more effort has been made with these profiles, which include information on nose shape and size. ('Sourpuss' was a surprising category entry. I have never knowingly seen a sourpuss nose.)

One donor writes passionately about her proficiency at table tennis. Another's photos include apparently authentic shots of her performing as a ballerina; I wonder what the hormonal and physical toll of ovarian stimulation feels like on opening night. Another, who has included several photos of her school-age daughter taken in a studio, says she is fluent in five languages. Some of the descriptions of their personalities have something that set them apart, but many are written in suspiciously correct, AI-sounding platitudes.

What differentiates these profiles from those on more reputable international donor databases I have browsed is the implausible healthiness of not only the donors themselves, but all their family members. Almost every single profile has zero family history of any ill health whatsoever; unchecked boxes listed a range of conditions from acne to suicide attempts via asthma, blood disorders, cancer, migraines, alcoholism and Alzheimer's. Boxes for siblings, parents or grandparents – all unchecked. It felt like I was looking at the medical records of the perfect genetic specimens in the sci-fi film *Gattaca* – and that they were equally fictional.

The absence of information is so uniform I assume the donors are advised to leave the boxes blank by their recruiters. Only one folder, stamped with a logo from a fertility agency based in St Petersburg, contained thorough and more honest-sounding information, including the birth and death dates of extended family members. Even in those, I found only one case of a grandparent who had died of cancer, versus two who had died in a car accident, and one of an electric shock.

As I looked through these health histories, I was reminded of a conversation with my friend 'Jessica Rabbit' (her choice of pseudonym), who, aged nearly forty and single, used her own eggs and sperm from a Danish donor to undergo successful IVF at a London clinic in 2023. She rejected one potential candidate on the basis of his family history of cancer, divulged in his profile.

'There was a guy that I quite liked in the US,' she told me, as she cradled her baby in an East London café. 'But his mother had died of cancer when she was thirty-nine. If I had a partner whose mother had died when she was thirty-nine, it would not have crossed my mind not to have a child with him. But when I'm actually purchasing sperm, for €4,000 . . . it put me off, massively.'

Jessica's sperm hunting helped me shed some light on the egg market. Despite some differences (for example, the fact that sperm donors are compensated much less than egg donors on the international market, even though sperm is easier to value in terms of its quality), there were commonalities for the consumer – like the higher prices associated with knowing more about your donor. Jessica's choice was limited by the fact that, in the UK, fertility clinics only work with specific banks. Her clinic worked with two banks in the UK at the time, two in the US and two in Europe. Jessica was given strict instructions about which kind of sperm to buy.

'At the clinic, they tell you, "Please don't buy shit sperm. Just spend the money on some good sperm because the likelihood of success is so much higher."'

'Shit sperm' is, of course, Jessica's characteristic turn of phrase, but it did strike me that 'shit eggs' sounds more aggressively sexist – I would later hear both terms used by industry professionals. Interestingly, it is much harder to differentiate 'shit eggs' from 'good eggs', which cannot specifically be tested for quality (it is only known that eggs deteriorate and deplete with age). Sperm samples can be tested for motility (how well they swim), and those with low motility are cheap; the cheapest are so poor they can only be used with the more expensive process of ICSI rather than regular IVF, which must result in some cases in a false economy. Sperm's motility rating gives it an easily quantifiable market value, distinct from the attributes of the donor.

I came to realise, however, that eggs are a more mysterious and risky purchase – with no motility rating, no metric beyond the number harvested at the last retrieval or the AMH level in the donor's blood. The quality is unknown, except in a general sense by any clinic that has successfully created embryos with them previously (embryos can be graded). The eggs' value on the open market is determined more by how well the donor presents herself – a rather obvious analogy for the value of women in society. Her looks have no scientific bearing on the health of her eggs, beyond the obvious: youth is relevant, but no guarantee of success. It seems obvious to me, surveying photos of grey-market donors, that the value of human eggs is in the eye of the beholder.

Jessica soon realised that once she had screened out the low-motility sperm, 'there is fuck all sperm available' – at least in the UK, where you are not allowed to buy from anonymous donors, and if you want certain criteria in looks.

'I filtered for blue eyes, like me, because I wanted people to not ask too many questions. I wanted the baby to look like me. There were two available men in the British banks, and hardly any info on them. Neither seemed very appealing.'

I asked Jessica why not. She winced slightly before answering.

'One was a bus driver. I know that sounds awful, but – am I choosing to buy the sperm of a bus driver whose photo I can't even see? No.'

Despairing, Jessica looked at the American banks, where she was struck by the extent to which you can pay to see more.

'I didn't actually want to pay extra to see an adult photo. I found that a bit off-putting in a way – it suddenly becomes way more about looks. They become more like a father than a donor.'

Finally, Jessica looked at the European banks, one of which particularly appealed to her because she had read that donor applicants had to undergo eighteen months of counselling before being allowed to donate (how rigorously this is applied is debatable). There were plenty of Danish donors, some of whom were blue-eyed. One of the banks offered good-motility sperm for around £3,000 (including transport), the other £4,000. Donor profiles included a handwritten note to any future children, photos of the donor as a baby, and voice recordings (in the US, some banks offer face-matching technology, to match the intended parent or a celebrity). Jessica was eventually left with seven candidates after she had applied her filters and decided she only wanted to pay £3,000.

For moral support in this lonely process, she headed over to a friend's house with her laptop to narrow down her shortlist and submit the forms. I asked her what the final choice involved. Her voice was flat as she answered.

'It was a process of elimination rather than a positive choice. Oh – this baby looks like it might grow up a bit weird-looking. Oh – this guy sounds like an arsehole, I don't want him. Oh – this guy seems fine . . . OK.

'So that's how I chose.'

FAKE EGGS

I started to wonder how easy it was to become a donor. At thirty-seven, I was too old to put myself forward as a genuine contender, so I experimented with a twenty-seven-year-old alter ego, with an entirely Caucasian-sounding name. I applied to one of the private hospitals that process donors in Northern Cyprus; on the online form, I answered questions about my menstrual cycle and general gynaecological health. Then the tricky bit: a photo taken within the last three months.

A paranoid part of me did not want to provide a real photo, not just because I do not look twenty-seven, but also because there are photos of me on the internet corresponding to my real name. Perhaps the clinic staff would use reverse Google

Images (unlikely), but the truth was, I just felt strange about using my real face – the same way I felt strange video-calling fertility reps when I was claiming to be an infertile, childless woman. It felt wrong, almost in a superstitious way; not like an abstract experiment but something more real, more potent – like when I gave my breast milk to a random man in the name of research. Something in my gut said no.

I pondered – very briefly – whether I knew a woman in her twenties who would consent to me using her photo, but this was a tricky one to broach. Then the obvious solution: I could use AI to create a fictional woman. I chose OpenArt, which creates portraits of various competing styles and of varying quality (most users want to create personalised avatars for online games, rather than photorealistic portraits). I typed into the prompt box to transform my idea into an image: 'Blonde young woman smiling on her couch, realistic, natural lighting.'

The first attempt was disastrous – clearly not a human at first glance. The second, using a different generative model, was much better – realistic, attractive, plausibly a woman of twenty-seven with no obvious glitches to give it away. I submitted it, along with a completed form, and the next day received a WhatsApp message from a representative from the hospital initiating a conversation. I panicked – what if she requested a video call? Clearly, I had failed to think this through.

Later, in Northern Cyprus, I felt bolder, presenting my physical self for inspection. I drove in a little hired car with squealing tyres to the largest and most prestigious university on the northern half of the island – a sprawling campus of brick student accommodation blocks, acres of manicured lawns and finally, after a few wrong turns, its campus hospital.

It loomed above me with glass-plated towers like a steely-blue Emerald City of Oz, its entrance shaped like a giant metal heart. I knew students were recruited as donors here. I passed through an extraordinary lobby featuring a futuristic golden sports car on a podium, found my way up to the IVF department and approached the desk, trying to look as young and fertile as possible. I introduced myself as a potential egg donor: thirty years old, with regular periods.

'OK,' said the woman at the desk, looking me up and down. Here, I was being clinically appraised as a potential investment, not seduced as a customer.

'When is your next period due?'

In two weeks, I told her.

'OK, come in then and we will scan you. Do you have an AMH test result?'

I chose a number – high, but not implausibly so.

'Good,' she said approvingly. 'Blood type?'

I told her; she made a note. I asked if I needed to bring any paperwork to the scan. She shrugged – I should just come with my printed AMH result.

Then I asked how much I would be compensated. The woman looked away and smiled slightly, as though this was a somewhat indelicate question.

'The more eggs you give us, the more money you receive.'

So how much might that be?

'It starts at €400 for minimum eight to twelve eggs, and goes up to €1,400. Some donors, they give us a lot of eggs – forty or more.'

I tried not to look surprised. This was the first I had heard of payment per eggs, and it took me a moment to digest – the more fertile you are, the higher your financial reward. This made business sense for the clinic, obviously, who want to maximise their return – they do not want to lose money paying a donor more than the amount they have invested in the retrieval and potential sale of their eggs. But €400 seemed very low to me, especially set against the roughly €1,000 compensation available to anonymous donors in altruistic markets like Spain and the UK. More than that, there seemed something very utilitarian about it. Later, I noted in donation-related guidelines published by the American Society for Reproductive Medicine (ASRM) that 'compensation should not vary according to [. . .] the number or quality of oocytes retrieved'.[12]

The donors here were young students, obviously needing the cash, going through the same hormonal and personal disruption as any other woman undergoing egg retrieval. Later, I mentioned this price range to T, the Turkish Cypriot fertility agent I had overheard talking in his distinctive accent at the Dublin Future Fertility Show. He had previously worked in Northern Cyprus but had since branched out to Georgia and Colombia. When I mentioned the compensation range I'd been offered, he looked shocked.

'What? That is the lowest compensation I've ever heard of. But I guess the Turkish lira is really weak at the moment – it's still attractive for students.'

I thought for a moment about the implications of payment per egg. Extremely fertile women – or those whose ovaries responded most strongly to hormonal stimulation – would not only be producing more eggs per retrieval, but would be more incentivised to donate in future. While egg retrievals are generally deemed to be safe, the data on the long-term effects of regular ovarian stimulation is not yet known. Another thought: the genetic offspring of these women could, theoretically at least, be significantly more numerous than their less fertile competitors, if you chose to see it in a Darwinian sense.

Later, I found out that while Northern Cypriot law limits donors to three retrievals per year, some cash-strapped donors do not 'rest' for the recommended three to four months between retrievals, donating again immediately at a different clinic, and then another. T told me that habitual donors produce progressively fewer and less viable eggs – they are therefore less reliable investments, and he avoids them. There is no overall limit of donations per donor in Northern Cyprus, and no limit to the number of families a single donor is allowed to create.

Before I left the hospital, I asked the egg recruiter if she needed any particular ethnicities of donor, if I were to spread the word among my friends.

'All of them, we are interested,' she said. 'We have too many patients on the waiting lists at the clinics. Just, it is important that they don't do drugs or alcohol.'

I nodded my agreement and turned to go.

'Text me on the first day of your period!' shouted the woman as the door swung behind me.

I felt flattered.

The very cursory vetting I received as a wannabe egg donor strengthened some doubts I was developing about donor identity. Some of the women I was looking at in the donor files appeared to have had so many cosmetic procedures done that it was hard to know what they – or their genes – really looked like, let alone whether they had the natural blonde hair I might be paying extra for. The filters did not help either. Even as a legitimate client, I would probably never meet these women and would have no way of identifying their eggs. It felt like I could be catfishing among the catfishers; these women seemed as ethereal as the crypto-currencies advertised for sale in Northern Cyprus.

At a clinic in Famagusta, the 'patient experience' manager I met told me that the clinic only used anonymous donors, in line with local laws, and warned me against buying 'known' donor eggs.

'Some of the [non-anonymous donors] are a scam – they can easily show you a girl's picture, but maybe she is not available. They will give you eggs from a woman who looks similar.'

The global human egg market is notoriously difficult to track in terms of its individual players, but it operates on a huge scale: a crack team of Bloomberg reporters in 2024 calculated that a human egg is extracted roughly every fifteen seconds somewhere in the world. Northern Cyprus is just one corner of an international network comprised of donors, clinics and a huge number of recruiters and middlemen. Some of the agencies now operating in Northern Cyprus moved from Ukraine soon after the outbreak of war in 2022, when cylinders of frozen human gametes were rushed out of the country like precious mini refugees.

One Ukrainian customer rep I speak to, 'Maks', tells me he is a doctor who has made a new life for himself and his family in Cyprus. His medical background, he says, informs his current job, although he seems to spend much of his day sending me emails with new offers of discounts, or simply pleading with me to answer his previous emails. The fact that he works on commission is painfully obvious. I have a stressful moment just before one of our scheduled video calls when I realise a photo of my infant daughter is visible behind my desk – I swivel my laptop away with seconds to spare.

Later, I learn that his particular agency has no physical presence on the island, no office – they are 'just a commissioning agency', sending cases to a separate agency for them to handle on the ground after preparing the contracts and taking their cut. While I doubt that this is explicitly illegal in Northern Cypriot law, it does make me worry about who is actually taking responsibility for the surrogates they employ.

Another rep tells me that I cannot import my own frozen eggs or embryos into Northern Cyprus from a London clinic because the laws have recently changed: I can only have new embryos created in a local Cypriot clinic. I ask other reps to confirm this; none of them have heard of the law, even when I follow up a few weeks later, and one rep notes it would be catastrophic for business. I wonder if it had been a genuine mistake (possibly the agent had become confused about a local law that makes it difficult for a patient's own eggs to be implanted in a surrogate, without a medical certificate of infertility) or a ploy to get extra business for the agency's affiliated IVF clinic.

Many of the reps I speak to seem to be slightly surprised that I am not a single woman or a lesbian. 'In Cyprus we usually help gay couples, single men and single women,' Maks tells me dubiously. I am advised by several of his rivals that I should go to their sister clinics in Georgia or Greece, because I am married and heterosexual – the process is the same price or even cheaper there than in Cyprus, and the paperwork is easier. 'No sense paying more,' 'Oksana' tells me helpfully.

It pays to be straight, even if you're infertile; Georgia does not permit IVF treatment to gay couples. Meanwhile, I discover that for Americans, the gay-friendly, cheap alternative countries are currently Mexico and Venezuela. Later, an international surrogacy expert tells me that Northern Cyprus is a favoured destination for Irish gay couples – something I am soon to see for myself.

Piece by piece, I am putting together an idea of what the customer base looks like for fertility treatments in Northern Cyprus. I notice a number of women in the older middle-age bracket in the waiting rooms of the clinics I visit, reflective of the laws that allow treatment for women aged up to fifty-five. I also notice that some of the egg donor profiles I have been sent have Mandarin translations alongside the English. In China, access to IVF is restricted to married, heterosexual couples, and donated eggs can only come from women undergoing IVF themselves, so there are almost none available – I was interested to see that Chinese patients are in the market for Caucasian donors.

Most agencies' webpages offer translations in Arabic, French and German, and I later find out that the biggest clinics here seek out patient coordinators fluent in these languages, plus Romanian and Albanian. In the IVF clinic in Famagusta, I am told that their Arab patients come mainly for egg and sperm donation, which is not allowed in their home countries, 'and because IVF is not very developed'.

Their many British patients come for just one thing: gender selection, which is illegal in the UK. I got a sense of this myself a couple of months after the Dublin fertility show, when I attended the London Fertility Show at Kensington Olympia. I asked an embryo courier company to quote me a price to transport my eggs from London to Northern Cyprus. 'Sex selection, right?' asked the rep, beaming widely.

I have not come across a single Black donor in the agency folders and wonder how much the agencies charge their Black clients to source one. One clinic rep tells me, 'We have some, but it is difficult to find them. We have many clients from West Africa who want them.' In a restaurant in Kyrenia later that day, I start chatting to a waitress, a business student from Cameroon, and ask her whether she has ever heard of the egg-donation scene at her university. She has not and asks how much is to be made. Feeling conflicted – I don't want to encourage her to embark on such a major procedure – I tell her. To my relief, she is not tempted. 'That seems like not very much money to sell your eggs.'

I am introduced via a contact to a local businessman, 'Latif', who has recently started up an IVF clinic on the outskirts of Lefkoşa. He knows I am a journalist and is just as interested in the information I can give him about his rivals as I am in his insider intel – I start to feel like I am getting involved in a cartel. He tells me he had a client who insisted on an Ethiopian donor, who could not be found. Latif shows me donor applicant files on his phone ('we will not accept them all'); out of maybe forty I scroll through, most with Turkish names, I spot one Black woman.

He tells me that he prefers not to offer non-anonymous donors to his clients because they become obsessed with the photos. 'They become very demanding. Sometimes they use an app to analyse the [donor's] face; they say, "You told me she is Ukrainian, but AI says she is from Moldova!" It is a big hassle. Or they search for her online, they send her a message on Facebook, make her feel uncomfortable – this is not good.'

Latif is also dissatisfied with local donors, he tells me; recently, embryos made from their eggs have been failing transfer attempts at his clinic. The fault is possibly with the technicians or doctors, but he has heard a rumour that local donors have been selling their egg-stimulating medications in Turkey (where most of them are produced anyway, and later sold to other markets like Georgia). The donors then buy cheap Chinese alternatives to take instead. I am somewhat impressed by the initiative of these women playing the system, and make a mental note that these black markets do not contribute to official fertility industry stats.

Once, as I speak to Latif on the phone, he sounds stressed and asks if he can call me back – he is passing through the checkpoint at the border, on his way back from buying medication in a clinic in the south of the island. He wanted to ensure that his recently hired donor, who has just started her period and is ready to start treatment, is injected with legitimate meds under supervision. At the London Fertility Show, I discussed medication protocol with a Georgian fertility agent and asked him whether he trusts his donors to inject themselves during the ten-day process. He scoffs.

'If I'm investing that much money in a donor, I'm supervising the hormone injections myself. She has to do it my way.'

KOSHER EGGS

One agent I spoke to, 'Helen', was noticeably more polished and credible than her competitors – warm, sympathetic, knowledgeable. She invited trust. She told me she'd had a child by surrogate years ago and felt strongly protective of parents in my situation (one of the many moments I felt guilty and uncomfortable in these conversations). She confirmed what I already knew – that even though Northern Cypriot law allows only anonymous egg donation, local clinics allow customers access to 'open' or 'ID-release' donors, meaning that as a customer, you pay extra to receive eggs from a donor whose contact details are kept and updated by the clinic (at least in theory), and who agrees to be contacted by any potential biological child on their eighteenth birthday.

While idly looking up where to donate my hypothetical eggs, I was surprised to find that Cryos, the world's largest international sperm and egg bank, had a local egg bank in Cyprus's capital Nicosia, but in the south, i.e. the Greek side of the city. Cryos, founded in 1987 in Denmark, ships sperm and eggs from both anonymous and open donors to over one hundred countries, but, until recently, it had only two clinics to process egg donations: one in Denmark, the other in Cyprus.

The bank was mired in controversy in 2021 after the *New York Times* reported on the lax international laws that meant the notorious 'super donor', Dutchman Jonathan Meijer (a veteran donor at Cryos and flagrant abuser of the national Dutch limit of twenty-five recipient families per donor), had fathered hundreds of children by donating to multiple sperm banks, unchecked. He continued to donate to Cryos, possibly under a pseudonym, even after being banned from donating by a court in the Hague in 2023. However, the *New York Times* reported that Cryos claimed to a recipient that they had destroyed existing stores of his sperm in 2019.[13] It is possible that such a large bank could not keep track of such vast quantities of one individual's sperm.

When I next checked the Cryos website, the egg donation centre in Cyprus had vanished from its listings. I got in touch; Kristine, a customer services representative, explained that they had stopped recruiting in Cyprus indefinitely because 'we now have a very large donor pool' and were only accepting new donors in Denmark. Knowing the extent of demand, I was only half convinced by this explanation, particularly when a sales consultant I'd emailed separately told me the reason for the closure was that they were preparing to open a fertility clinic instead.

I wondered if Cryos had strayed too close to the wind with their open-ID donor programme in a country whose anonymity laws are more strictly enforced. If they were a less well-known company, I imagine they would have been better off running their bank north of the border, where, as I had now established, local laws also prohibit non-anonymous donation but are lax in implementation.

When I asked Helen how she circumvented the Northern Cypriot laws, she cheerfully explained a 'go-around'.

'We can't offer an open donor to you directly from the clinic, so if you want one we show you the open donors, you choose one and send it to us, and say, "We want this." And we can go with that. It is an extra €4,000 to €20,000 or more, depending on criteria. These donors are giving you names, contact details, some are even willing to meet before the donation, and then to be part of your child's life.'

With a degree of honesty I did not encounter from anyone else, she pointed out the drawbacks of this extra cost. Nothing is guaranteed — the donor might agree to be contacted but then disappear off the face of the earth. 'You're paying tens of thousands of dollars for this woman's eggs, and she might vanish. She will also have all of your information. If it's open on one end, it's open on the other. She might be wonderful, but we never know where anyone is going to be in ten to twenty years' time; we don't know if you would actually want her in your life.'

I asked Helen what kind of donors are available for €20,000.

'[Those from] a credited modelling agency. Extremely beautiful donors will be charging quite a bit. Or donors who are in medical or law school . . . certain types of ethnicities . . . Jewish donors, some kind of "kosher" donors – they do some ceremony to bless the eggs, I think?'

At this point, my faith in this agent faltered and a spot of research confirmed my doubts. Rather than egg-blessing ceremonies, Jewish agencies like the Chosen Egg Bank have much more stringent checks at source. They guarantee to clients that all their donors undergo a test by a rabbinical court (*beth din*) to ensure they are Jewish and single – something that is important for Orthodox Jews who want to ensure the maternal lineage of their child (in some strict interpretations, the donor must be single so that she could theoretically be considered married to the father). The donor's egg harvesting is then overseen by a member of the PUAH Institute, an Israel-based organisation that ensures fertility treatments comply with Jewish law.

I tried to imagine the reality of this particular security check: a representative in an operating room, watching doctors insert a long needle through an unconscious woman's vagina. When the eggs are unfrozen in the lab, that is also supervised by one of PUAH's 150 'discreet' female supervisors.[14] It seems – at face value at least – to be the most rigorous third-party checking process on the market.

EGGS

The majority of the international human egg market does not work along the lines of the Chosen Egg Bank, or even pretend to. Most agencies working to get donor eggs to the highest-paying clinics and patient-clients available work around the parameters of what is legal, and many have no online presence at all, sourcing donors via word of mouth. Others present respectable facades to the world, while sourcing their eggs via agents who in some cases prey on women desperate for money, and who are in no position to advocate for decent medical care. These women risk being paid much less than the promised sum, or nothing at all.

Some of these agencies' activities are definitely illegal, some legally grey, and much of what they do is unpoliced, certainly in terms of international checks (as was the case with Jonathan Meijer's donations). Travelling donors stopped by immigration officers at airports are trained by their handlers not to state their real reason for travel, but to claim instead that they are visiting friends. In 2024, as part of an investigation by Bloomberg – which has consistently been at the forefront of reporting in this area – the journalist Jessica Brice personally followed two shipments of frozen eggs on a nearly 8,000-mile journey from Buenos Aires to California.[15] Only one shipment was registered (and valued at $135, despite the donor being paid $35,000 for the eggs). The FDA admitted they held no record of the other shipment. (I can only imagine the disgusted reaction of my contact, M, the suave operations officer at the bespoke embryo courier service.)

The Bloomberg investigation also uncovered an underground network of agents and clinics operating in the northern Indian city of Varanasi and in the southern state of Tamil Nadu, which preyed on impoverished women – and in some cases underage girls – by offering the equivalent of a couple of hundred dollars for a round of eggs worth thousands to the clinics collecting them. The greed involved in this was staggering to me. A network of fertility clinics in India called Nova, implicated in the egg retrievals of underage girls and women in Varanasi, was founded by a New York-based private equity firm and is worth around $11 million; Goldman Sachs is one of the main stakeholders. Later, I would discover just how heavily private equity and venture capital firms have invested in the fertility industry as a whole.

One thing I had come to realise by this point was that women are rarely the primary beneficiary, in financial terms, of their own eggs. In a capitalist world, this was not particularly surprising – what interested me was how differently certain cultures view women 'selling' versus 'donating' their eggs. In the competitive market of the US, I discovered, the language of altruism euphemistically cloaks any suggestion of commerce.

A GIFT MORE PRECIOUS THAN GOLD

'Should I donate my eggs for money? Are there other reasons?'

The website of the Pacific Fertility Center in San Francisco poses deep existential questions. Women interested in donating to this particular agency might be motivated by the upper echelon of $20,000 offered per cycle of egg retrieval (the US average is around $5,000 to $10,000). Other women with perhaps a hefty student loan to pay off might gravitate towards Elite Fertility Solutions in Southern California, which is one of the clinics in the area that offer substantial compensation to women with high SAT scores or an Ivy League degree, or who are of a particular ethnicity or phenotype – or both (Asian and Jewish donors are in particularly high demand; a doctor at one New York clinic told me she was scheduled to perform an egg retrieval on a Jewish donor charging $50,000 – a cost ultimately borne by the intended parents). Other agencies claim to pay their most desirable egg donors up to $100,000, a striking comparison to the strict cap of €250 received by Finnish donors.[16]

In the US, unlike in the UK, it is legal for fertility clinics to offer any amount of money in exchange for a single cycle of 'donated' eggs. The eggs extracted from an individual by a clinic or hospital are always referred to as 'donations'; the individual is always a 'donor' and the money they receive is always 'compensation' or 'reimbursement', never payment. When I started looking into fertility clinics in the US, this euphemism was so prevalent that I was compelled, even as a native English speaker, to double check the definition of 'donate' ('*to make a gift of*, especially *to contribute to a public or charitable cause*' according to Merriam-Webster).

In 2011, an unexpected legal battle put the value of human eggs in the spotlight. Before this point, the guidelines of the American Society for Reproductive Medicine (ASRM) specified a limit of $5,000 (or up to $10,000 in exceptional cases) per cycle to be given in compensation to egg donors. In April that year, however, an American woman called Lindsay Kamakahi sued the ASRM, claiming that its guidelines were a form of illegal price-fixing in violation of US anti-trust laws.[17] A motion from the ASRM to dismiss the case was denied, and four years later, Kamakahi was victorious: the ASRM lifted their guidelines on price.

It was not, however, the start of some kind of egg-related gold rush. For scholars of medical ethics and anti-competition lawyers – and me – the case is a fascinating one, particularly as the standard compensation given by most donation-processing clinics in the US is still around $5,000 to $10,000, around a decade later.[18] Some clinics, as mentioned above, far exceed that offer, but there seems to be a natural squeamishness when it comes to exchanging large amounts of money for human eggs, even in the US.

In many parts of the world, such as Europe, that squeamishness is very much baked in to law. In Germany, although sperm donation is legal, egg donation is not because of the perceived problem of 'split motherhood' (the existence of a genetic mother as well as a birth mother), meaning patients who need donor eggs to conceive are forced to travel abroad.[19] In the UK and in EU countries, the compensation for egg and sperm donation is capped relatively low, and is intended not to act as a financial incentive but to cover expenses – the cost of travel, days taken off work. In the UK, the cap is £985 per egg cycle, and £45 for sperm. The cap in European countries for egg donation is around €1,000, but Finland offers the lowest amount in Europe at €250 per egg cycle. According to one Finnish agency, 'for the recipient, the donated egg is a gift more precious than gold, and in reality, its value cannot be measured in money at all'.[20]

Yet abstract value has a way of being measured, even in the world of altruistic donation. Private clinics and hospitals in London offer 'egg-sharing' schemes where women are offered IVF for free in return for donating half their harvested eggs to the hospital, to be used by other patients.

Theoretically, this is a pragmatic, win-win opportunity. In practice, it can lead to some painful decisions. According to the rules of one London clinic's egg-sharing scheme, for example, if a woman produces fewer than eight eggs (the minimum required for a fifty-fifty share), she can keep them all if she agrees to pay for full-price IVF, or donate four, and be left with an almost negligible chance of success.

One of the reasons the UK does not have a flourishing egg- or sperm-banking industry is that anonymous gamete donation has been illegal since 2005. Now, children in the UK born via donated eggs or sperm have the right to learn the identity of their biological parents when they turn eighteen, and donors are legally obliged to update the clinics with their contact details. There is also a cap on donations; donated sperm or eggs can only be used to create up to ten families. But even in countries where there is a legal limit, super donors can get round the rules by making informal donations via private websites and chat rooms, or simply by donating to clinics all over the world, which do not cross-check with each other. In the US, there is no limit at all.

In Spain, where only anonymous gamete donation is legal, there are, unsurprisingly, no national shortages of sperm or eggs. By contrast, the UK has to import three-quarters of its donor sperm from abroad – from countries like Denmark, which supplies banks and clinics worldwide with both anonymous and non-anonymous sperm and eggs.[21] Given the prevalence of DNA testing kits and databases like Ancestry, it is relatively easy to track down an anonymous donor, but anonymous donation takes away the legal right to do so.

Spain, despite its law of anonymity, runs a national register to keep track of all gamete donations from the more than 300 clinics across the country, with each batch of sperm, eggs or embryos given an ID number.[22] Part of the rationale to this is to ensure that no one over-donates, and that potential hereditary diseases are tracked in donor children. Its cost is perhaps why other countries like the US do not follow suit, but a more cynical explanation is that it is extremely lucrative for clinics *not* to limit the number of donations they use from a single donor, given how costly especially egg retrievals are.

Sperm and egg banks can also use donor limits to their financial advantage. For very high-paying clients, some banks offer IVF clients the chance to pay tens of thousands of euros or dollars for 'donor exclusivity' – i.e. to be the only recipient of a particular donor's eggs or sperm.[23] Usually the 'exclusive' donor gets none of that lump sum; they are paid a standard fee per donation. In the UK, the agencies that match donors and intended parents have to be non-profit too. But at sperm and egg banks in some countries in Europe, and in Canada, although donors are unpaid, the agencies can profit.

EGGS

This seems difficult to square – how can it be right that donation works altruistically within an otherwise monetised industry; that the woman supplying her eggs at significant physical cost is not remunerated, while others are? When I started my research for this book, the naked commercialism of the American donation model repelled me, but I gradually began to change my mind. In some ways, a system where everyone profits is fairer; it is certainly simpler to treat it as a transaction from start to finish, than a hybrid of profit-making and altruism.

Lewis and Andre are a British–Portuguese couple based between Rome and Lisbon. In 2019, they had embryos frozen in Lviv, Ukraine – a country that, before the war, had been a major hub of fertility treatments in Europe. At the time of writing, Ukrainian egg donors receive roughly $1,000 to $2,000 per cycle, providing what one Israeli father (featured in the next section of the book) memorably referred to as the 'cheap, white eggs' favoured by himself and other clients on the global market.

Lewis and Andre bought eggs from a twenty-seven-year-old Ukrainian woman, an open-ID donor who agreed to meet their future child as an adult (a more expensive option than a standard anonymous donor). At the outbreak of war in February 2022, the clinic offered to move the embryos to one of their affiliated clinics in Eastern Europe, all of whom declined because Lewis and Andre are gay. The embryos were, in Lewis's words, 'caught between Putin's war and Eastern Europe's homophobia'. Eventually, they managed to transfer the embryos to Canada, where they began their search for an altruistic surrogate.

While Lewis and Andre became victims of the unpredictable and volatile nature of the global egg market, there has always been a safer, more predictable alternative for those who can afford it. French–American couple Ivan and Bryan, introduced to me by a friend of theirs in Madrid, represent the top-paying clients who had the funds to choose an egg donor in the US. Now separated, and co-parenting their twins, they spoke to me individually by video call and later in person about how they chose their egg donor and surrogate.

I was particularly interested in how they described their anxiety to vet as thoroughly as possible – from afar – their egg donor, a woman who would always remain nameless to them and to their shared biological children, and whom they would never meet. It highlighted an obsession with genes that most people, deep down, seem to share, particularly when it comes to their own children.

To get two different perspectives on the same experience was eye-opening. Most parents I spoke to talked to me just as one representative or as a pair, but this was the first time I interviewed both parents individually, almost like a mediator. I spoke to Ivan first. He is a tall, fast-talking Parisian with thick grey hair who was living in New York on a green card when we first talked, pacing the streets of Manhattan between meetings – the consummate corporate high-flier. He is the CEO of a global health consultancy and his salary contributed significantly to the surrogacy journey, which eventually amounted to $186,000 over the course of several years.

Ivan was factual at first, running me through the key chronology of his story at lightning speed in a heavy French accent laden with Americanisms. An hour or so into our second conversation, he reflected more expansively on some of the moral points that nagged at him, even eight years later. By the time we met in person, I felt that we had gone deep together into a very intimate period of his life. I had probed his feelings on parenthood in a way that I will probably never be asked or allowed to do by another random acquaintance, and that in fact is rare even among close friends. There is something unmistakably taboo about asking someone why or how they had their children, but the book provided a reason – a fig leaf – that made it seem normal.

Ivan told me that he and his American ex-husband Bryan were living in Miami in 2015 when they decided to have children.

'First, we looked at adoption, but those children come from very complex backgrounds, and they are older,' Ivan said, instinctively answering a question he knew I would be thinking. He spoke without defensiveness.

'The authorities check your papers every time you cross state lines. You can also adopt from a mother who is pregnant but doesn't want the baby. They put up their baby for adoption in advance, but they can change their mind until the last minute.'

Pre-birth adoption, popularised in the cult 2007 film *Juno*, has received intense public scrutiny for obvious reasons. The practice relies on the birth mother signing away her maternal rights after birthing her baby, as agreed with the adoptive parents, via a broker. Not all do, even after receiving money from the prospective parents (technically, this money is framed as pregnancy-related expenses).

'We read a lot of horror stories,' said Ivan.

Eventually, the couple decided to pursue the more expensive and (in some ways) predictable option of surrogacy. They were able to take advantage of the legalisation of gay marriage in the US in 2015, which paved the way for the legalisation of two male parents on a birth certificate. The two states in which their chosen agency looked to engage a surrogate were North Carolina and Texas, but first, they needed an egg donor.

'We had to choose – frozen or fresh? The quality is the same, but the problem of the frozen eggs is that they come with donor profiles. You swipe through and choose – it looks like online dating. Then I realised that none of these profiles are verified. Those donors fill out a form on their own and they are not checked. I have [close friends] who have had children from totally anonymous donation, and it has made me question the mental health of the donors.'

Ivan was figuring out that there is a limit to what prospective parents can find out about their egg donor, especially about frozen egg donors, who have already signed a contract with an agency and cannot be contacted. Finding a 'live' donor (meaning a woman who provides fresh eggs after being matched with the parents), means that you find 'a woman who is willing to go through the process with you'.

So was it more difficult to find a fresh egg donor?

'Yes. They are more *à la carte*' – this was pronounced with particular French-ness – 'and a bit more expensive – you create fresh eggs with a fresh contract, and sometimes they are more willing to have contact. Usually they are in their twenties and already have donated – you can find out how many eggs they usually produce at each harvest. We went through two egg donors that the agency found.'

Ivan knew he and his husband wouldn't be able to meet their donor in person, but they managed to negotiate a video call with a willing candidate – who would still remain nameless, and would not be contactable after the donation.

'It took a few months with the first one. We paid for the first visit to the clinic, then when she started the hormone treatment she disappeared, stopped responding to us. We don't know what happened.'

I asked him how that felt – what is it like to start to bond with someone who might be the biological mother of your children, and then she disappears?

'It was disappointing. It was the first time. You don't know how long to wait for them to reappear before trying with someone else.'

Was it hard to keep hopeful and positive throughout the process?

'You keep comparing the profiles, you spend a lot of time choosing . . . Now we don't care. We have our kids and they are perfect, but at the time when you're doing the search, it seems so important. You find one you really like, and you lose it; you go to your second choice. It's not like there are new profiles every day. Now you realise, I was stupid, it doesn't matter.'

Luckily, Ivan and Bryan fell in love with their second donor.

'We were not paying per egg donor – the agency keeps searching until you have a result. And the second donor, we loved her. After fifteen minutes into a very weird Zoom call we were laughing. We don't know her name, we have the picture from the profile somewhere. She gave forty-seven eggs from one retrieval [a very high number]; not all were viable – maybe twenty viables, and we were left with eight embryos.'

Ivan and Bryan used two of the embryos. 'We wanted a boy and a girl, and we just happened to get one from my husband and one from me. We implanted them both at the same time in the surrogate, so they are twins.'

This, as I was to discover, is common – the cost of a surrogate carrying an extra baby is only $5,000 more (a cost that has remained unchanged for nearly a decade), an enormous saving on a whole new surrogacy process costing upwards of $100,000. I asked him what happened to the rest of the embryos.

'I'm not sure – good question – I think the clinic sent me a bill for storage; I forgot to pay. Then they said do you want them donated to other couples, donated to science or destroyed? I'm 80 per cent sure I said destroy. Or maybe donate to science. It would be awkward if our kids had little brothers and sisters out there.'

As we finished our call, I was struck by the difference in how intensely Ivan described the anxiety and investment of hope in finding the eggs that helped create his children, and how vague he had been about the surplus frozen embryos held by the clinic. The value of those embryos – created at the cost of around $75,000, including agency fees, egg donor compensation and IVF treatments – had plummeted to nothing.

I voiced this to Ivan, knowing he would not be offended. He agreed – 'Once you have your kids, nothing matters.' Ivan had reservations and regrets about the surrogacy process – more on which later – and I came to realise that this was relatively unusual among intended parents (or, at least, unusual to voice to a third party). Ivan was a happy recipient of assisted reproduction but also a critic.

I also spoke to Ivan's American ex-husband Bryan by video call. He was living in Lisbon with the twins at the time, but happened to be in Paris for the 2024 Olympics, looking relaxed and smiley as he wandered the streets on a sunny July day. He struck me as taking life at a more sedate pace than Ivan.

'It was a long process – you feel the length of it. For us gay couples, everything has to be planned out. Not only do you have the task of the process itself, but you have all the emotions. You're thinking – what if the donor is crazy, what if the eggs don't work out? You have to be able to relax, take a breath, not get too emotionally involved in every single aspect, because there are so many variables along the way. Some things are not in your control.'

Bryan mentioned a friend of his who wanted to have a child alone and the embryo split in three – three identical girls, born severely premature. The babies spent four months in hospital, and Bryan's friend became a single father of three children 'when he was just trying to have one child', as Bryan put it.

'You're playing with nature – it doesn't have a set of rules that it follows.'

'Playing with nature' was a phrase that stuck with me – it is often used by critics of IVF, particularly by religious conservatives who oppose same-sex parenting as against nature's norms. Here, a gay man was transforming it into a philosophical maxim to relax and go with the flow.

Although Ivan and Bryan went through two egg donors, Bryan viewed this as a stroke of luck.

'It changed my perspective on what I was looking for. The most important thing wasn't the beautiful model girl – I thought I wanted the six-foot Scandinavian model. We ended up finding an egg donor who was very smart and accomplished, and one thing that finalised the deal was that she told me her husband was trans – this was like eight years ago, remember.

'I thought the story of how she met her husband was so mature and beautiful. She said she wanted to be an egg donor because her sister was a lesbian and she saw the difficult process that gay people went through. I thought, OK – this is who I want to be the mother of my children.'

The experiences of Bryan and Ivan, and my friend Jessica, in choosing their donors had seemed to me – initially, at least – to be based on superficialities. But I wondered if the process was as different to choosing a 'mate' the old-fashioned way as I'd first assumed. To see someone's educational achievements and physical characteristics noted down would be awkward, in your face. But when we meet someone we are attracted to, someone we might like to date, perhaps to marry, to make babies with – all but the most romantic of us are assessing them in a similar way.

Underneath the supposedly ethereal chemistry and meeting of souls, we are attracted to the way our partner looks, to their talents, to the details of their background and their achievements as we uncover those nuggets of information along the way. We do not usually, however, know anything about their ovarian reserves or their sperm motility. Perhaps that information is coming to elite dating sites in the US in the not-too-distant future.

MONETISING THE CLOCK

While the global egg market grows, wealthy women are being encouraged to 'bank' their own eggs to avoid having to buy donated ones in future. Navigating social media as a woman in your thirties, it is impossible not to feel like a lucrative battery hen as you scroll past adverts for ovulation apps, fertility tests and egg freezing. Anxiety about infertility is ubiquitous and highly profitable, even before any infertility has been diagnosed. At-home fertility tests costing around £50 are increasingly available online, while those with a higher budget can visit private clinics which require you to undergo a 'Fit for Fertility' assessment for around £500 prior to treatment. The growth of egg freezing is part of an increasing societal preoccupation with infertility that is partly justified and partly hyped by a flourishing market, which relies on that anxiety.

CASH COW

Now, it's everywhere, but commercial egg freezing started in 2014 in corporate America. Half a century after the contraceptive pill ushered in a sexual revolution, the April 2014 cover of *Bloomberg Businessweek* welcomed a new era of choice for women: 'Freeze Your Eggs, Free Your Career.' Two years earlier, the American Society for Reproductive Medicine had officially stopped considering egg freezing an 'experimental' medical procedure. Private clinics in the US and abroad started urging women to 'bank' their eggs for a future point at which they might be unable to naturally conceive. Advertising campaigns featured cute babies or metaphorical graphics – eggs nestled in more than one basket, or 'golden egg hunt' promotions.

As ever, the golden goose (or cash cow) was – and remains – the customer herself. Money from private equity and venture capital firms started pouring in to egg-freezing clinics as well as the wider industry of assisted reproduction. Six months after the Bloomberg cover, Apple and Facebook announced cash gifts of $20,000 to their female employees to cover egg freezing.[24] The news split feminist opinion – welcomed by many (and spearheaded by Sheryl Sandberg, then-COO of Facebook and author of *Lean In*), it was also criticised as a form of cleverly marketed pressure on women to remain in work and postpone motherhood.

That cynicism has largely disappeared, and financial support for employees' egg-freezing treatments is now widely adopted corporate policy – several of my friends, in the UK and the States, both partnered and single, have gratefully taken advantage of such offers. Interestingly, the vista of professional opportunity heralded by *Bloomberg Businessweek* was overshadowed in the following decade by the high numbers of women who have frozen their eggs not to prioritise their career, but because they have yet to find a suitable partner – the academic Marcia C. Inhorn calls this 'the mating gap'.[25]

(Perhaps unsurprisingly, women in physical lines of work – even high-earning ones – have been less privileged in terms of career support. More than a decade after Sandberg spearheaded corporate support for employee egg-freezing, the Women's Tennis Association announced it would protect players' ranking if they chose to pursue egg-freezing, reducing the pressures to return to court.[26])

Elective egg-freezing undoubtedly offers women options, but there has been a growing realisation that many clinics mis-sell their services in an aggressively competitive market – playing down medical risks, playing up success rates and charging confusing, pay-as-you-go fees (for 'extra' but essential services such as medication and storage fees), which end up spiralling beyond customers' expectations.

Is it immoral to exploit women's fear of being childless or is it a market like any other? In private healthcare, to what extent should a patient be treated as a customer, and vice versa? Is an optional procedure like egg-freezing primarily a luxury or a medical service? What ethical standards should fertility clinics be held to? These are questions that I kept returning to, particularly as I met women whose lives had been radically changed by freezing their eggs.

It is worth emphasising that the opportunity to 'extend' one's fertility is, currently, an investment that a relatively lucky few can afford, despite the various loans and payment schemes that many of the major providers offer. It is the preserve of financially secure, generally white women. To these women, it is marketed as a form of insurance policy against childlessness, despite its unpredictability. One campaign by Kindbody, a hugely popular New York-based chain of nationwide fertility clinics, featured the dubious slogan 'Own Your Future'.[27] The vast majority of eggs commercially frozen to date have not been used, which is part of the reason why success rates are hard to determine. Broadly speaking, frozen eggs have around an 18 per cent chance of making it to a live birth – hence the need to preserve upwards of ten for a decent chance of success (the older the woman, the more eggs are needed – the success rate falls to 5 per cent for women aged forty).

Many clinics do not make this clear; a BBC investigation in 2024 found that 42 per cent of clinics in the UK could be breaching guidelines by failing to explain the chances of a successful pregnancy.[28] The likelihood of having a high-risk pregnancy also increases with age, something that is often glossed over in the promotional brochures.

When I was talking to high-earning career women in the US about their egg-freezing and IVF treatments, I was struck by the level of financial desperation they had experienced. One female psychiatrist, who explained that even with decent health insurance she and her husband got into considerable debt after just a couple of rounds of IVF, told me about Facebook groups that exist solely to share tips on getting access to jobs with favourable insurance.

EGGS

I found one called 'Amazon Infertility Journey: IUI/IVF – for people who are interested in working at amazon for the Ivf/infertility coverage'.[29] It had more than 6,000 members exchanging information about how to play the system by working at Amazon for the minimum number of days before quitting (benefits usually kick in by day seven, for those interested). It was a sobering insight into the American insurance system, and particularly striking viewed alongside the enormous profits to be made by companies investing in the clinics that so many struggle to afford.

The early 2020s were big years for venture capital and private equity investment in fertility tech. One venture capitalist in London I spoke to, who was pitched by a couple of fertility chains but decided against investing in them, described his bewilderment that so many of his competitors were keen.

'These clinics presented as software-like businesses, but they were just slapping website and Insta ads on traditional IVF clinics. We never understood why they were getting these crazy investments. Between 2020 and 2021 there was a lot more money than sense – investors were investing in tailwinds, in things they didn't understand.'

By 2024, however, there were signs that some of the biggest fertility chains were in danger of overreaching themselves. The most major of these was Kindbody, which was valued at $1.8 billion in 2023, a figure ten times its forecasted revenue that year.[30] The chain set itself apart with its spa-like clinic spaces, all floral bouquets and plush sofas, and an ethos that the focus was on *you*, the customer. Just a year after its $1.8 billion valuation, financial news outlets were reporting that the company was trying to raise money to keep afloat as it closed clinics across the country, its CEO departed – twice – and its valuation fell to an estimated $400 million (Kindbody disputed this valuation).[31]

According to the venture capitalist I spoke to, the profit margins for most fertility businesses hover around 20 per cent – this sounded like a lot to me, but compared to software companies, which can generate around 70 per cent, this is apparently 'low-margin' territory for tech investors like him. The business model of a company like Kindbody requires a high turnover to keep profits ticking over – i.e. as many women and couples undergoing procedures and treatments as possible. At Kindbody, there were also scandals including reports of embryo mishandling and mix-ups that may have precipitated its fall, and which might also have been connected to the speed of its expansion.

Adam Wolf, a top US attorney of the firm Peiffer Wolf Carr Kane Conway & Wise LLP, represents victims of fertility-related negligence, often at high-volume clinics. He gave an interview in which he described clinics with a very high turnover as 'just doing a ton of procedures. And it's all happening very quickly. And there's pressure to get it done. And it leads to mistakes.'[32]

Embryo mix-ups are increasingly common as the industry grows. In 2025, a white American woman called Krystena Murray sued the Coastal Fertility Specialists, instructing none other than Adam Wolf to represent her, after she gave birth to a Black baby.[33] She gave up custody of the child she still wanted to consider her own when DNA tests confirmed they shared no genetic link, and the biological parents sued for custody. She still does not know whether another woman was impregnated with her embryo.

The UK appears to be more aware of the industry's problems than the US. The US has no regulatory body equivalent to the UK's Human Fertilisation & Embryology Authority (HFEA), something that has long been recognised as a problem. In 2023, the HFEA called for an urgent update to the laws around egg-freezing, which were made over thirty years previously, to reflect changes in clinical practices and the need to regulate and inspect these.[34] Concerns raised by other authorities in recent years include the Competition and Markets Authority on clinics' marketing practices, and reports from medical authorities such as the Nuffield Council on Bioethics.

Meanwhile, the bankability of the US fertility industry, despite dramatic examples like Kindbody, remains strong. It was only mildly disturbed by the repercussions of the overturning of *Roe vs Wade* in 2022, for example, which called into question the legality of destroying unused or non-viable embryos that might be deemed to have 'personhood' and be regarded as children, as the Alabama Supreme Court decided in 2024. (Alabama was relatively late to the party, compared to the 1986 Louisiana statute, which defined an embryo as 'a juridical person'.)

The reluctance of authorities to interfere in the thorny issue of the legal status of IVF clinics has had a key part to play in the industry's lack of regulation. After the 2022 overturning, IVF clinics continued to function more or less as normal and business continued to boom: the US market is projected to reach $8.69 billion by 2033,[35] although previous predictions have underestimated its speed of growth (a 2020 report suggested it would be worth $5.56 billion by 2027; it exceeded that by 2023).

To some people's surprise, especially outside the US, the industry had an additional boost in the form of Donald Trump, who instigated the *Roe vs Wade* overturning. He proved to be, perhaps counterintuitively, a huge fan of IVF, signing an executive order in 2025 – less than a month into his second term as president – in which he expanded access to IVF by 'aggressively' reducing out-of-pocket and health-plan costs for fertility treatments.[36] Trump called himself 'the fertilisation president' and explained his executive order succinctly: 'Because we want more babies, to put it very nicely.'

I was interested to learn that the overturning of *Roe vs Wade* created ripple effects in the fertility market beyond the US. I learned about an ovulation tracking company headquartered in Germany that had a major boost following 2022, when women living in US states that had criminalised abortion turned to European alternatives instead because of privacy concerns: they were scared that American ovulation tracking apps might share their data with authorities (including possible pregnancies and terminations).

I was beginning to get a picture of the lucrativeness of women's limited fertility window – the confusion of choice, cost and risk that women face, often alone – while trying to anticipate their personal and biological futures. While egg-freezing, in the right context, can legitimately be viewed as offering women 'optionality', as one management consultant described it to me, I was increasingly troubled by the industry as a whole. Adverts for egg-freezing play on a fear of childlessness, selling hope in parallel to the diet and cosmetics industries that have targeted women's insecurities since the dawn of advertising. Again, I thought of the Future Beauty Show seamlessly merging with the Future Fertility Show in Dublin – same women, same messaging, same cash cow.

TAKING ADVANTAGE

'ARGC are next level! Thank you so much for making our dreams come true' 5 stars

'They treat women like money-making objects' 1 star

'How do I review a place that gave me two lives?' 5 stars

'They make you feel like cattle' 1 star

The Google reviews for the Assisted Reproduction and Gynaecology Centre (ARGC) in central London, which offers IVF treatment and egg-freezing, vacillate wildly between five stars and one star. An example of the more widespread phenomenon of 'J curve' ratings (reflecting the fact that reviewers are generally motivated by either strongly positive or negative feelings), this response is perhaps particularly unsurprising for medical services heavily reliant on individual biological luck, and is steeped in emotion.

Many of the one-star reviews speak of tragedy: miscarriages and unsympathetic doctors, eggs badly thawed and destroyed, thousands of pounds wasted. The five-star reviews give thanks for creating life, and many imply that the clinic is a last resort for women and couples who have failed elsewhere; it boasts the UK's highest IVF success rate 'per treatment cycle started' and is also one of the most expensive.

This reputation attracted Saskia, who completed a round of egg-freezing at the clinic in 2021, just before she turned thirty-five – the much-dreaded (though disputed) 'cliff edge' of female fertility. I have known Saskia, a relentless high achiever, since we both released our first eggs at our all-girls' London day school; her cool fashionista exterior hides a true geek within. She has always excelled at homework, and her search for the best London clinic landed squarely on the ARGC.

When I visited the clinic, I was struck by the unassuming door and scuffed brass sign on Upper Wimpole Street, a smart address in London's central hub of private health providers. The interior was surprisingly drab and dark, enlivened only by photographs of clients' babies lining the walls of the reception hall – all the marketing a fertility clinic really needs. It seemed impossible to socially profile the clientele in the waiting room. Much like a row of commuters in a train carriage, here was a truly London scene of women of all races glued to their phones, avoiding eye contact.

I asked an unsmiling receptionist if I could book myself a blood test to measure my AMH levels – not because I had suddenly decided to find out, but as an indicator of how easy the process would be. She told me I could not, because I had no patient number (which could not be obtained without a consultation, costing around £100), and could therefore not be processed. I realised this clinic was trading off its reputation for results rather than luring customers with shiny surfaces and attentive staff; it was the exact opposite of the clinics I had visited in Northern Cyprus, and of Kindbody's mobile clinics offering free AMH tests to potential customers. Later, I discovered that in 2016 the clinic unsuccessfully sued the HFEA for changing the metrics of published IVF success rates in the UK, because the changes made the ARGC's rates look slightly less impressive (they are still the best in London).[37] This place was not messing about.

Here, Saskia went through the usual process for retrieving and freezing her eggs: first, a fertility assessment, including an AMH test, and an ultrasound of her ovaries (as I had been offered as a candidate for egg donation). Then the intensity ramped up: for ten days she woke up at 5 a.m. to self-inject hormones to stimulate her ovaries into producing eggs. These were harvested under sedation – Saskia produced fourteen, of which twelve were selected as mature (viable) and frozen.

Close monitoring in the run-up to the egg retrieval, in the form of almost daily blood tests and frequent ultrasound scans, are expensive but a crucial factor in the success rate of ARGC and its main competitors. I wanted to get a decent assessment of the competitive landscape; one private gynaecologist's personal assistant told me, on condition of strict anonymity, that one London clinic is notorious for pushing treatments on their patients.

'They let patients do round after round of IVF – it's like a treadmill,' she told me, in a locked store cupboard (I do not exaggerate). 'We had one patient who had done thirteen rounds [I calculated this must have cost around £100,000]. Whereas somewhere like the CRGH [the Centre for Reproductive & Genetic Health, a nearby competitor] will say, "OK, let's do three; we are not going to put you on that treadmill." They're a bit gentler.'

(The CRGH was bought in 2022 by FutureLife, a European fertility group backed by two private equity companies, which two years later bought the Bristol Centre for Reproductive Medicine – examples of the fertility investment boom in the UK mirroring the US.)

Two close friends of mine, Jessica and Kath, froze their eggs at the treadmill London clinic, and both now have children as a result. Both told me they 'felt like a number', but according to Jessica, who is still connected to an informal community of women in their late thirties and early forties navigating the UK's IVF clinics, the clinic is not an outlier.

'I don't know a single person who found egg-freezing a good experience,' she said, characteristically not mincing her words. 'Everyone seems to deal with staff who don't know their details, you never see the same doctor twice. You can't believe you're handing over all this money to be treated this badly.'

Saskia paid a flurry of invoices and felt lucky that she got away with a mere six months of hormonal imbalance and sleep disruption after the retrieval. I was interested to compare the invoice she shared with me and the prices listed on the ARGC website; while the website quotes £2,850 for egg-freezing, Saskia's itemised bill, which included all her meds and monitoring, came to £8,475.

On top of that, she pays ongoing storage costs – some of my interviewees told me they agonise over the question of how long to keep paying these costs. One noted that she chooses to pay around £800 per year for storage of her eggs and embryos, but foregoes private health insurance in order to afford it. 'Insuring' the possibility of a future child is more valuable to her than her own health.

There is a new, low-cost model emerging, with bright citrus intensity, from the old guard of London IVF clinics: an ambitious easyJet challenger to the British Airways incumbents. Avenues, licensed by the HFEA in 2024, operates from a townhouse in north Euston, near the nightclubs of Camden Town. A glass viewing wall into the lab reveals an overwhelmingly yellow floor to match its branding. I first encountered the clinic at the London Fertility Show, where its stand was literally unmissable, and busy.

Avenues promises a radically different service, AI-driven technologies and a fair pricing model. 'The UK fertility system is broken,' its website declares. 'High IVF costs, financial barriers, and postcode lotteries deny too many the chance to start a family on their terms #ThisIsNotFairIVF.'[38]

Only relatively young and fertile couples qualify for its 'Fair IVF' programme (which is certainly cheap at just under £3,000 with medication and monitoring included): the female partner must be younger than thirty-five and have an AMH level of more than 10 pmol/L, and the male partner must have a sperm count of more than 1 million/ml (both these fertility thresholds are modest). Together, they must have 'fewer than two previous consecutive miscarriages' ('fewer than two' struck me as only isolated miscarriages, by definition), and no previous IVF cycles. The pricing model makes sense for customers who will not be effectively subsidising less fertile people by paying the same as them. But it also struck me that the clinic benefits by attracting more fertile people, who will contribute to its overall success rates (which, in the absence of a personal recommendation, seems to be how most people choose their clinic).

On average, women in their thirties produce eight to fifteen mature eggs per retrieval (and need to retrieve more than younger women for the same chance of a successful pregnancy, as fewer of theirs will be viable). Saskia had felt fairly happy about the twelve mature eggs she had produced, but when she discovered that a friend of hers had produced a significantly higher number, she experienced a crisis of confidence – something I had been afraid of feeling with my hypothetical AMH results. She considered coughing up another £8,475 for a second round – and ended up spending a similar amount two years later, at a rival clinic, to create some embryos with her partner.

This sentiment of panicked inadequacy is familiar to Carol, a Harvard-trained cognitive neuroscientist who in early 2019 founded a consultancy in New York advising a global client base on the best and cheapest egg-freezing clinics in Europe. Her top country recommendation was Spain, which was the first country to fast-freeze eggs and remains something of a market leader; it is the biggest provider of donor eggs in Europe, carrying out 45 per cent of all cycles per year[39] – all egg donors remain anonymous. Some of her clients were from countries like Turkey or China, where single women are not allowed to freeze their eggs or access IVF (though this is being reconsidered in China due to the country's declining population).[40] Around 70 per cent, however, were American women seeking a better deal abroad.

When I spoke to Carol over video call she told me how she struggled to manage 'difficult patient populations' with unreasonable expectations. 'I've dealt with very high-achieving New Yorkers who have high-powered jobs and have never failed. They think if you put in the hours, you can make it – so they find it incredibly frustrating that they can't just fix their AMH levels.'

Carol's sympathies lay ultimately with these women. 'In the US, it's not a pro-patient market. It exploits people's desperation,' she told me. I was interested that she used the word 'exploit' – it was a word that had occurred to me, but I had not heard or seen it used within the industry.

I wondered if there was a cultural clash – whether, as a Brit, I was simply struggling to get my head around the ultra-privatised US health system. The egg-freezing market is perhaps no different to other parts of the system, where it is not unusual for doctors to be paid to promote drugs that are more expensive than identical alternatives. Arguably, it is incumbent on anyone who spends money on a medical procedure or drug to do their own research, to decide if the treatment is worth the physical and financial toll, and which are the best competitors in the market. In the US, a patient is fundamentally a consumer. And yet, reflecting on the experiences of women desperate to have children and the big promises of the clinics involved, I couldn't help feeling there was an extra vulnerability to this 'patient population', a more disturbing tinge to their exploitation.

Carol seemed to think so too. She experienced moral qualms marketing her own company's services, which, along with the challenges of global travel brought by the pandemic, meant she ended up closing down her consultancy. It was the first of its kind, though others now exist. I encountered a British firm at the London Fertility Show, which offers an IVF concierge service in several countries (with bespoke sightseeing tours included) where I was invited to scan a QR code to enter a competition to win a free round of IVF at a clinic in Turkey – I politely declined.

A Canadian fertility clinic rep I spoke to said there is currently a glut in these concierge services, which are unregulated in the UK, unlike fertility clinics themselves. In 2025, the popular online concierge company Apricity Fertility went bust, owing money to fifty-two of their clients who were left without treatments despite having paid commissions to the company to arrange their IVF. Yet in a confusing global market, it's easy to see why people would want an agent or middleman to help them find the best deal.

One of Carol's first clients was my friend Gillian, a thirty-nine-year-old tech consultant who lives in Puerto Rico. In 2019, she froze nine of her eggs in Madrid at a prestigious fertility clinic called the Clínica Tambre. Two years later her tech-company employer paid for a second round at a clinic in New York costing $15,000 – three times as expensive as her Spanish freezing round, she says, using much higher levels of hormones. (I'd heard European clinics' attitudes to ovarian stimulation described as 'conservative' by American standards; a higher intensity of stimulation generally results in a higher number of eggs, and is favoured in the US and Canada, but carries a greater risk of serious side effects, such as ovarian torsion and haemorrhage.)

Gillian's second round left her with just eight viable eggs and painful dental problems that are linked to the hormone surges of fertility treatments and pregnancy. She couldn't sleep for three nights because she was not allowed anaesthetic before her egg retrieval. After her eggs were removed, so were her teeth.

Around the time of my conversation with Gillian, I read *The Tale of Jemima Puddle-Duck* to my daughter: the story rests on the determination of a goose to lay and hatch her own eggs. I thought of a female patient re-laying and re-laying, an exercise in hope. I also thought of how a retrieval is referred to as 'harvesting' – suddenly, the whole process seemed distinctly farm-like: cash cow, battery hen, high or low yield.

There are much more harrowing stories than Gillian's, some of which involve indisputable medical malpractice, as opposed to potential side effects voluntarily taken on. In 2021, a nurse at Yale Fertility Clinic stole vials of fentanyl intended for women undergoing egg retrievals, replacing the vials with saline solution.[41] When the women who had endured their egg extraction without fentanyl complained of excruciating pain, doctors ignored them or told them that their pain was normal – a statistically more common outcome for women than men in medical settings.[42] Three years later, the women were awarded undisclosed damages after suing the clinic.

The systemic poor treatment of female patients is not particular to the US, and neither is the fierce commercialism of the egg-freezing industry. But the latter is particularly acute there, and I was interested in what an American professional in the business might have to say about the exploitative nature of the industry – or whether all is fair in love, war and baby-making.

While researching surrogacy in the US for the latter part of this book I talked to a family and fertility lawyer in California who represents intended parents entering into surrogacy agreements. He has been in the business since the 1990s, and talked to me from his sunny office – after our conversation he was off trick-or-treating with his child.

We talked for over an hour, much to my grateful surprise – I know how much an hour is worth to an American lawyer. As we wrapped up, he asked me – as many people do – whether I was 'pro' or 'anti' the fertility industry in general, and whether my book would be a 'skewering'. I told him it would not be, but that I did have concerns about exploitation, particularly in terms of the overselling that some IVF clinics engage in, and the marketing that is carefully aimed at desperate women.

The fertility lawyer leapt to defend his professional territory and, again to my surprise, we soon found ourselves in a philosophical tussle. Yes, he said, 'there are bad actors in any business', and there are unethical doctors and clinics who overmedicate and oversell their services, but that is not endemic to the fertility industry. I asked him whether there is not an extra and specific vulnerability to fertility patients, desperate to have children and overpaying for any chances offered to them.

'I don't think the doctor created that vulnerability,' he replied.

'But is it right to exploit it?'

He paused before asking thoughtfully, 'Are they exploiting or just taking advantage?'

When I play back the recording of our interview, I can hear myself suppressing nervous laughter at this juncture.

'There is a difference,' insisted the lawyer. 'Exploitation is – you are intentionally charging higher prices and preying on these women to just make money, as opposed to [thinking], *There is a market there, and we should market ourselves to them.*'

I burst out laughing. 'That is such an American way of looking at things!'

I realised that I had been attaching an entirely negative meaning to 'taking advantage', ignoring its positive connotation in a business context. I was struggling with this overlap, while the lawyer warmed to his theme.

'Exploitation denotes something more nefarious than just taking advantage of a market that exists.'

Yes – the market exists, and will only grow. But that didn't stop a nagging feeling I had that this man was arguing about semantics, and that something 'nefarious', as he put it, was indeed at play in a systemic way, not just in a few bad actors.

Dr Rahi Victory, the Canadian fertility doctor I met at the Dublin Future Fertility Show, is an expert in his field; his clinic boasts impressive success rates; he has more than twenty-six thousand Instagram followers and he is ambitious to expand his practice internationally. He is also very clear about the difference between running a profitable clinic and 'taking advantage' of vulnerable patients. He told me that egg-freezing is sometimes offered to women for whom it would be a total waste of time and money.

'[For women in their] forties and above – egg-freezing is total nonsense. Late thirties you need many eggs, but it's an option, just not a great one.'

I thought about women who freeze their eggs, perhaps not really being able to afford it, encouraged by clinics to believe that it would give them a baby. More than the wasted expense and time, it was the false hope that seemed so cruel. After our conversation, Dr Victory told me in an email follow-up that he believes 'the business industry has invaded the fertility world and the drive is often for financial reasons rather than for the patients'.

This was the first time, other than my conversation with Carol, the former egg-freezing broker, that my instincts had been explicitly echoed by someone within the industry. Dr Victory continued.

'I believe that we must repurpose ourselves to address the fact that we are helping women and men in their most intimate anatomy in their most vulnerable position physically, mentally and emotionally. All their hopes and dreams are vested in us. We should be held responsible for that trust.

'I do think we need to answer to a higher motivation than financial reasons. For me, it's God.'

I wondered how big a part his religious beliefs played in his assertion that there should be a 'higher motivation' than profit for fertility doctors (is the Hippocratic Oath not sufficient?). Later, we would have another conversation about the notorious God complex that many male fertility doctors seem to suffer from.

Meanwhile, I had a flight to Madrid to catch.

HOW MANY BABIES DO YOU WANT?

The Clínica Tambre in Madrid, where Gillian first froze her eggs in 2017, kept cropping up in my conversations with friends. I knew it was one of the world's first fertility clinics, founded in 1978, and had retained an impressive reputation, even in the context of Spain's pre-eminence in the field. I wanted to see it for myself. My friend Elinor, another American and a Madrid resident, had frozen her eggs there in 2023. A year later, she wanted to explore a potential second round. Hearing about my research, she booked a consultation and invited me to tag along.

The night I arrived in Madrid I slept in a bed with Elinor, who had just got her period. The next day, I started bleeding, although I was on a form of birth control that usually prevents it. 'I caught your period off you,' I said to her, half-jokingly.

'I know,' she said. 'Sorry about that.'

It seems fitting that my first day in the European capital of fertility treatment was marked by unexpected menstruation. Science has ruled out the possibility of 'period synching' – the phenomenon of women spending time in close proximity getting their periods at the same time – yet anecdotally it is a popular theory. Over coffee and pan con tomate, Elinor and I speculated about the under-researched power of pheromones. She is a great believer in the power and mystery of the female body, and is convinced the phenomenon is real. I want to believe in it too – the idea of some sort of force field of sisterhood that science cannot explain is attractive. But it is perhaps even nicer to consider it a manifestation of people noticing their commonalities as well as their differences, seeking to be in harmony.

Elinor and I take a taxi through a wealthy neighbourhood of gated houses just outside central Madrid to reach the Clínica Tambre. Its entrance manages to be simultaneously discreet and opulent, with a manicured courtyard and fountain, and a sweeping double staircase leading to the entrance. Its sleek reception and waiting room are reminiscent of a first-class cabin on British Airways – private booths behind curved screens 'to ensure patients' privacy' as the clinic's marketing rep, Eliana, would inform me.

Eliana offers us some cucumber-infused water and takes us on a tour. We pass consultation rooms with names like

'Serenidad' (serenity), 'Esperanza' (hope) and, less explicably, both the Roman and Greek names of the virgin goddess Minerva/Athena, as well as – more explicably – Hera, goddess of childbirth. I peer into the andrology lab, where semen is stored and analysed: big cylinders of liquid nitrogen, and lab assistants in front of computers.

'We have many sperm donors,' says Eliana proudly (they and their donations are received in a separate clinic downtown). I'm not allowed in the IVF lab or the operating rooms but am shown into an outdoor waiting room that looks like a fashionable Mykonos bar, all minimalist sandstone benches, pebbles and cacti, where we sit for our interview.

Eliana's answers to my questions are moderated later by the clinic's PR team – one of the conditions of my visit. For example, in the Mykonos-style waiting room she tells me about an enticing deal offered to some prospective international patients, but I am told afterwards I am not allowed to write about the details (I later encountered the clinic's representatives at the London Fertility Show, where these promotions to international clients are made). I am allowed to note that around 68 per cent of people coming to the clinic are not from Spain (they are mostly other Europeans, though increasing numbers are from the US), and that numbers are rising year on year. This does not surprise me, especially when I reviewed the price of medications used for egg retrievals in Spain versus elsewhere – one of them, Decapeptyl, is currently nearly five times more expensive in the US than it is in Spain, and about three times more expensive in the UK, though medication prices fluctuate.[43]

I am also allowed to note that the clinic employs a plethora of multilingual staff to ensure that every patient can communicate with doctors in their native tongue (much like the clinics in Northern Cyprus). More single women are freezing their eggs now, apparently, and doing so at a younger age – closer to thirty-five than the previous average of thirty-seven.

I am chastised for referring to their 'clients'. The clinic only uses the term 'patients' – because, apparently, 'they have medical needs to achieve their pregnancy'. I am not sure this is always correct, since most cases of egg-freezing are speculative rather than medically necessary – a hedge against a possible future scenario of not being able to have a child naturally. Where is the line between medical necessity and choice when it comes to fertility preservation? I judge that an argument would not be productive in this particular setting.

After the interview with Eliana, I follow Elinor into a consulting room where Dr Angela Llaneza is waiting, a kind, tired-looking gynaecologist who oversaw Elinor's retrieval the previous year. I later learn that today's consultation and a blood test to check her hormone levels will cost €295.

Elinor and Dr Llaneza discuss the pros and cons of another round of egg retrieval and freezing, while I sit awkwardly jotting things down on my notepad like an over-officious chaperone. Dr Llaneza advises Elinor not to have an AMH test performed to check her ovarian reserve – 'it will only stress you out', she says, which, personally, I find a little stressful.

'I already have fourteen eggs,' says Elinor, coming straight to the point. 'I am thirty-six, single. Should I do it again?'

EGGS

Dr Llaneza looks at her screen, then at Elinor. 'How many babies do you want?'

'Hundreds,' says Elinor. All of us smile weakly; there is a pause. Dr Llaneza sighs and suggests that Elinor might like to do an egg retrieval involving a weaker hormonal dose this time – 200 to 250IU of Pergoveris, a synthetic version of FHS, or follicle-stimulating hormone, to avoid side effects – 'we can go for eight, maybe twelve eggs this time, see how it goes'.

Elinor's INSEAD-trained business mind whirrs into action. She points out that this would cost nearly the same as the first time around, when she was prescribed 300IU per day (alongside other medications), because the medication is dispensed in pre-filled 900IU 'pens'. Should she get her money's worth and optimise her chances of more eggs by going for the whole dose again? Later, in the taxi, Elinor and I note the grimness of weighing up her health against the cost-effectiveness of the procedure.

During Elinor's previous round of egg-freezing, she had to inject herself exactly thirty-six hours before she went in for the retrieval. This was a different medication, Decapeptyl, to prevent her ovaries releasing her eggs too early. Elinor remembers it being sold in a multi-pack despite only a single dose being required, so she accepted the offer of a friend in Madrid who had recently been through the process and kept her valuable surplus meds in the fridge. The process of mixing the powder and liquid precisely and using a specific syringe is notoriously difficult – Elinor ended up wasting the first dose, so she rang her doctor cousin in New York for syringe advice for the next attempt.

CASH COW

Listening to this story, I remembered the fertility agent who told me that he would not dream of allowing his donors to self-administer the medications, because the entire retrieval could be jeopardised if anything goes wrong.

'If I'm investing that much money in a donor, I'm supervising the hormone injections myself. She has to do it my way.'

The donor is an investment; the customer is not.

Gillian had also told me about a Facebook group she had used to find women giving away their leftover medication to help other women save money. 'I saved $800 that way,' she said, with satisfaction. I found something very touching about this altruistic sisterhood playing out alongside the vast costs of individual fertility treatments; at the same time, it did not seem right that it should be left to individuals to do this. When women use their friends' or strangers' leftover drugs to save money, they are taking a risk, sometimes unknowingly. Elinor's doctor cousin made her check that they were still in date, had been stored in the fridge, and that there hadn't been an electricity outage in the time they were stored. Some women might not consider this, or take a chance if they really needed to save the money.

I wanted to get to the bottom of why these medications are so unnecessarily expensive. I contacted Clínica Tambre to question their prescription protocol, and was told that independent pharmacies sell the medication to their patients. I reviewed Elinor's personal treatment plan; she had correctly remembered that she was prescribed Decapeptyl in a multi-pack of seven doses of 0.1mg, despite the fact that she only needed to take one dose of 0.2mg – this is the only format in which the medication is sold, according to Spain's regulatory body for medicine and medical devices, the Agencia Española de Medicamentos y Productos Sanitarios (AEMPS).[44]

The drug's manufacturer, the global biopharmaceutical company Ipsen Global (represented as Ipsen Pharma in Spain), did not respond to my request for an explanation as to why this has been the case since its introduction to the market in 1999, meaning that women undergoing egg retrievals have to pay for extra medication they will never use. I assume there is no decent explanation: it is more profitable that way.

At the end of Elinor's consultation, I asked Dr Llaneza how she calculates each of her patient's chances of having a baby.

'We work with odds,' said Dr Llaneza wearily. She gestured at a graph on her computer screen that predicted the chances of a live birth from the frozen eggs of variously aged women – big, bold rainbows of colour plotted confidently against the axes.

'Age is the biggest factor, and cumulative attempts. But it is a lottery.'

'A lottery' – here, again, was an admission of the randomness of fertility: a testament to its persistent unknowability, despite decades of research and multibillion-dollar attendant industries.

The next day, I am on the phone to the PR representative of the Clínica Tambre when I spot the woman I have arranged to meet, Samira, striding towards me down a Madrid side street, a huge, muscular mastiff straining on the lead in front of her. She is dressed in black leather and has the dramatic, glossy black fringe and piercings I recognise from her online photo; her posture is upright, limbs long – the movements of a yoga teacher. As I watch her, I am chastised by the Clínica Tambre rep because I have referred yet again to their 'clients' rather than 'patients'. I apologise and wrap up the conversation.

Samira – a thirty-nine-year-old American woman from Detroit who could pass as Spanish – embraces me warmly. We settle ourselves onto bar stools in a chic café, her dog stretched out below us. We have already talked at length over the phone; Samira has told me about her bizarre life trajectory from working as a private doula in Los Angeles a decade ago to working as a part-time estate agent and yoga teacher here in Madrid, trapped in an unhappy marriage to a Spanish man she knows little about, suddenly anxious about her biological clock.

Samira was one of several people I talked to on the phone for this book before meeting in person, someone I tracked down from afar to tell me about the most emotional and painful episodes of her life. I share most people's reservations about phone conversations; there is a literal and communicative distance that usually inhibits real trust and disclosure. To my surprise, however, there seemed to be something about this subject matter – fertility, the desire to have a child, and particularly the anxieties and taboos involved in assisted reproduction – that actually seemed to work over the phone.

I sensed my subjects shared more with me more quickly than they might have done in person; maybe it was like speaking to an anonymous voice on a helpline, or more simply the old-fashioned Freudian principle of 'free association' encouraged by a lack of eye contact. Either way, the ironic result was that there was perhaps more initial awkwardness when we finally met than there otherwise would have been, especially with the men. It is no small thing to smile and shake hands, as if with a stranger, with someone who already knows some of the most intimate details of your life.

This seemed not to be a problem, however, with Samira, who overflowed with chattiness and warmth. Our conversation was very much *'hermana a hermana'* – she grasped my hands at several points as she talked; she cried; we embraced frequently. Samira was going through a crisis far from home, and she needed a friend.

Samira has spent her entire adult life working with birthing mothers, first as a well-paid doula in Los Angeles, charging $3,000 for her antenatal and birth services. 'The money was good for me, but I knew most families could not afford me. I wanted to give back.' So she started working in an inner-city hospital maternity ward back in Detroit.

What did she see there?

'Babies withdrawing. Single moms giving birth alone. Women who had had miscarriages were in my care, women giving up their child for adoption. The youngest girl I saw was sixteen.'

Samira had two abortions, in her late twenties and early thirties, something she still feels deeply uncomfortable about – especially having worked as a doula. Now, finally, Samira felt ready for a child at the age of thirty-nine. The problem was that, just a couple of months into her marriage, she strongly suspected her husband of cheating on her. So she decided to freeze her eggs alone.

She told me she went to Clínica Fivmadrid, a rival clinic to Tambre, and was asked why, as a married woman, her husband was not there. Did he consent to this? Samira was confused; she just wanted to freeze her own eggs, not embryos. A receptionist checked with the clinic director, who confirmed that no consent was needed from a patient's husband. (When I followed up with the clinic, they confirmed that this was their official policy, in line with Spanish law.)

Samira could have continued but, she said, the episode 'left a bad taste in my mouth'. She left without signing up for a retrieval.

When I talked to Samira nine months later, she told me she had returned home from a trip to the States the previous summer and caught her husband cheating on her on their one-year wedding anniversary, like something out of a cheap telenovela. They had separated but remained married, both living in Madrid. Samira entered into a casual relationship with a thirty-one-year-old man. They fell in love; the relationship became more intense. 'The only thing stopping us from having a future was . . . reproduction,' she told me sadly. 'I felt my age was something to be ashamed of.'

Now, Samira is forty and single – 'I have about two years left, max.' Her experience with Fivmadrid had involved a misunderstanding that was at best unfortunate and at worst an indication of the patriarchal norms that persist even in the most women-oriented of medical settings. It had put her off freezing her eggs at a crucial juncture in her closing fertility window; even if she had frozen them, that was of course no indication of future success.

As I was discovering, laws are just one part of the picture when it comes to the well-marketed field of 'fertility preservation'. Local cultures, expectations of success from both patients and market competitors, and varying attitudes to regulation affect both the intensity of medical treatment and the personal treatment of the women who pay for it. Some of the most aggressively competitive, highly priced markets treat their patients much worse than I had expected.

One of these patients was the next-door neighbour of Gillian, the egg-freezing pioneer among my friends, who lives in the same apartment block in San Juan, Puerto Rico. Aged thirty-one, Rosa froze her eggs in Chicago to donate to her cousin, who was struggling to get pregnant. Rosa underwent the procedure at a well-respected teaching hospital in the US but still suffered major internal bleeding, necessitating two blood transfusions. When I spoke to her over Zoom, she showed me a large, dark bruise on her arm that lingered several months later.

'They told me nothing about the risks. The whole process was about: "Are you viable as a donor?" It was so impersonal.'

Listening to Rosa, I thought of that one-star ARGC review: '*They make you feel like cattle.*'

CASH COW

IVF: LOTTERIES AND GODS

Several years ago, my friend Virginia was standing in a queue at a hospital pharmacy waiting to buy the IVF medication her doctor had just prescribed, wondering how much it would all cost. When she reached the front and tried to pay, her credit card was declined. Flustered, she backed away from the till – now she had to figure out how to transfer £1,200 to the account she could access on her card.

Later, she told me the story not as a traumatic experience but like 'an impossible game of *Mario Kart* – you think you've completed all the levels, but there's always another, more difficult level. Embarking on IVF is such an emotional, physical, visceral thing – then the logistical challenges on top of that. You have to compartmentalise all your emotions to get through it.'

Her experience echoes that of some of my other friends, who describe the steep learning curve from total novice at the outset of an IVF journey to relative expert by the end. Virginia had a striking analogy for figuring out the various costs, budgeting decisions and risk assessments required when making choices about your own treatment.

'Your body is a business, basically, and you're the CEO of that business.'

Something about the pharmacy scene Virginia described to me, the idea of spending an unpredictable amount of money on a treatment that may or may not work, made me think again of the relationship between fertility treatment and institutionalised risk. Specifically, I thought of a gambler buying chips at a casino, preparing for another throw of the dice. Embarking on IVF has historically been a relatively uncalculated risk, because the statistical chances of success are so hard to pinpoint, although that is now changing with AI. Much more than money is at stake, but most people must have private funds to pursue it.

Two of my friends – my thirty-five-year-old girlfriend F, and her partner in his fifties – applied for, and were denied, IVF on the UK's National Health Service (NHS) on two grounds. First, F's partner was considered too old to help. Secondly, although they had no children together, F's partner had existing children from his previous relationship. So while my friend, at thirty-five, desperately wanted children, her choice of partner excluded her from help from the state.

A vast amount of money is made from infertile women and couples in the private healthcare sector, but there is a different pot of money – its use under constant debate, although rarely in the public arena – that is spent on helping them in a public health service. The ability to conceive is a matter of luck – biological, economic, even residential. Currently, people living in adjacent postcodes can be entitled to completely different opportunities to access IVF. Local integrated care boards (ICBs) decide who is and is not entitled to free treatment, and how many rounds to offer. Some ICBs will not treat women over thirty-five, or women with a high BMI, single women, lesbian couples, a heterosexual couple in which either partner has a child from a previous relationship (like my friends) or women who have not already tried self-funded intrauterine insemination. Ironically, single women or couples who have already paid privately for IVF (and then run out of money, perhaps) are automatically ineligible.

The result is not exactly a random lottery, but one that resembles the ancient female Fates representing birth, life and death in Greek mythology. The primary Fate, Clothos, spins the thread of life for every baby in utero – an unseen but powerful force dealing out good and bad fortune according to her own, mysterious logic. The ICBs make decisions that are, at least in theory, meant to provide the most cost-effective care to the most needful – a huge responsibility that necessarily excludes some infertile women and prioritises others. These local departments do what is, in their eyes, affordable and fair. How does it feel to make those decisions, to play God?

When people are not entitled to IVF on the NHS because they do not fall into the qualifying category of their area, or are denied it outright on ethical grounds (usually relating to their age or pre-existing conditions), they can choose to take matters into their own hands. As I discovered, Northern Cyprus is one of the most popular of these low-cost fertility hubs among Brits, given its relative familiarity as a tourist destination, its plethora of donors and its willingness to treat women up to the age of fifty-five. One NHS obstetrician told me, with palpable frustration, about her experiences of treating women in their fifties who return from overseas IVF hotspots pregnant with twins or triplets, often with serious pregnancy complications.

I started to think about the economic forces that result in young women in Russia, Ukraine, Central Asia and Turkey selling their eggs to impregnate, among others, older, well-off British women. These women will never meet face to face. Their transaction is brokered by clinics that profit two ways: from the younger women's relative poverty and from the older women's desperation to become a mother.

The power that resides in doctors and nurses to create life can manifest itself not only in a straightforward profit-making sense, but in stranger, more disturbing ways. The specific kind of God complex or narcissism that some (male) fertility doctors seem to suffer from fascinates me, and is relatively well documented – Dr Karbaat in the Netherlands, and Dr Cline and Dr Fortier in the US, to name some of the most well known, impregnated dozens of their unwitting female patients with their own sperm.

Other Genghis Khan wannabes will have inevitably gone under the radar, but even the known stats are striking – the *New York Times* reported in 2022 that more than fifty fertility doctors in the US alone have been accused of fraud in connection with donating sperm.[45] Many of these cases were uncovered when home DNA testing kits hit the market, particularly with the spike in use during the Covid-19 pandemic.

Sometimes the God complex is more subtle, and would have gone completely undetected if not for some chance remark or strange exchange. Seven years ago, in a popular fertility clinic in Vancouver, a distinguished Canadian doctor hugged my friend Lisa as he congratulated her on her pregnancy following the IVF treatment he had overseen. Holding her close, he whispered in her ear: 'I did what your husband wasn't able to.' In shock, she said nothing as he warmly embraced her husband.

Later, she complained and inferred from the clinic's embarrassed but seemingly unsurprised response that he had made similar comments to other patients – but there has been no scandal, no exposure. My friend and her husband considered escalating their complaint, but ultimately decided, as soon-to-be-parents, that they did not have the time or energy. Instead, they complained directly to the doctor and received this response:

> Dear Lisa,
> Thank you for the comments that you made. You are absolutely correct in what you have said. I have no idea why those words came out of my mouth. I have never said that before and have no idea why I even spoke them. I realize how hurtful they are and I can only apologize for my stupidity and thoughtlessness. Regardless of the cause of your failure to conceive, my remark was uncalled for, insensitive and of no relevance. I can only guess that on the spur of the moment and my joy of what I saw on the ultrasound, my thought processes were overshadowed by my happiness with the findings on the scan.

Lisa forwarded the email to the partners of the clinic, suspecting that parts of it were a copy-and-paste job. Apparently, none of the staff was surprised, and 'they all bent over backwards to help us after this'.

When I met Dr Rahi Victory, a fellow Canadian fertility doctor, at the Dublin Future Fertility Show, he had agreed that the God complex seemed to be prevalent in male fertility doctors. He was not talking about the urge to secretly inseminate patients, or eclipse a patient's husband, and he did not agree that it was necessarily a bad phenomenon. In his eyes, as he explained in a later email to me, the God complex was harmful when 'you're so sure of yourself you fail to grow, or focus on patients'.

He referenced the performance of actor Alec Baldwin playing a highly qualified, repellently arrogant gynaecologist in the 1993 film noir *Malice*. During a scene reminiscent of Jack Nicholson's court scene in *A Few Good Men* – another Aaron Sorkin script – Baldwin's doctor is accused of having a God complex, and answers with total defiance:

'You ask me if I have a God complex? Let me tell you something: I *am* God.'

In the right context, Dr Victory explained to me, the God complex can be 'a desire to be the best, it can actually incentivise learning, excellence and patient care. It depends on what is most important to the physician. To be perfectly honest, this is me to some extent. I actively want to be better than everyone else. It's important to me to be the best. I don't see this as necessarily me *thinking* I'm better than everyone else, but I definitely *want* to be better than everyone else.'

I appreciated his honesty. In a later email, he qualified his own self-assessment: 'I don't really think I have a God complex, but I do believe I am very good at what I do. Better than others? Yes, I would say that. But in my case it is my drive to be the best. I always listen, I'm always willing to learn, but I will never stop trying to strive for number one.'

CASH COW

Reading this, I wondered how different this was to normal ambition and competitiveness in any field of life – is any desire to be the best a 'God complex'? Surely it is significant that fertility doctors are not just caring for their patients but creating life – the most God-like of powers vested in medical practice? And what about the undeniable whiff of machismo? Victory admitted that he doesn't 'really see the competitiveness in female colleagues. Perhaps in a rare few, but it is very common among the males.

'Maybe it's just our prehistoric selves coming to the fore? But I think used wisely it can actually benefit patients. Used improperly, it can be a great tool for evil.'

There is an obvious fact of human biology that is worth emphasising: women could never act on a God complex in the way a man can, by which I mean the most dramatic scenario of secret mass conception. There are egg donors who have donated many times, producing tens if not hundreds of eggs over the course of several retrievals, of which a portion might be used successfully. But there could be no one akin to the fertility doctors like Dr Karbaat and Dr Cline, or to anonymous super-donors.

One high-profile sperm donor in the US has actually complained of the emotional toll involved in becoming the biological father of far too many children. Dylan Stone-Miller tried to meet the ninety-six children he produced after donating for several years as a student to earn some cash.[46] Now, he lobbies for a national cap on sperm donation. But he is unusual; most super-donors seem to be either indifferent or to get a kick out of the many children they produce, and that is possible because donating costs them very little indeed.

Egg donors and women who have their own eggs retrieved for IVF or freezing take on health risks that include, in the most extreme cases, death with every retrieval, earning or paying up to thousands of dollars while doing so. This is a relatively high-risk, high-reward market, urgently in need of greater regulation and enforcement – as is the case with so many markets that revolve around women and their bodies. I was yet to discover how bad it could get.

Sam Everingham is a busy man, and he lives in a wildly different time zone to me. Before we met at the Dublin Future Fertility Show, I had found myself talking to him on Zoom at 8 p.m. his time, 9 a.m. mine, as he finished off dinner on his sofa in Sydney. I'd found his name in an article in the *Irish Independent* from 2023, reporting on Irish and Australian couples affected by a huge fertility scandal in Crete.

Everingham has an unusual expertise, increasingly in demand. His organisation, Growing Families, provides advice and assistance to couples undergoing surrogacy overseas, these days mainly in the US, Colombia, Georgia and Mexico. He learned first-hand about the industry when he and his partner had two girls by surrogate in India in 2011, during what he calls the surrogacy 'gold rush' there. (Four years later commercial surrogacy was outlawed in India, first for international clients, and then for domestic clients.)

Talking to Everingham confirmed my growing realisation that paying for any donor – anonymous or (allegedly) non-anonymous – is an extreme exercise in trust and hope, and perhaps ultimately a doomed one. Even knowing everything it is possible to know about the person you choose to procreate with, you have no way of predicting how the genetic lottery will play out. Yet in a desperate enough position, people will take a chance on anything, and pay as much as they can possibly afford, to people offering them the world.

What I didn't know before speaking to Everingham was the extent of fertility fraud possible in an EU country with regulations regarding surrogacy. Greece, specifically the island of Crete, hit the news spectacularly in August 2023 when the organised crime unit of national police busted the Mediterranean Fertility Institute (MFI) in Chania, in the west of the island.[47] They arrested eight staff, including the institute's founder, and exposed a human-trafficking ring, which had been bringing vulnerable women from Georgia and Bulgaria to Crete to 'donate' their eggs, and to act as surrogates, housed in what local news outlets described as squalid conditions.

Sam, who seems to have seen it all, passed on one particular thread of this story with genuine horror in his voice. Doctors at the MFI, to save money in their IVF treatments, had apparently used the harvested eggs of scores of women paying for treatment to create embryos to impregnate other women. Many of these cases of egg theft were impossible to trace, but at least one local Cretan woman was informed by police that her eggs had been stolen and implanted in another woman.[48] Because of confidentiality laws, they could not tell her who had received her eggs, or whether the transfer had resulted in any children.

EGGS

This was mind-blowing to hear about from Everingham (Growing Families had coordinated embryo shipping for some of these parents), but what I also did not realise, until a later exchange with him, was that the episode was uncomfortably close to home for Everingham himself. Having been told that their two daughters came from the eggs of a single donor at the Indian clinic and were therefore half-sisters, Everingham and his partner had doubts that grew as the years passed. In 2023, when the girls were twelve, the couple grew sick of wondering and ordered DNA tests. The girls' results did not match.

I soon realised that cases of egg theft are as old as mainstream IVF itself. In 1996, the Californian fertility doctors Ricardo Asch and José Balmaceda Riera (father of the actor Pedro Pascal), both highly successful and sought-after, were indicted by a federal grand jury for crimes committed between 1986 and 1995 that included using secretly harvested eggs in their fertility treatments.[49] They were also investigated for tax fraud; Asch subsequently fled to Mexico, Balmaceda to Chile.

In the late 1990s, an Israeli gynaecologist called Professor Zion Ben-Rafael was accused of doing something similar on possibly a greater scale, stealing hundreds of eggs from unconscious women in his care – sometimes overstimulating their ovaries – with which he impregnated scores of his other patients.[50] Prosecutors alleged he stole 232 eggs from one woman alone and used 155 of them for the IVF treatments of 33 infertile women. In 2000, he was apparently caught paying $20,000 to have his criminal file closed. In the end, the case never went to trial but the judge noted that a doctor's code of ethics had been blatantly violated. In 2007, Ben-Rafael confessed to the crimes as part of a plea bargain which meant that his medical license was suspended for two and a half years; the judge said he was treated with leniency because of his 'impressive service' in the Israeli Defense Forces.

Today, he publishes papers on new reproductive practices and is the founder and chair of the annual World Congress on Controversies in Obstetrics, Gynecology & Infertility. I met him in November 2025 in Rome at the 33rd Congress; he was friendly and warm, clearly on top of his game at the age of 76, and hugely respected by the other experts present. When I interviewed him, he did not want to go on record with his side of the story, but implied that the case had been a witch hunt. Perhaps the truth cannot be known; meeting him certainly made me understand why he maintains a brilliant reputation despite his convictions.

BLIGHTED EGGS

While writing this section of the book, I started seeing eggs everywhere. I looked at my daughter and imagined the millions of eggs in her tiny body, gradually depleting from puberty onwards. I thought of the Russian dolls that exist within mothers and daughters, the eggs hidden away in the ovaries of female foetuses from gestation, tiny fertile babies growing in their mothers' wombs. I knew that the egg that eventually became my daughter was already nestled in my body as I grew in my mother's belly; my mother had carried her own granddaughter. I wondered if I had carried mine too.

I read my daughter books my mother had kept through several house moves from when I was a little girl – classic fairy tales like *Rapunzel* and *Sleeping Beauty*, in which a childless king and queen, longing for a baby, are eventually granted one, which is then stolen away by a jealous old childless witch. I realised I had grown up on stories of infertility and magic alongside the earthy realism of Beatrix Potter and characters like Jemima Puddle-Duck, desperate to hatch her eggs but thwarted by powers beyond her control. I was handing these stories down to my daughter in turn, shaping her ideas about female fertility and agency, about babies as mysterious and mercurial gifts.

I imagined my own ovaries like symmetrical bunches of grapes, gently withering on the vine; I wondered whether the body gives any sign before it releases its very last egg, for the very last time. I thought about the finality of menopause – not a pause at all, but maybe a liberation as well as a kind of death. I thought about all my periods, a flood of blood and pain transformed, eventually, by some hormonal alchemy, into something I was afraid of: stasis. The postpartum period of fertility itself.

I became pregnant again, and after a couple of months experienced what is known as a missed miscarriage; my body gave no sign that the embryo inside me had stopped developing. In the hospital, I stared at an ultrasound image of a yolk sac that was too small, with no heartbeat, and wondered what I had been doing the moment it died.

'An anembryonic miscarriage,' the sonographer said. 'Otherwise known as a blighted egg.' I knew, rationally, that maybe it was a blighted sperm but silently accepted the term, letting its ugliness burrow into my brain like a sperm penetrating an egg. My womb had held the invisible foetus for weeks, slowly, patiently growing a sac while the heartbeat failed to materialise.

I waited to bleed, and thought of all the women who had experienced this, and worse. Eventually, when I failed to miscarry, I had surgery to remove what was left of the pregnancy. I chose to be conscious during the procedure. Lying with my feet in stirrups, I felt a kindly nurse stroke my hand as a local anaesthetic was injected into my cervix. I thought of the countless backstreet abortions and miscarriages that women have undergone, without any of the pain relief or kindness I was offered. I thought of the women paying to have their eggs harvested by the most rapacious private clinics, women desperate for children, mourning their miscarriages, pumped full of hormones and sold a little percentage of hope. And because I had now glimpsed some of that world myself, I became angry, I am ashamed to say, in a way that I had not been before.

PLACENTA

Organ attached to womb lining and foetus via umbilical cord, weight approximately 500g at birth, length approximately 22cm

Cost to producer of delivery: from $0 (public health service) to $30,000–$50,000 (uncomplicated vaginal or caesarean delivery, respectively, in the US without insurance)

Cost of commercial surrogate programme: from $16,000 (Iran) to $250,000 (US)

Surrogate receives: from $0 (strictly altruistic service) to > $90,000 (US)

Processing of own placenta for consumption: approximately $350–$900 (UK and US)

A BUSINESS TRANSACTION

'I am the most experienced surrogate in the US – my lawyers will tell you.'

With calm confidence, Stephenie sips soda through a straw in her parked car, sunlight flooding her face as she talks to me over video call. It is midday in Idaho, evening for me in the UK. She is waiting to meet her mother, who apparently didn't like her being a surrogate so many times – 'didn't like the risk'. Stephenie is friendly and open about the joys and pitfalls of carrying twelve surrogate children, after having two children of her own.

Twelve? My ears and brain struggle to process this.

'Yes! Four singletons and four sets of twins,' says Stephenie with a proud smile. She gave birth to them all vaginally apart from the last two sets of twins, who needed caesarean sections. In 2023, aged forty-three, she had a hysterectomy.

Stephenie describes herself as the kind of person 'who couldn't say no to more pregnancies. During my last surrogacy – I was pregnant with twins at forty-two – I was crying to my doctor, saying, "Don't let me do this again!" My body was like: *enough*.'

Instinctively, my hand reaches for my tummy; I can almost hear my womb howling in sympathy. After my conversation with Stephenie, I contacted several fertility lawyers in the UK,

Europe and the US, as well as her own, asking them if they knew of any surrogates who had carried twelve or more babies. None of them had, and one American lawyer elaborated, with a squirmy-eyed emoji, that he 'wouldn't want to. That is too many babies and too much risk in my opinion. Let me know when her uterus falls out.' I wondered if I found his last comment jarring because he is a man, without a uterus to worry about, or because a seasoned lawyer can talk flippantly about almost anything. With thirteen surrogate births, Carole Harlock from the UK claims to be the most prolific surrogate in the world, but Stephenie appears to remain unchallenged in the commercial market of the US.

Until her hysterectomy, Stephenie had carried one or two babies almost every year for the last decade, earning between $20,000 and $60,000 during each pregnancy. Settled in a small town near Boise, Idaho, where she'd lived since the age of nine, she and her husband had two children by the time she was thirty.

'Then I was happy, and I was done. But after my son was born, I realised I love being pregnant, I absolutely love it!' She signed up to act as a surrogate with her husband's full support, and has no regrets.

For those who can afford it, the US has always been the biggest market for commercial surrogacy in the world. While the practice appears and disappears in other countries like a legal hot potato, the US has been steadily legalising and expanding access to surrogacy state by state, year on year. In the Midwest in general, but in particular in Stephenie's home state of Idaho, which has a relatively low average income, the high availability of surrogates plus relaxed regulation has led to a booming cottage industry. Until 2023, there were no relevant regulations at all in Idaho – in April that year, its House of Representatives passed a house bill that allowed pre-birth validation of surrogacy agreements, encouraging legal representation for all parties involved.

Stephenie says that there is still not enough supply to meet demand for surrogacy in Boise, even though she estimates that about 50 per cent of the pregnant women where she lives – a 1,200-person town just outside of Boise – are already surrogates.

'I say to any pregnant woman I see around town, "Oh, is it your own or a surrogacy?" I'd say about half the time they say surrogacy. Two women in the courthouse where I work are both pregnant with surrogate babies right now.'

A few years ago, Stephenie started her own agency, matching surrogates with intended parents. Now, with her potentially record-breaking experience behind her, she runs the agency alongside her other day job as a courthouse clerk; she charges domestic clients $12,000 per successful match, while foreign clients are charged more. One of the biggest sources of her foreign clients is Spain, where surrogacy is not only illegal but classed as a crime against women – and where both left-wing and right-wing political factions are, unusually, united in their opposition to it. While most of the US surrogacy market is domestic, a substantial proportion of intended parents are foreign (an estimated 32 per cent in 2020, and anecdotally, closer to 40 per cent currently).[1]

Despite the apparently plentiful supply of active surrogates in Boise, Stephenie says she is always trying to recruit more local women, sharing her own experiences to allay their concerns. One of the misconceptions Stephenie has to correct with these women is that their own eggs are going to be used.

'I tell them, no, it's not your egg, not your embryo. Not your baby. Completely genetically different.'

Stephenie, like every surrogate I interviewed or have heard interviewed, insisted she has never felt that any of the babies she carried for others were 'hers'.

'They were never mine.' Did you ever feel any emotional bond? 'No.'

I believe her, even though I cannot help wondering if I would feel the same way. I have only carried my own biological children, to whom I felt an intense bond while pregnant – they were an extension of me both physically and existentially, in every sense 'mine', and I knew the bond would continue for the rest of my life. Imagining anything else is a difficult thought experiment – one of many I had during my conversations for this book.

It seemed understandable to me that Stephenie's prospective surrogates were confused about their biological connection to the baby. 'Traditional' surrogacy, in which the surrogate's own egg is fertilised by sperm from an intended father, was the only way surrogacy was done for millennia. Women carrying babies for others – voluntarily or coerced, paid or unpaid – is not new. In the Book of Genesis, Sarah, the infertile wife of Abraham, orders him to sleep with her Egyptian slave Hagar to conceive a child for them. This upending and abuse of power, steeped in jealousy, is reflected in the dystopian

PLACENTA

Gilead of Margaret Atwood's *The Handmaid's Tale*, in which fertile women are used as birthing slaves by wealthy families in a largely infertile future society – a popular comparison among surrogacy critics. Ruling dynasties have long depended on concubines bearing male babies to be raised as potential heirs. Historically, surrogacy has often been seen as an extension of rape.

So traditional surrogacy, with its emotive perception of babies either being 'taken' from their biological mothers, or their mothers 'giving them up', influences many people's feelings towards surrogacy today, even after fertility treatments have changed the game – genetically speaking at least. Since the first successful birth via in vitro fertilisation in 1978, advances in reproductive technology have allowed independently created embryos to be implanted into the womb of a surrogate, or 'gestational carrier', the legal term ('sounds like a pigeon', as one industry professional put it). Gestational as opposed to traditional surrogacy is now the standard in commercial arrangements, particularly in countries like the US, where the embryo is treated as distinctly as possible from the surrogate as a matter of law.

Whether a surrogate should be paid or unpaid – or allowed to do it at all – are questions interpreted in wildly different ways, especially in Europe. One American fertility lawyer I interviewed was surprised that I was treating surrogacy as a controversial subject, while for some of my European and British interviewees, any suggestion that paid surrogacy might be OK was completely revolting, or, at best, unsettling. Feminists in particular are deeply divided about whether surrogacy is primarily exploitative or empowering for women. Some countries reflect their cultural attitudes in their laws – either explicitly legalising or criminalising the practice – while others choose to maintain an enigmatic and usually problematic silence on the issue.

In countries like the UK, New Zealand, Australia, the Netherlands and Canada, only altruistic surrogacy is legal, and both traditional and gestational are practised – I spoke to one British surrogate, for example, Jemma, who carried her own biological daughter for a gay couple. (She used one of the couple's sperm to inseminate herself with a syringe.) 'Contracts' governing altruistic surrogacy in the UK cannot be enforced, and birth mothers are recognised as legal mothers on UK birth certificates, which can lead to obvious worries for intended parents: will the surrogate hand over the child if she is not obliged to do so? Often, this uncertainty, coupled with a scarcity of surrogates, drives them to the US, despite the high price tag – or to cheaper destinations abroad, as I was to discover.

Stephenie told me she would never act as a surrogate unpaid, and 'no one should' – something that I heard echoed by other American surrogates. She has extensive experience of the legal and medical protocols that each surrogacy entails, and feels well placed to give candidates advice, some of which sounds slightly alarming.

'I tell them, put everything in the contract – like whether you will want to breastfeed or not – and sometimes they don't listen, and it's frustrating. My advice to prospective surrogates is this: everything will seem great before the birth, but the gloves will come off after the birth. The parents won't be the same. Put everything in the contract.'

Despite a generally easy and happy run of surrogacies, her first attempt in 2009 was disappointing. 'The embryo didn't take [after transfer to her womb]; I thought I was done. Then I tried again in 2011. I did three embryo transfers for a couple from California, and we were successful at the third transfer. Baby H was born in April 2012.'

I ask how much she was paid per transfer. 'One thousand dollars.'

Her first surrogacy also involved a huge disappointment in terms of her relationship with the intended parents. After an initially promising start, towards the end of the pregnancy the dad became 'such a jerk'.

Stephenie had let the couple stay in her home as her due date approached. The day before that date, she and her husband were on the sofa watching TV, when the dad-to-be came into the room and berated her.

'He said: "What are you doing just sitting there? Get up and do some jumping jacks [to induce labour], I want my child."

'As soon as the baby was born he said, "This is a business transaction." They didn't thank me the day of the birth.'

Listening to this, I am already appalled, but the litany of bad behaviour continues. The 'jerk' dad used Stephenie's food-allowance token in hospital, and did not allow her to hold the baby even momentarily. She was paid $20,000 for this first surrogacy in 2012 – 'nothing in today's market', she notes.

'At the beginning of the journey with them, I said I'd do it for the same price again. But they were such jerks that when they contacted me again asking me to carry for them a second time, I refused to do it for $20,000 again. I said, "This is a business transaction" – the husband's words. I charged them $30,000.'

I pause to take in everything Stephenie has told me, particularly the $10,000 jerk penalty. One obvious question has to be asked – why did she do it again after such an upsetting experience?

'I love being pregnant,' comes her reply, unhesitating. 'And the money was good. We were paying off our debt. I don't think anyone should do it for free.

'After that first journey, I thought, *OK, I'll try it again, but I'll do it with a Christian couple.* I am a Christian woman. So this second journey was twins for a Christian couple. I delivered May 17th, 2013. Then I carried for the Californian couple again.'

As I discovered when I started reading agency paperwork matching surrogates with intended parents, most agencies allow both to express a preference (or aversion) for any particular religion, ethnicity or sexuality in the other. One form I read offered potential surrogates the following category boxes to tick or cross: *Same sex couple, Single male, Single female, Couple using an egg donor, Couple using a sperm donor, An older couple, A couple with children, An African American couple, A Jewish couple, A Caucasian couple, An Indian couple, A Hispanic couple, An international couple (Living outside of the US), A non-English speaking couple with a translator.* A blank space also allowed candidates to request any other preferences or restrictions.

Stephenie tells me that the base payment for a first-time surrogate is now $50,000 in Idaho (slightly above the state's average annual income at the time), while an experienced surrogate gets an additional $10,000 (plus $5,000 extra for twins). This is roughly average, nationwide, at the time of my research – some agencies start at $30,000, while top-end agencies pay their experienced surrogates $90,000 or more. Slightly to my surprise, agencies rarely specify upper age limits for their surrogates (though the guidelines of the American Society for Reproductive Medicine advise forty-two) – a lot of value is placed on successful previous pregnancies, reflected in the bonus payment, despite the extra monitoring needed for older women.

(One of the very few common stipulations in commercial arrangements worldwide is that a surrogate must already have carried at least one child of her own to term – even the least ethical outfits do not want to waste their time with a woman who has not proved herself physically capable of doing so.)

Shopping various US agency websites through the eyes of a discerning wannabe surrogate, I discovered that most of them offer to cover lost wages (sometimes capped, sometimes not, and usually offered for the surrogate's partner as well), bed rest, miscellaneous monthly expenses and, in some cases, surprise bonuses at pregnancy milestones. The elite Californian agency Growing Generations, which offers base pay starting at $75,000 for first-time surrogates, increases this by $10,000 for every subsequent successful pregnancy, while suggesting that the right candidates can name their price: 'Experienced surrogates are invited to discuss setting their own compensation with us.'[2]

'It all depends,' agrees Stephenie. 'I had a surrogate at my agency here who wanted $70,000 for twins, which is $20,000 more than the usual price [for a singleton]. It's a case-by-case basis. Maybe they'll want extra for a potential hysterectomy – it's usually about $3,500 or $5,000 – and they will put that in the contract, and the parents will accept it or not.'

I reflect that $3,500 seems a very small price for losing one's womb, as does an extra $5,000 for carrying twins – accepting the first figure is a bet on something relatively unlikely to happen, while the other is compensation for almost guaranteed extra discomfort and possible pregnancy complications. (One US lawyer told me 'we do everything in our power to prevent triplets' – multiples were common in the early days of IVF, when doctors tried to maximise the chances of at least one embryo 'taking'.) While reading another interviewee's surrogacy contract, I noticed that the loss of one fallopian tube would be reimbursed to the tune of $1,500, but the loss of both would result in only $2,500. I questioned what logic resulted in this decision – particularly given that the loss of both fallopian tubes would result in infertility.

Reading surrogacy contracts, I discovered a major attraction of the income involved: it is tax free, and in wealthy states like California the saving is even greater than in a state like Idaho. An experienced surrogate based in Southern California can earn a base payment of $90,000 (for nine months of pregnancy plus roughly three months of embryo transfer preparation), rather than the rough $60,000 she would earn on a $90,000-a-year salary.[3] Contracts typically do not refer to surrogacy payments as a 'fee', or even 'compensation' (both of which are taxable), but as 'reimbursement' (which is not). In some contracts, the payments are simply referred to as 'living expenses', which struck me as the most elegant solution. The whole transaction is often presented as an altruistic endeavour, with terms like 'gratitude' cited as the official motivation for transferring money; I discovered that this is to emphasise the point that in legal terms, paying a surrogate is not the same thing as buying a baby, which is a federal offence.

I found myself wondering what Stephenie had done with the hundreds of thousands of dollars she had earned from a decade of surrogacy work. (Surrogates in the US are required to demonstrate financial stability before entering into any agreement, which means the ability to cover monthly household costs without the help of surrogacy payments. Women receiving government assistance like welfare payments or public housing are usually excluded.) My British hesitation in talking about money held me back, but I steeled myself – she said she used it to pay off the debt on her family house. 'We are financially independent, and the surrogacies have definitely helped with that. I wouldn't do it for free, definitely not.'

I also found myself thinking about the 'pain and suffering' specified in the contract. While Stephenie herself had easy pregnancies, 'bar a few headaches', she is all too aware of the medical risks involved. A friend of hers had delivered a few days before we spoke; she had suffered from placenta accreta, a dangerous condition in which the placenta embeds into the womb, leading to haemorrhage. Stephenie's friend ended up having a hysterectomy. Tragically, she had wanted more kids of her own (surrogates are usually encouraged to wait until they have completed their own family before embarking on surrogacy).

This brought our conversation naturally back to the hysterectomy that Stephenie had begged her doctor to perform on her. Was it a drastic form of self-help, a cure for an instinct she couldn't help responding to? Stephenie tacitly agreed.

'When I help match parents with surrogates, if I like the parents and can't find them a surrogate, I want to carry for them myself. So I begged my doctor to do the operation once I'd finished my last surrogacy. No regrets – I wish I had done it twenty years ago.'

Another obvious question sprang to mind – that would have meant she couldn't have acted as a surrogate?

'I love not having periods, if I'm honest. That's probably why I did surrogacy so much, I love not having periods – I would be pregnant and then breastfeeding, each journey [lasting] a year, no periods.'

The American Society for Reproductive Medicine (ASRM) guidelines advise a limit of five pregnancies for surrogates.[4] After Stephenie's fifth surrogate pregnancy (and sixth surrogate child – her second journey produced twins), she matched with a couple who took her to see their fertility doctor to check her medical eligibility for another pregnancy. As Stephenie recalled, this doctor was unfazed at a potential breach of the ASRM rules. 'He told me, "I don't give a damn, you can rock it.'" Stephenie laughed as she told the story. 'So we side-stepped the guidelines.'

Stephenie has a firm 'favourite intended mother I've carried for': Ali, a Jewish woman from New York who was diagnosed with a genetic condition that caused infertility, after suffering repeated miscarriages during IVF treatment with her husband. The closeness of this relationship came as something of a surprise for Stephenie.

'At first, I was so sceptical about Ali, because my first set of parents were from California. I thought, *She'll be the same, she's from New York*. I 100 per cent did that one for the money. I remember thinking, *I don't care if they like me or not – they're gonna be jerks anyway*. But the day I met Ali, she made dinner for us, she was fantastic from the start. I remember thinking I would do this for her for free. I love her so much.'

Ali wanted Stephenie to breastfeed and pump milk for the babies, despite being warned by her lawyer that the sight of another woman feeding her babies would only upset her. After Stephenie's first disastrous surrogacy with the Californian couple, when she was not allowed to hold let alone breastfeed the baby she had delivered, she realised how important this contact was to her. With Ali's twins, she stipulated that she wanted two hours alone with the babies.

'I put it in my contract and I got it, and I got my closure. I felt great emotionally. And when I had Baby R [the Californian couple's second son] I was breastfeeding that baby, and I felt a lot better.'

This was very interesting to me; Stephenie said she did not think of any of her surrogate babies as 'hers', and yet she needed this postpartum contact as closure – an experience so important it required legal protection.

I thought about the hormonal fireworks of childbirth and early lactation – so dramatic and overwhelming that it was impossible, for me at least, to disentangle my emotions from the biochemical changes going on in my body. Did I experience primarily a physical or emotional need to hold my baby? I had assumed it was both, and it is likely that Stephenie's was too – but for her, contact with the babies she had carried was a form of closure, rather than the beginning of something, as it was for me.

In a contract I later read in Northern Cyprus, I noticed that the surrogate was strictly prohibited from breastfeeding or having contact with the baby, and was ordered to take 'lactation-cessation medication' prescribed by a doctor. While this sounded grim, I reflected that I would probably prefer not to hold and risk bonding with a baby that was not mine to keep. The sooner the milk stopped, the sooner you could move on.

I wondered about how contact with the baby affects a surrogate's emotional bond with the baby's parents, and about the difference, for example, between Stephenie's relationship with Ali, and with the Californian jerk couple. I asked her how close she is to the other parents she has carried for. She described a spectrum ranging from sporadic Instagram messaging, frequent chats with the gay couple in Switzerland for whom she carried two sets of twins ('I'm their "tummy mummy" and I think that's adorable'), and a sad, intermittent communication with a single mother in Connecticut, whose partner died a year after Stephenie delivered twins for them.

She has no contact with the 'jerks' from California. She says she is not particularly bothered about maintaining a relationship with the children she has carried, but does care about a continued bond with their parents. Ali's kids 'didn't want anything to do with me when I visited them. I was like, "Oh, that's a bummer!" But it didn't really bother me.'

I asked her about her own family – how did they feel about her frequent surrogate pregnancies?

'My kids absolutely hated me being a surrogate. I would ask them for help all the time, and didn't have any energy, and they would say, "Oh, you're so grumpy." They're so happy I've finished now. My husband liked the money; he would have let me do it twenty more times if I wanted to.'

She laughed.

'Now it's his turn to work hard.'

These words – spoken half in jest – stayed with me. There is no doubt that pregnancy is 'hard work'; the labour involved in birthing a baby is, literally, labour (certainly the hardest my body has ever worked, and the nearest I have come to death). Like Silvia Federici in the 1970s, surrogacy advocates argue that carrying a baby is essentially no different from any other form of work, or – to use the legal terminology – a form of pain and suffering for which one should be reimbursed. All the US surrogates I interviewed told me that, although they did not become surrogates 'for the money', they would not consider doing it for free. I came to realise that payment was important to them not just as cash, but as a form of recognition and respect.

The altruistic surrogates I interviewed in the UK and Canada were equally insistent that, to them, carrying someone else's child for money would feel 'dirty', even though the money itself would be welcome. Two of them, strangely, described it as the potential 'cherry on the cake' that they would nevertheless not accept. (It is worth noting that, in practice, UK-based surrogates can and do receive money from intended parents that is not strictly to cover pregnancy-related expenses.)

The power of cultural context to shape a personal value system had never seemed so stark to me — this idea of money as 'dirty' or not — yet there were also similarities in how passionately all these surrogates felt about shifting the public perception of surrogacy as 'womb renting'. They were all enthusiastic about sharing their stories — they were aware there is an ideological battle going on, and wanted to do their part.

PICK YOUR SIDE

It seems important, in many circles, to have the 'right' take on surrogacy, and for it to be fundamental, not dependent on context or circumstance, almost Kantian. I began to feel rather alone in my fluctuating feelings.

I never had the sense that any of the surrogates I interviewed were not being transparent with me. They gave me a full spectrum of positive and negative experiences; there was no hard sell of surrogacy as a perfect, problem-free arrangement. Yet their stories had a beauty to them — stories of trust and intimacy between total strangers, and the miraculous arrival of longed-for babies. These were all women acting with autonomy, proud of their ability to help others while financially supporting their own families. I admired them, in many ways. The challenge for me was imagining their experiences and emotions, when mine were so vividly different to theirs, while also imagining the experiences of other women less fortunate than them.

It is undeniable that the growth of altruistic surrogacy in wealthy countries like Canada challenges the idea that it is a practice only entered into by vulnerable and exploited women, or by those attracted by the high fees offered in parts of the US. But, notably, I was speaking to surrogates in countries where the practice is legal, and these women were happy to open up to a complete stranger. I had not yet begun to look into countries where surrogacy can involve shame, abuse and coercion.

Over the next decade, the value of the global surrogacy market is projected to increase almost tenfold, but surrogates are becoming harder to access. Commercial surrogacy for foreigners is legal only in the US, Ukraine, Georgia and, surprisingly, Iran – in a handful of other countries (like Mexico, Colombia, Northern Cyprus, Uganda, Kenya, Armenia and Nigeria) it operates without explicit laws, and in many countries it has been outright banned – hence the surge in demand for the current top destinations. The US, although by far the most expensive option, is popular in large part because it caters for gay parents, a significant proportion of the market (and because of the bonus of a US passport, at least currently). Ukrainian surrogacy is not offered to gay couples or single parents, and neither is Georgian; Putin's government banned commercial surrogacy for foreigners in December 2022, and in 2024, Argentina made it all but impossible for foreigners to access. Affordable options are drying up, particularly for gay couples, and prospective parents are turning to problematic alternatives.

In many emerging markets, surrogacy operates with a worrying culture of anonymity between surrogates and intended parents; no one but the agents know how the women are treated, or how much they are actually paid. Nigeria is on the UK's list of illegal adoption countries and concerns of child trafficking there are real; 'baby factories', in which underage girls are raped and kept against their will, provide children for the adoption market.[5] Reputable-looking fertility clinics with branches in multiple cities openly advertise for surrogates on their websites, despite the practice not being legal.[6] A 2025 High Court judgment in the UK dealt with a case where no records could be found of either the Nigerian surrogate used by a couple resident in the UK, or the payments made to her. She was assumed to be the biological mother of the child conceived with the intended father's sperm but could not be contacted for her permission to hand over parental responsibility. The judge granted the parental order anyway.[7]

In India, commercial surrogacy, previously a huge market, was banned in 2015 after the country became notorious for the exploitation of very poor women. Ukraine has been a leading market since the ban in India, but, similarly, the financial instability of some surrogates has led to concerns of exploitation, particularly since the Russian invasion.[8] In Georgia, where the market benefited from Ukraine's invasion in 2022, a lack of domestic surrogates has led to less expensive, 'travelling' surrogates yo-yoing between Central Asia and Georgia for embryo transfers and birth – a situation mirrored in Northern Cyprus.

As I continued my research, I started building a picture of a vast, ethically complex industry about which we do not know as much as we should, and in which surrogacy advocates and critics hold very little common ground, even with all the facts available. I wondered why there is no national conversation about surrogacy in the UK, no discussion of its nuances. I was not yet born when the practice was legalised in 1985, but the 2017 Law Reform Commission inquiry also passed me by. This apparently featured an 'open public consultation' about surrogacy law, to which only 340 members of the public responded.[9] The current government has announced that it will not prioritise surrogacy law reform, which is not surprising – there is no appetite to engage in the so-called culture wars that any vaguely centrist party struggles to navigate.

As I write, there has recently been a huge national debate in the UK about the legalisation of assisted dying, the informally named 'Suicide Bill'. It has dominated Parliament and the media – a rightfully urgent conversation. The ethics and legality of sex work, a more comparable topic to surrogacy, are discussed in polite society. Surrogacy rarely is, even as the practice becomes more common across the world. I started to realise that there is a particular kind of taboo attached to carrying other people's children that runs deeper than paid-for sex or legally getting state-sanctioned help to kill yourself. While newspaper columnists publish their hot takes, many people are hesitant to air their views, not knowing what to think or how to express tentative feelings on the subject. I realised I had to scrutinise my own feelings – as a woman and as a mother – before coming down too hard on anyone else's opinions or lack thereof.

LEAP OF FAITH

After my conversation with Stephenie, I realised that I was struggling to comprehend her experience, constantly comparing it to my own 'matrescence' (a term popularised by the writer Lucy Jones), or the process of becoming a mother. This was like trying to imagine breastfeeding another woman's child for money – my own lived experience was in some ways hindering my imagination. Stephenie had done something I could not conceive of doing – not once but many times – with a totally pragmatic attitude, and in doing so she had contributed substantially to her family's income. I felt a sense of awe for what her body had done, as well as a kind of gulf between us. What did it actually feel like to sign that first contract? Or to prepare contracts for others to sign, as Stephenie does running her surrogacy agency – recruiting and guiding other women into the work, connecting them with parents seeking their perfect match, taking responsibility for rejecting and accepting applicants?

One of these applicants was Shelby, a twenty-eight-year-old mother of four, with dreams of working as a law-enforcement officer or FBI agent. Stephenie recruited her as a surrogate in

Boise in 2023, and she delivered a baby girl in April 2024. She said it was a 'beautiful' journey and was eager to do it again. We spoke via a protracted exchange of voice notes, which led to a stream of consciousness from Shelby as she reflected on her route to surrogacy.

'I always knew – ever since I was already pregnant with my first child – I knew that if I could bear children and someone else couldn't, why not give them that gift?' Here, Shelby's voice cracked with emotion. 'When Stephenie and I met for coffee, I didn't even hesitate, I just signed the paperwork.'

Now, Shelby is ready to meet some more intended parents, with all the energy and positivity of someone fresh on the dating scene again. She told me she would like to continue her journey of helping people until her doctor tells her she 'physically can't any more'. The way she described her motivations chimed with other surrogates I'd spoken to – a huge appreciation for gratitude from the parents, an anticipation of a lifelong bond, a sense of pride.

'I want to be that person at the end of the day, where they thank you and they hug you and tell you, "I'm so incredibly grateful for this gift, and I couldn't ask for anyone else to give me this gift."'

Like Stephenie, Shelby also seems to be on some level religiously motivated, which interested me.

'There's so much anger and hate in the world and no love any more,' she said passionately, towards the end of her last voice note. 'God is telling me I need to do my part.'

I wondered what it would feel like to be one of the other signatories on a contract, someone who was willing to navigate a relationship with a stranger that is both transactional and dependent on a deep level of trust.

Ali, the New Yorker for whom Stephenie had accepted to act as a surrogate '100 per cent for the money', particularly intrigued me. Stephenie assumed Ali would be 'a jerk', but she ended up becoming extremely close to her. Ali is a busy woman – a celebrated chef, TV host and author. She spoke to me between editorial meetings from her New York apartment, opening up immediately about what it felt like not to carry her own children, to entrust them to another woman – 'it was something I really had to grieve'. She described the weirdness of the medical side of the process, especially having had the experience of carrying her first child – a son – herself.

'My daughters were literally built in a lab. They are biologically ours; they share the same biological connection to me as my son. But I worried I wouldn't feel the same connection.'

She and her husband suffered repeated miscarriages and failed IVF rounds after the birth of their first child, before doctors discovered the reason: Ali is a genetic carrier of HY-restricting HLA class II alleles, a rare condition that means that after she gave birth to her son, his Y chromosome lingered in her womb and attacked all subsequent pregnancies. This diagnosis – which Ali explained briskly, like a doctor – sounded to me like a Biblical curse couched in the language of sci-fi. As Ali pointed out, if she'd had her daughters first, she could have conceived and carried her son, never knowing about her genetic condition.

I asked Ali what it was like to receive the diagnosis.

'Everyone kept asking me if I was upset, and actually I was relieved,' she answered. 'When we started doing IVF, the embryos were good. I knew from the beginning that something else was wrong.'

We mused on the mysteries of infertility, the terrifying limits to what doctors know, and how much can go wrong. Ali, reflecting on how difficult it was to get her diagnosis, said she was amazed how little pregnancy-related illnesses have been studied. I wondered about the roots of this relative black hole in medical knowledge, typical of a general lack of investment in women's health – is it down to the ethical boundaries that limit tests on pregnant women, or on women trying to conceive? Is it also more lucrative to continue to develop IVF treatments – increasingly in demand – than to plough money into researching the mysteries of the female body? Yet again, I found myself thinking about to whose cost and to whose profit the fertility industry functions in the ways that it does.

Ali's sister-in-law, who gave birth to her second child in New York a few months before Ali's twin girls were born, donated litres of her breastmilk to her nieces in February and March of 2020, before the pandemic hit. She was one of many donors who helped Ali but was the only one she knew, or even met. The others came from a Facebook group called Human Milk 4 Human Babies, which facilitates mothers donating to each other in a strictly non-commercial arrangement.

'You're not allowed to pay more than the cost of the bags. My husband was dashing around New York getting milk from these total strangers. It's one of the most pure instances of altruism I have ever encountered.'

The privacy and intimacy of these donations were at odds with Ali's relative celebrity in the US. She and her husband were financially secure enough to pursue commercial surrogacy when doctors told them that Ali was extremely unlikely to carry any pregnancy to term. She spoke to me on the record, initially, to combat what she sees as the ignorance and prejudice around surrogacy.

'Surrogacy is still seen as this taboo thing. But it was incredible to have someone else who had none of my issues, who could carry my children. I look at my daughters and I think, *If we had tried to put them in me, they wouldn't exist*. My girls are four and a half now. The thought that "they weren't meant to be" is unfathomable to me at this point.'

Ali says she has always been fully transparent with her daughters about how they came into the world.

'The greatest gift I can give to my daughters is to talk about surrogacy – I don't think that they should ever feel any shame or weirdness about how they came into the world.'

At the time that Ali and her husband made their decision, paid surrogacy was illegal in New York (it was legalised in 2021 and New York is now the only state which requires agencies to be licensed). They asked a New Jersey-based agency to find them a surrogate in another state, and were matched with Stephenie in Idaho. Laws around surrogacy in the US differ by state – in some, parents can get a pre-birth order, which establishes them as legal parents before the birth. In other states, parentage is declared post-birth, and in some states a biological connection to at least one intended parent is required. Ali and her husband, as a heterosexual, married couple with their own embryos, had more freedom to choose than most, but their agency still required a multitude of steps:

a background check, home visit, and psychiatric and medical evaluations.

The IVF clinic performed one transfer with two embryos, which was successful. Although Ali worried about not feeling a connection with her girls, she ended up being more 'present' with them after their birth because she was not recovering from surgery, as she had been with her son.

Ali voiced something I had already wondered: was this what it felt like to be a father? I remember, during my own pregnancies, pondering my husband's experience of having his genetic offspring gestated by someone else. At one point in our conversation, Ali revealed that a close friend had offered to carry her children for free, but that she turned down the offer.

'I wanted everyone to know what they were getting, and I wanted it to be compensated. I knew what [the surrogate's] expectations were and vice versa. There was a legal framework and a financial value.'

I was initially surprised, even shocked by this – I had always imagined that if I were ever to enter into a surrogacy arrangement, I'd want someone very close to me to carry my child; a private, familial arrangement, unsullied by money. But when I thought about it in the days that followed our conversation, I came closer to understanding the desire for a transaction, rather than for a gift so vast as to be almost overwhelming in its generosity, and a power imbalance that might easily threaten the original relationship, and possibly your relationship with your own children. I knew that unofficial arrangements between friends or family can involve a connection sometimes too close and too complex for comfort – a sense that intensified when I later interviewed my friend Kath, whose sister-in-law carried her twins.

'I was morally twisted up about surrogacy initially,' Ali admitted. 'Then, when I talked to Stephenie, I thought: *She really likes being pregnant.* She'd had all these natural surrogate births – she's had twins before. It's this amazing thing she can do for people, and also it pays for her kids' school fees.

'I thought: *This is actually not weird in any way.*'

Yet she also admitted that there were some uncomfortable moments when she had to take a leap of faith. When Stephenie was five months pregnant with the twins, she rang Ali and asked for permission to go white-water rafting with her own family. Privately, Ali was uncomfortable about this but told Stephenie to go ahead if she felt safe.

'That was her family life, her parenting of her own kids,' explained Ali. 'She could have not asked me, and I would never have known. You have to profoundly trust this person you don't really know.'

I asked Ali what the birth was like.

'I pulled one of my daughters out of her. It was amazing for me – it had been very emotional to not be able to carry them. She let me be there. I just adore her; I don't care what people say about surrogacy. How can you think that this beautiful person, who had given me the greatest gift on earth, is bad? When done in the right way, for the right reasons on both sides, surrogacy is beautiful.'

Stephenie told me the two continue to have a close relationship – 'like a cousin or an aunt – she's part of our family'.

PLACENTA

Ali, like many parents who use a surrogate, is a liberal, wealthy, East Coast American. She also happens to be Jewish. She delights in the closeness that exists between her and Stephenie, despite their differences. As Ali described her, 'she's a very religious Christian and she believes this is what she's meant to do. Before us, Stephenie had never met a Jewish person before. She had never met a gay person before, then she carried for gay parents. She travelled to Switzerland to visit them . . . in what other world would these people be friends?'

In this polarised world it is, indeed, a striking question. According to Ali, the hospital in Idaho where Stephenie gave birth to the twins was a snapshot of a localised culture of surrogacy. Ali found herself chatting to many of the nurses, and discovered that nearly all of them had been a surrogate. 'A lot of surrogates are evangelical Christians – it ends up being a religious thing for many of them; it's their gift to bring children into the world.' The hospital, apparently, 'was this interesting Christian sub-culture, but with an understanding of medical issues. They were not anti-abortion.'

Even with some assurances that basic values were aligned, I speculated that it must have felt like a huge decision to pay a stranger to carry your children – what did it feel like to trust the agency to find the right person, and to vet that person yourself?

Ali smiled, remembering the agents asking her and husband to declare any 'racist' preferences for their surrogate at the outset.

'I just wanted someone who had been a surrogate before, who would be comfortable "giving them away".'

Ali told me that she and Stephenie had 'every single uncomfortable conversation possible' via their lawyers, or through the agency, including how comfortable both parties would be carrying out a doctor's recommendation to terminate. Abortion can often be a sticking point, especially if genetic testing has not been carried out on the embryos (although this is routinely done by fertility clinics in the US).

I was interested that Ali – who is firmly pro-surrogacy, for obvious reasons – constructs her argument from an ideological standpoint as well as a personal one.

'It's amazing to me how many feminists are anti-surrogacy. It's really insulting to the surrogate. Like they're too stupid to know what they're doing; there are so many better ways of earning money.'

Finally, I thought to myself: *the feminist angle*. I'd already discovered that, like sex work, surrogacy divides feminists over women's freedom of choice to do what they want with their bodies. Like sex work, the undercurrent of discourse is emotional, on both sides. Surrogacy remains taboo for some people even in countries where it is legal, and several of my interviewees for this section did not want to be named (even by their first name).

Activist groups like Nordic Model Now!, originally formed to advocate for the criminalisation of paying for sex (but not charging for it), argue that even without payment, surrogacy exploits the female body, as well as the unborn child. They argue that existing regulations are inadequate, pointing to the stricter laws that govern the breeding of dogs in countries such as the UK, which limit the number of pregnancies per dog and prohibit puppies being taken from their birth mothers before eight weeks – a comparison that pro-surrogacy campaigners find offensive.[10]

I did not put forward the puppy-farming angle to Ali but was interested to know what she had to say about money as a principal attraction for some surrogates.

'Our surrogate was required to be financially stable – not destitute – and have children of her own,' she says, with finality. 'I'm yet to meet anyone who does it for the money.' (Ironically, Stephenie herself had admitted she initially agreed to their match '100 per cent for the money'. In Ali's defence, that attitude soon changed.)

For me, as with many of my interviewees, this was a tricky part of our conversation – the difficulty of separating personal convictions, born of a particular experience, from a wider moral debate. I pointed out that there are parts of the world where women become surrogates because they are in dire financial need – which she readily acknowledged (it was obvious she'd been challenged on this before). We talked about the exploitation of surrogates in black and grey markets like India and Nigeria.

'Sure,' said Ali, with the assurance of someone who is used to defending a controversial take. 'Not caring about the humanity of the person on the other side of it [i.e. the surrogate] . . . it's like *The Handmaid's Tale*. As with anything, when it's consensual on both sides it's a beautiful thing. When it's not consensual, or coerced, it's the opposite.'

We agreed that there is, like it or not, a sexual element to surrogacy, even though sex is notably absent from proceedings – it is a process that takes place in a woman's reproductive organs, fundamentally affecting her body and her sex life both during and after the pregnancy. That sexual element, especially when applied to women and coupled with any hint of coercion, makes some cases of surrogacy 'disturbing', as Ali described it. But she referenced more dangerous jobs, entered into by both women and men, that no one argues should be illegal.

'We allow people to be soldiers. Or astronauts. Or work on an oil rig. There are many jobs that have a higher fatality rate than surrogacies.'

Statistically, Ali is right. Yet as I listened to her, there was something that made the comparison seem not quite appropriate, to my mind at least. Only women can do this job, and they put their health at risk for individuals who are paying them to do exactly that. Surrogate pregnancies are statistically more dangerous than other pregnancies; a 2024 study of nearly a million Canadian women found that surrogates faced a severe maternal morbidity rate of 7.1 per cent – much higher than the rate in unassisted conceptions (2.4 per cent) and, interestingly, also more than women who conceive their own children through IVF (4.6 per cent).[11]

This is a very gendered and specifically compensated form of risk-taking, rather than a job with generic risks attached – that does not make it exploitative per se, but there is a difference. This difference came home to me when I actually read a surrogacy contract.

PLACENTA

BABY CONTRACTS

In 1986 in New Jersey, a traditional surrogate called Mary Beth Whitehead broke a private contract with the intended parents by kidnapping the baby she insisted was hers shortly after giving birth to it.[12] Foregoing the $10,000 that had been promised to her, she and her husband went on the run with the baby. Warrants were issued for their arrest. A legal battle first upheld and then invalidated the surrogacy contract. A new financial settlement was reached and, eventually, the intended parents were awarded custody of 'Baby M'.

The dramatic case of Baby M captured the American public's imagination, and since then, most news stories about surrogates focus on details of celebrity parents, wealth and privilege. The tabloids stoke our horror at the idea of a wealthy and apparently selfish woman choosing to pay another woman to go through pregnancy for her – so that she can preserve her figure, or because she is afraid of childbirth, or because she is simply too old to bear children herself – even as the practice becomes more mainstream for both infertile heterosexual and gay parents, more affordable with the rise of altruistic and transnational surrogacy, and less about privilege.

When baby contracts do come into the public eye, they are, like Baby M, generally of a nightmarish quality – for example, the 2016 case of an agreement made in the UK between a same-sex couple and a surrogate with learning difficulties who met on Facebook, signed a template agreement in a fast-food outlet and flew to Northern Cyprus, where the surrogate was impregnated with two embryos conceived with donor eggs and one of the couple's sperm.[13] After the couple fell out with the surrogate, she miscarried one of the twins and falsely claimed she had miscarried both; instead, she kept the remaining baby. The couple applied to court for custody, which was ultimately awarded to the surrogate – the judge considered her in a better position to meet the baby's emotional needs. The baby was also legally represented in court, as Baby M was not – a sign of how the rights of the babies have been increasingly recognised in the last few decades.

Surrogacy law is a new frontier in constant flux, and while some parts of the world are becoming more surrogacy-friendly, others are going the other way. In Italy, surrogacy has been illegal since 2004, but there have never been any criminal convictions, and using a surrogate abroad was not a crime. However, in 2024, the right-wing Fratelli d'Italia government passed a law to punish couples who use an overseas surrogate with up to two years in jail and fines of up to a million euros.[14] Existing birth certificates that named two men or two women as parents were changed in some parts of the country, to remove the non-biological parent's name. I can barely imagine what it must feel like to be legally struck off as a parent.

In 2025, the Spanish government also cracked down on its citizens pursuing surrogacy abroad, making it impossible to register surrogate-born babies at its embassies abroad. When I read the news, I wondered if it had been partially triggered by the 2023 scandal of a sixty-eight-year-old Spanish actor, Ana Obregón, who had a baby by surrogate in Miami using her dead son's sperm and a donor egg.[15] I also wondered how the change would affect Stephenie's business in Idaho.

Most of the gay couples I interviewed for the book were of different nationalities. Most had to navigate different countries' laws, choosing where to live according to which governments recognise joint same-sex paternity of surrogate-born children, or even same-sex marriage. The choices became even more thorny when considering separation or divorce, tipping the power balance more sharply towards the parent with the greater biological and therefore legal claims to the children, and to their country of residence or birth. It is the usual mess of divorce, exponentially complicated. I went to talk to a couple in the midst of such a separation, to find out more about the hurdles they had encountered and the contract that had brought their children into the world.

In October 2024, a few months after our initial conversations, I flew to Lisbon to meet Ivan and Bryan, the estranged couple who had – unusually – negotiated a video call with their 'live' egg donor. Ivan had moved from New York to Lisbon to be closer to their children. I was meeting them separately. Both suggested the same meeting place – a popular salad bar in the Príncipe Real neighbourhood – so I had to warn them that they might run into each other if timings went awry. We were on a strict schedule to discuss how they found their surrogate and how the contract was negotiated.

I arrive early in a cavernous New York-style salad bar with high ceilings, loud house music, enormous potted plants and austere wooden chairs. A mix of well-heeled ex-pats and locals eat salads of pickled wakame and pomegranate seeds. As I sit here in front of my laptop, like several other diners, I realise the place looks familiar – it's part of a chain, and I've been to a branch in Madrid, chosen by another of my ex-pat fertility-related interviewees. Suddenly the world of (legal) surrogacy does seem very small, and very privileged.

Bryan arrives flustered, having tried for thirty minutes to find parking, and gratefully drinks the double macchiato I've ordered for him. He is a tall, muscular American in a tight white polo shirt, with perfect skin and a quiet demeanour. He tears up when he talks about how proud he is of his children, and how grateful he is to the surrogate who brought them into existence.

'The surrogate is the most important part of the whole journey,' he says emphatically. 'You'd think it would be the donor, but no.'

This was interesting to me – the assumption that the woman who produces the genetic material would be of more importance than the woman who merely carries your child, but I could see that perspective. In any case, Bryan had come round to the opposite view.

'I think Taylor is an angel. She is truly an amazing woman. With a surrogate, it's a spiritual bond, an emotional bond. You go through so much with them.'

Like Ali, Bryan got the impression from the many profiles he'd viewed that there was a commonality to surrogates in the US market. Most were from the Midwest, with jobs as nurses, school teachers – 'something in the social service realm' as Bryan put it. They had often been inspired by gay or infertile friends or family members to help strangers in similar positions.

Bryan and Ivan created their embryos in a clinic run by Dallas-Fort Worth Fertility Associates, and were subsequently offered several surrogate candidates in Texas. The couple travelled from Miami to meet one of them, but she had put on too much weight since her initial assessment.

'We couldn't use her,' said Bryan, reminding me that fertility clinics are acutely aware of their success ratings. Using a surrogate who may not carry a pregnancy to term, adversely affecting the clinic's rating, is not a good business decision. With a roughly 30 per cent chance that this particular pregnancy would fail, the overweight candidate was also not a good 'investment' for Bryan and Ivan, as the doctor advised them. Instinctively, the terminology seemed jarring to me, but a lot of money was at stake, and no one was pretending otherwise.

A few minutes after Bryan left the café to go and collect the twins from school, Ivan entered, and we headed up to the rooftop bar. I was beginning to feel a bit like a couples' therapist, even though both men were being pointedly careful not to say anything negative about the other. There was obviously a code of discretion, but I had now talked to both of them for several hours and formed an impression, both from what was said and what was unsaid, of a very difficult juggling act. I felt for both of them, and for their children. Sometimes it was difficult to focus purely on the logistics of their story.

In person, Ivan was as open as he had been on our video calls, giving my questions careful thought before answering at high speed in his heavy French accent. He confirmed what

Bryan had just told me about the Texan doctor's advice not to pursue an embryo transfer with the overweight surrogate.

'I remember the doctor said, "With the amount of money and time you are investing, I would not advise this one. If it was your wife I would do it, but if you can choose whoever you want, I would not pick this one."'

Ivan paid a total of $185,327 for twins in 2017 – today, that amount would likely be higher. His budgetary calculations had come to $142,784, so he overspent by around $42,000 – more than the price of the cheapest, entry-level surrogacy programme in Northern Cyprus, as I was to discover later. I was initially overwhelmed by the complexity of the spreadsheet he shared with me, detailing the costs for egg donation, IVF, embryo storage, fees for the surrogate, lawyers and agencies, plus travel costs. After other parents shared their documents with me, I realised it was totally standard.

The first candidate found by Ivan and Bryan's surrogacy agency did not respond well to the hormones during her preparation for IVF; the second was the 'bad investment', and the third was going well until negotiations hit a stumbling block. She refused to sign the contract because of a clause that prohibited travel outside her state after the sixth month of pregnancy, in line with insurance requirements. '"This is becoming too transactional,"' Ivan remembers her saying.

'These contracts are scary, so some women, they read it and pull out.'

Like Bryan, Ivan feels a deep sense of gratitude to Taylor, their eventual surrogate. His tone changes when he talks about her, telling me about her visit to meet the twins in New York when they were around three years old. He tells me he has encountered more curiosity than criticism from strangers (particularly in the US, and the liberal, ex-pat echelons of Lisbon where he lives). Some initial concerns from his family were quickly overcome when they saw how well he and Bryan parent their children. His main interrogators are taxi drivers, who often ask him where his wife is. 'Some become very curious, and I spend thirty minutes explaining to them. I like to explain.'

Similarly, I had spent an hour's drive to Lisbon chatting about surrogacy with my Portuguese friend Diogo, who had given me a lift from a town up the coast. Diogo listened in silence as I explained Ivan and Bryan's story. When I asked him what he thought, he took his time, weighing his words before saying that, on balance, he supported his government's reluctance to legalise even altruistic surrogacy (pro-surrogacy legislation has been introduced several times and rejected as unconstitutional by the Constitutional Court).[16] He saw it less from the perspective of the surrogate and more from that of parents everywhere. He and his wife had lost an infant daughter some years ago, and the biological ill luck that caused this, along with the thought that perhaps more expensive medical care could have saved her, had made a deep impression on him. In his eyes, surrogacy would only be right if state healthcare could provide it to all who want it.

This made me think about the right to biological parenthood. Relatively few people can afford IVF, and even fewer can afford surrogacy – even the altruistic kind. Surrogacy is the preserve of the rich, and probably will be for the foreseeable future – especially when state healthcare providers are already stretched to breaking point. Ivan and Bryan had what could be viewed as the biological ill luck of not being able to procreate without science's help, but they had the economic luck of being able to get that help.

Ivan told me that he and Bryan could not fly to attend the twins' birth, stuck in blizzards in New York as Taylor went into labour four weeks early in Austin, Texas. The hospital staff had stopped Taylor's husband from entering the birthing room because they knew that Taylor was a surrogate and that he was therefore not the father.

'We had to call the hospital and tell them to let him in,' remembers Ivan. It is one of several moments when he expresses something akin to sadness, or a wish that things had gone slightly differently. When I ask him if he has any advice for parents pursuing surrogacy, his answer is immediate.

'Be careful with twins. I didn't know you put the woman's life in danger – as soon as you transfer two embryos, it becomes a high-risk pregnancy. I just thought, *Cool, we will have twins*. I love our twins, but I wouldn't do that again. I think it is wrong.'

(Bryan also admitted to 'completely underestimating' the complications and risks of a multiples pregnancy but, unlike Ivan, said that even hinting at regretting twins felt like 'blasphemy' to him. Taylor later told me that she also underestimated how difficult carrying twins would be.)

As we chatted, I realised Ivan was under the impression that you can no longer transfer two embryos into the same surrogate. I put him right – it is still an option in most surrogacy arrangements, at an extra cost of around $5,000, though some surrogates ask for more. Many clinics in the US are now less willing to transfer multiple embryos, looking for particularly robust surrogacy candidates and even stipulating a minimum height requirement. Colombia's evolving and refreshingly sensible surrogacy laws – all dictated by the Constitutional Court – actively discourage multiple embryo transfers. While not strictly illegal, it is rarely done, according to a Colombian lawyer I spoke to, because of the threat to the surrogate's health.

The cost-effectiveness of choosing twins over two separate surrogacies from a parent's perspective is obvious – $5,000 was a drop in the ocean of Ivan's overall bill. Yet, to my surprise, he was very self-critical about the ethics of that choice, not just in relation to putting Taylor's health at risk but from a societal perspective.

His and Bryan's babies, like many premature twins, spent time in intensive care, which, according to Ivan, was 'a huge cost to society – I think it was $6,000 or $7,000 per day per child; they were there for fifteen days. It cost my insurance company hundreds of thousands of dollars. I don't think it's fair that, just because I wanted children, other policy holders in our insurance company had to cover that.'

This again made me think of the concept of 'the right to parenthood' – I was slightly surprised that Ivan had given the matter so much objective thought, but perhaps I should not have been. He had already told me that when he read the first surrogacy contract presented to him he had nearly cried.

'I remember bits like: what happens if you need to do a DNA test to check the baby is yours because maybe she had sex with her husband the same night as the embryo transfer? What happens if she gets drunk and dies in a car crash, do you get reimbursed because it was her fault? What happens if me and my husband die – the baby is not hers so who looks after it?

'I hated those paragraphs because you could tell these things had happened to people – the lawyer could not have thought of all these things. You felt like you were reading the life stories of these people. Every time something goes wrong, they add a clause.'

I read through the fifty-two-page contract he subsequently sent me with increasing amazement and some horror. Some of the clauses initially confused me, like the one that specified that women with Native American blood are not allowed to act as surrogates. After some research, I discovered that in 1978, Congress passed the Indian Child Welfare Act 'in an effort to protect the best interests of Indian children'. Before that point, an estimated 35 per cent of Native Indian children had been removed from their families, often forcibly, and placed in adoptive or foster homes with non-Indian families, or in religious institutions. I was horrified that I had not known this part of American history, and that I might never have known it if I had not read this almost completely unrelated document.

Other clauses I found so upsetting that I was still thinking about them weeks later. One forbade the surrogate's husband (who was also a signatory of the contract) from hitting, kicking, pushing, abusing, harassing or committing any act of domestic violence on his wife, because any such abuse would be considered a 'material breach of this agreement'. The husband would be liable for any and all financial 'damages' incurred by the intended parents that would result from the pregnancy being threatened. I was not surprised, exactly, that the contract dealt only with the financial repercussions of a criminal act of violence, but it was disgusting – to my eyes, at least – to see it set out that way, in isolation.

The surrogate's husband featured heavily in other parts of the contract; he was forbidden from deciding as next of kin to terminate life support for his wife, as long as the pregnancy remained viable. If his wife decided to terminate or not terminate the pregnancy against the wishes of the parents, he would also be liable for reimbursing the parents for what they had already paid, or paying for further costs. Reasonably enough, he had to undergo psychological evaluations and DNA tests along with the other parties. I asked Ivan if he and Bryan had read Taylor's psychological evaluation, as the contract stated. Ivan could not remember, but he did remember his and Bryan's own evaluation as perfunctory – 'We had a thirty-minute meeting to check we were sane and knew what we were doing.'

One particularly unpleasant section of the contract dealt with the question of stillbirth, explaining how, if the child was stillborn before the thirty-second week of pregnancy, the usual monthly instalment of $3,500 paid by the parents to the surrogate would be stopped and a prorated fee of $166.66 per day would be paid from the last instalment up until the day of the stillbirth. Even more complicated were the calculations involved in case of multiples. If one child died in the womb, the instalments of the extra $5,000 the surrogate should have received for a multiples pregnancy would also be prorated, so that she would receive $23.80 per day after the day of the stillbirth for the inconvenience of carrying a dead foetus alongside a living one.

Money, obviously, featured heavily throughout, and I was particularly struck by the clause detailing the first payment after the embryo transfer payment: '$3,500.00 within five (5) days following Intended Parents' and Agency's receipt of written confirmation from physician of fetal heartbeat via ultrasound.'

I could not help thinking of my miscarriage. Imagining that moment of stillness in the sonographer's room as representative of a financial dead end was surreal and, to me, grotesque – but also, I recognised, a completely different context. The contract reminded the parents that they had to pay the final instalment within four weeks of the birth, 'regardless of the child being stillborn, being born with a defect, or not surviving after discharge from the hospital'.

I found some clauses aggravatingly petty – for example, the one that forbade a surrogate who had experienced a miscarriage, and who had already received the $800 allowance for maternity clothes, from claiming it again if she undertook more embryo transfers with the same intended parents. Others, while upsetting to read, were – I had to admit – extremely practical and necessary, like the ones that required the names and addresses of two 'successors' to step in if the intended parents died before the baby was born (one as the primary choice, one as back-up). Much like a will, this was something that all parents should probably decide when they have a child, perhaps within a more relaxed time frame. The contract also demanded to know which of Ivan or Bryan would take responsibility for receiving the twins from hospital if the couple separated before their babies were born.

I tried to figure out why the clauses featuring money upset me so much – would I feel differently as an intended parent signing this contract? I think if anything I would feel uncomfortable at such an obvious and seemingly disproportionate effort to protect my financial interests, but perhaps not. From my conversations with surrogates, I was convinced that money – while not unimportant – was not usually the primary factor in their decision, so why did the contracts give such an overwhelming impression of the potential scope for fraud? It was true that the financial interests of the surrogate were also addressed – the escrow arrangement to ensure her payments, the timings of those payments laid out clearly, and so on – but the impression was that the surrogate held all the power, and could abuse it.

Was this true, I reflected? Who really held the power? Yes, a lot could go wrong for the parent, while the escrow arrangement ensured the surrogate would get her money, if the pregnancy went to plan. Yet the very real, life-changing risks for the surrogate seemed to be accounted for in a strikingly miserly way. While reading the section of the contract addressing compensation for medical risks, I thought back to my conversation with Stephenie, and to her friend who'd had to undergo an emergency hysterectomy after delivering a surrogate baby, despite wanting more children of her own.

CASH COW

The average compensation for the loss of a reproductive organ (fallopian tube or ovary) in the event of a complication is around $1,000 to $2,500, while the loss of a uterus varies between $3,500 and $10,000. Growing Generations (which pays first-time surrogates $70,000 to $75,0000) seems to have mysteriously built in the cost of potential complications into their overall payment plan: 'We don't believe women bold enough to help others create a family should only be compensated in the event of an actual complication.'[17] I wondered what this meant if one of their surrogates did lose a uterus – the agency did not respond to my email asking for clarification.

Even putting aside the tragedy of undergoing a hysterectomy while wanting more children of your own, and putting aside the physical risks of such a major operation, it seemed to me the compensation was not fair from a long-term financial perspective either. A surrogate who did choose to carry other people's babies primarily for the money could be deprived of her future earning potential – tens or hundreds of thousands of dollars – for a few thousand dollars in compensation.

I was unsurprised that some potential surrogates baulk after reading this kind of contract. I was even more intrigued to meet the women who had said yes, and in particular, the woman who had carried Bryan and Ivan's twins.

PLACENTA

WALKING THE WALK

When I dialled in to my video call with Taylor, I already knew some key details about her that set her apart from other surrogates I'd spoken to. I knew she was an anti-Trump gay ally with two lesbian sisters, living in Texas, a conservative state that prohibits abortion but welcomes surrogacy. I suspected that money was pretty far down her list of reasons for wanting to carry surrogate babies.

She appeared on my laptop screen, a smiling, forty-one-year-old woman wearing a rainbow bracelet, who described her decision to carry twins for a gay couple as 'walking the walk'.

'I've always thought there's not really a lot of pathways to parenthood for gay men. I can talk all about rights and access and justice and equality, but to really walk the walk and help the gay community – that really meant a lot to me. It was such a good lesson for my kids.'

I was impressed at such a radical embodiment of support, particularly when Taylor told me that both her own parents and her husband's parents were 'not pleased' about her decision. (I reflected that none of the surrogates I'd interviewed had reported their mothers being thrilled by their decision, and several were in strong opposition.)

'My mum was never supportive of my surrogacy journey; she was embarrassed about it. She still doesn't talk about it. It was very weird at the time; I was thirty weeks pregnant with twins and nobody talked about it. She didn't like that there was money involved; she didn't like how obvious it was to outsiders.'

Taylor goes to a progressive Methodist church, where the congregation was proud and supportive of her decision. The pastor wanted to mention the news in a sermon, which worried Taylor's mother, who didn't want her friends to find out.

I was fascinated by the mother–daughter dynamic Taylor was describing, particularly with religion, shame and generational differences coming into play. It made me wonder what my own mother would say if I announced I was going to become a surrogate, or what I would say to my daughter in thirty years' time. Apparently, when Taylor's mother had first found out what Taylor was planning to do, she rushed to her daughter's house.

'She asked me, "How much will you get?" and I said I didn't know, but online I'd seen $32,000 or $35,000. She said, "Please don't do it – I'll write you a cheque right now for $50,000." It was an immediate no from me.'

I asked Taylor if that was a lot of money for her mother. 'It was not an enormous amount of money for her, but it would have been an enormous amount of money for me.'

Despite her family's wealth, Taylor says she paid for her own college course, graduating with a degree in human development and family studies. She is now a second-grade schoolteacher, and had previously worked in a kindergarten. After giving birth to her first son, she had to go back to work after six weeks of unpaid maternity leave: 'It's awful – AWFUL – how early we have to go back.' She and her husband are not well-off, but she insists she did not do the surrogacy for the money, which she remembers as '$35,000 base pay, $800 when we transferred [the embryos] and $12,000 for twins' (Ivan had initially budgeted a standard $5,000 for twins) – the total amounting to around the number on the cheque offered by her mother.

When Taylor decided to become a surrogate – something her sister and husband fully supported – she realised that many women in her position turn to informal groups on Facebook to match with intended parents, rather than to agencies.

'There's no psych valuation, there's rarely a contract, sometimes it's done without pay – it always seems sketchy. So I chose an agency that was good at protecting surrogates' rights.'

I was curious about the Facebook world of surrogacy, particularly in a state like Texas – what was Taylor's impression of her fellow surrogates? Was religion a motivating factor for them?

'I do think there is a very conservative religious component in the surrogate community,' she said carefully. 'Maybe it's just in Texas, but I didn't really find my people there – I think there's an ick factor to some of these surrogates. For me, it was not a religious calling that way. I am Christian, but I think I'm probably not the same Christian as some of the other surrogates. I think it probably was part of God's plan that I helped Ivan and Bryan, but [I didn't do it as] evangelism – for me, it was about doing good.'

Warming to her theme, she noted that, while she is a 'proud' surrogate, she has never posted publicly about her experience. 'There's a lot of attention-grabbing about it. Wanting attention for being a surrogate. For me, it was about helping somebody and being a model for my own children.'

I wondered about the social differences between what Taylor called the 'very conservative, religious' surrogates of Texas, and the parents – gay couples or immigrants like Ivan and Bryan, for example – that they match with. Taylor said she had wondered about this too.

'Do these intended parents know what they're dealing with? They're using a surrogate who may have voted against their rights; against their right to be in the country, for example.'

At this point I am reminded of the enigmatic views of conservatives on surrogacy in the US. Many right-wing groups are loudly anti-abortion, and the Trump administration rejoined the controversial Geneva Consensus Declaration, an international document signed by forty signatories, which 'defends the unborn and reiterates the vital importance of the family' – but this focuses on the abolition of abortion rather than on surrogacy. As Trump himself said in relation to his executive order granting wider access to IVF: 'We want more babies.'

Taylor told me she did not want to donate her eggs. 'I just wanted to be a gestational surrogate. And I did pump [milk] for Bryan and Ivan. I did it for six months, I think; they paid for all the breastmilk to be shipped to New York. I got mastitis three times. It was horrible. I was never able to pump enough to sustain the twins.'

Somewhat to my surprise, Taylor said there were plenty of single men on her 'stack' of potential parents offered by the agency she joined. 'I didn't want to do that; I always pictured a gay couple. I knew I was only going to do it one time.'

PLACENTA

After matching with Ivan and Bryan, a video call was arranged, with a rep from the agency present but not speaking on the call ('a bit weird'), and all three hit it off. Like all the surrogates I interviewed, Taylor said she felt no emotional attachment to the twins she carried: 'For me, it was very easy. They were never my kids.'

My mind turned to practicalities – Ivan and Byran are both tall men. I asked Taylor what it was like to carry their babies.

'Oh my God, it was hard. They were big babies. Z was breech on top, and she would kick and dislocate my ribs at the back and every week I had to go to the chiropractor to get them put back in line. But I birthed them both vaginally. They were 6 pounds 7 and 6 pounds 10. They were ready to come at thirty-five weeks. It worked out beautifully, couldn't have gone better – but knowing what I know now, I wouldn't carry twins again.'

What I particularly admired about Taylor – apart from her willingness and ability to carry a combined total of nearly 14 pounds of babies as an act of solidarity with the gay community – was how upfront she was about the commercial side of it all. I believed that she did not do it for the money, yet she did not pretend that the money was not useful and important.

'Yes, the money helped me a lot. In the last two weeks of the pregnancy, my husband lost his job. Not because of the surrogacy, but the money really helped. And even pumping [milk] helped – I got paid $125 a week for pumping.'

At various points in our conversation, Taylor expressed her frustration at the hypocritical attitudes towards women's bodies and childbearing in Texas, a state where abortion is illegal after six weeks, but where surrogacy is legal. 'It blows my mind,' said Taylor. 'They have so much to say about women's bodies in Texas.'

As I was reading the clauses relating to abortion in the contracts that had been shared with me, I thought that, as a parent, I would be extremely wary of using a surrogate in a state that prohibits abortion. I had read a 2019 contract that had stated:

> All Parties acknowledge that the Gestational Carrier has a CONSTITUTIONAL right to make a determination regarding whether or not to abort or reduce any pregnancy she is carrying regardless of the terms herein, however the Gestational Carrier may be liable for monetary damages in the event of a breach.

That contract was written before the overturning of *Roe vs Wade* in 2022. Now, no such constitutional right exists, and each state makes its own rules on abortion – Texas being a prime example. I needed a lawyer to help me decode the implications for the surrogacy industry, and to help me understand whether my gut reactions to the contracts I'd read were sentimental or just uninformed.

PLACENTA

DON'T HANDLE A REPTILE, DON'T EAT SUSHI

I had many rookie questions for the busy Californian fertility lawyer and he answered them with impressive patience. I jumped straight in with abortion: what would happen if the intended parents find out their baby has a genetic abnormality and ask the surrogate to terminate, and she doesn't?

'The only two times that the surrogate has refused to terminate, the baby died anyway,' said the lawyer matter-of-factly. 'So it didn't come down to who is going to pay the health bills, or look after this baby.' Nevertheless, he takes no chances, and advises his clients not to go to Texas or any abortion-unfriendly state. He thinks the abortion ban has already had an effect on the surrogacy market there; in the years since the ban, he reckons 'business is down like 25 per cent' – but because there is such a time lag between finding a surrogate and having the baby, the drop has not been apparent until recently.

Before our conversation, I'd had a vague idea that surrogacy disputes might end up in court, and might even involve law enforcement, but the lawyer soon dispelled those sensationalist ideas.

'Once there is a breach [by the surrogate], the remedy is the parents don't pay the next instalment.'

He told me that the scope for surrogacy arrangements to go wrong is in practice very limited – he estimates instances of a 'significant material breach' of contract as less than 1 per cent. However, he explained another 'non-major' kind of breach that crops up more regularly.

'In the thirty years I've been doing it I've seen several types of breach. Little breaches like toasting champagne or sitting outside when someone is smoking. In our contract there is a very long list: don't go to a nail salon, don't handle a reptile, don't eat sushi. These are non-material breaches. There has never been a lawsuit [in his practice] which has sued someone for breach.'

I quickly thought back to my own pregnancies; I had avoided sushi, and luckily it had never occurred to me to handle a reptile (which carries a risk of transmitting salmonella to the baby, apparently). I wondered how it would feel to get into legal trouble for breaking the rules, rather than experiencing a little spike of maternal panic. The lawyer described how his clients discover 'little breaches' by looking at their surrogate's social media posts. 'We just call the surrogate's lawyer and tell them: "Please tell your client not to eat sushi." We always figure it out.'

I noted that his firm's website claims they have never had a surrogate change her mind after entering an agreement – what about the parents?

'I've had some IPs [intended parents] change their mind, but we talked them down.'

I wanted to know more about this, but I also wanted to know what would theoretically happen if they had not been talked down – I was aware how literally precious this man's time was, so I asked the second question.

'Nowadays their money is paid upfront in escrow before the IVF starts,' he replied, his patience perhaps a little strained at this point. 'So unless there is a real breach by the surrogate and lawyers get involved, that money will be paid to her. You have to wire in like $130,000 [upfront]. We [lawyers] won't send the letter until the trust fund is funded.'

Yet again, I marvelled at the wealth required to pursue surrogacy in the US. I asked him about the legal terminology used to describe surrogate payments – how does he word his own contracts?

'All of our contracts call it "reimbursement for pain and suffering". It's illegal to buy yourself a baby. You're not buying a baby. Secondly, for tax purposes, if you're reimbursing people for suffering and pain, it's not income – it's not taxable.'

I mentioned a North Carolina contract I read, which referred to the surrogate payments as 'child support in utero' – was that unusual? He said it was.

'The law says that the child doesn't come into being until birth, so how would you have child support? Maybe there is some arcane North Carolina law about it . . . You can't fight over custody costs of a child that has not been born.'

I was interested in how this lawyer got to where he is today; what was it like starting his firm in 1994? 'We probably had like five cases that year. In 2004, we had a hundred cases. Now, we probably have four hundred cases. There are fifteen or twenty other lawyers in California that have like two hundred to four hundred cases.' (I totted this up as roughly 5,400 cases per year in California.)

'I don't know if it grows year after year because our firm is growing, or because surrogacy demand is growing; I think the latter. People are waiting longer to have babies.'

I asked him about the global market – how many of his clients are international?

'Forty per cent. It goes with the economy and laws of the various countries. In 2009, after our financial crisis, I went and started getting clients from Europe and the euro was strong. Then the crisis moved to Europe, and our business picked up in the US.'

When I started my research, I found the naked commercialism of the American model of surrogacy disturbing. There are still elements that disturb me and always will – the almost psychopathic language of contracts, the callousness of some parents, and the normalisation of 'cost-effective' hacks like putting two embryos in the same womb.

I also reflected that less than 1 per cent of surrogacies involving a 'significant material breach of contract' could still amount to scores of cases per year in California alone. My instinct that the surrogate ultimately wields less power than the parents was confirmed by the horrifying case of a surrogate baby who was stillborn in 2024 and the blame game that followed. The journalist Emi Nietfeld has brilliantly reported on the legal action taken by the wealthy mother against her surrogate (who also nearly died during the stillbirth), the hospital and the California-based surrogacy agency, who stopped making escrow payments to the surrogate. She had to rely on pro bono lawyers, has hundreds of thousands of dollars in medical bills in her name, and lives in fear of online vigilantes after the mother doxed her.[18]

The worst case scenario of a surrogacy gone wrong is almost unimaginably grim, but it is potentially even worse in countries where the surrogate has no legal protections at all. The US, at least, has protections that largely work. If you agree that women should be allowed to be paid for the labour of bearing a child – and even countries like the UK, whose model is supposedly 'altruistic', allows this in practice – then it makes sense for all aspects of the practice to be above board and subject to regulation. I was to find out just how exploitative and dangerous surrogacy could be in other parts of the world, from South Asia to much closer to home.

CHEAP SURROGACY

On 25 April 2015, an earthquake of 7.8 magnitude hit Kathmandu in Nepal, killing nearly 9,000 people. In the chaotic footage that was broadcast to the world, some incongruous scenes stood out: panic-stricken Israeli men clutching very newly born babies, desperately trying to make their way to their consulate. In total, the Israeli government arranged for the evacuation of twenty-six surrogate-born babies and their gay parents back to Tel Aviv in the days following the earthquake. The postpartum surrogates were left behind, but other pregnant surrogates, due to give birth to Israeli citizens any day, were evacuated along with the rest.

The earthquake drew unexpected attention to a thriving industry that sprang up in Nepal after 2013, when neighbouring India, which had previously been the most popular low-cost centre for international commercial surrogacy, tightened regulations to prohibit gay intended parents. In 2015, India had banned commercial surrogacy for all foreigners, but it remained popular with local intended parents even after more bans were introduced in 2018 and 2022. The practice continues in some areas under the guise of altruistic surrogacy, as it does in Cambodia.

Many of the surrogates discovered in Kathmandu after the earthquake were in fact Indian women taken across the border for embryo transfers and their ensuing pregnancies. Despite the fact that some of these women were Muslim, and Judaism practises matrilineal lineage, Israeli parents made up the majority of the clients of the Nepalese market.

An extraordinary joint investigation by Israeli, Indian, Nepalese and American journalists published in 2015 by Radiolab dug deep into the story. It found that the sums paid to the surrogates – around $5,000 – were far less than the intended parents had been led to believe by the Israeli agency involved, which, along with numerous middlemen, pocketed the majority of the overall fee.[19]

Listening to this story, I found myself thinking of the Cambodian women who had been paid a fraction of the sale price of their milk by the Utah-based company Ambrosia Labs, before the practice was banned: a clear-cut case of exploitation that was, nevertheless, more complex than first appeared. The Indian surrogates interviewed by Radiolab said $5,000 was still a life-changing sum for them, allowing them to pay for their daughters' future dowries, or to build a house or a small business. One woman, who had miscarried and missed out on her anticipated fee, was devastated that after the Nepalese government outlawed commercial surrogacy in the wake of the outcry, she would never again have the chance to earn that kind of sum. Again, I thought of the Cambodian women who missed their regular pay cheques from Ambrosia Labs.

I had strong emotions listening to two of the gay Israeli parents interviewed for the story (one of whom had unforgettably described Ukrainian donor eggs as 'cheap, white eggs'). They had met their chaperoned surrogate in Kathmandu and managed to slip her a couple of hundred dollars when the chaperone's back was turned (he would otherwise have taken a cut). The thought of 'tipping' the woman who gave birth to your child seemed completely grotesque to me, yet I also had to recognise that the parents were trying to make some (small) amends. The surrogate had not been expecting the extra cash, and gratefully accepted, pressing her hands to her heart in silence. How did the parents feel, slipping her that money, and how did they decide how much to give her? They told their interviewers that they had been horrified to find out how little the surrogate really received from the agency – had this 'tip' assuaged their conscience? I wondered how much (if any) of the details of the story they have shared or intend to share with their children.

Two truths can, very uncomfortably, coexist – this Indian surrogate had been exploited, but she was still materially better off than if she had not been. The usual answer to the problem of exploitation is legalisation and regulation, which might ensure fairer pay for the women who otherwise seek out surrogacy work on the black market. But regulations are often ignored and unenforced, and even when they are not, they cannot deal with all eventualities: plague and war, for example.

Before the Russian invasion in 2022, Ukraine was the European centre for cheap IVF, egg donation and commercial surrogacy; the latter was particularly popular because intended parents can be named as legal parents on the birth certificate, and in theory the industry is regulated. But the outbreak of the Covid-19 pandemic in 2020 exposed cases of sloppy medical practice like test-tube mix-ups (definitely not unique to Ukraine), and mistreatment of surrogates by profit-hungry clinics (ditto).[20] The pandemic itself added extra challenges: some surrogates found themselves looking after the babies they had birthed, waiting indefinitely for intended parents to navigate closed borders, trying not to bond with babies that were not theirs. Some babies were never collected. Fees went unpaid. Medical conditions resulting from surrogate pregnancy complications went untreated as clinics focused on the valuable end products: the babies themselves.

Two years later, when Russia invaded the country, pregnant Ukrainian surrogates found themselves escaping bombardments; intended parents lost the means to communicate with them, and, as in the pandemic, they could not travel to collect their babies, some of whom were cared for in bomb shelters by the surrogates themselves, or by nurses. (Alongside the nightmare scenarios, I came across stories of intended parents evacuating their surrogates out of Ukraine, and inviting them to live with them – model and author Rosanna Davison is one high-profile woman in Ireland who sponsored not just her surrogate, but the surrogate's family to relocate to Ireland.[21])

The industry in Ukraine was shaken but is slowly picking up again (although one very experienced UK family lawyer I spoke to, Cara Nuttall, said she now receives almost no enquiries from parents thinking of pursuing surrogacy there, compared to around 'one a week' pre-war). Similarly, the US, which experienced a drop in women willing to act as surrogates during the pandemic, is back to business. Despite the worst-case scenarios that a pandemic and war cast into the spotlight, the urge to have one's own genetic babies – by surrogate if necessary – is unquenchable.

Researching international reproductive law, I found my expectations regularly overturned when it came to liberal and conservative tendencies, country by country, even state by state. I also came across what seemed to be some intriguing commonalities. With the major exception of the US, where everything is available for the correct price, it seemed that the legality of surrogacy and non-anonymous donation are loosely aligned, at least in Europe. For example, in the UK, where altruistic surrogacy is legal, only non-anonymous gamete donation is legal. Ditto in the Netherlands. But in Spain, only anonymous gamete donation is legal, and all forms of surrogacy are illegal. Similarly, in Italy – another Catholic country – surrogacy is illegal, and was described by a lawmaker in 2023 as 'worse than paedophilia'. As in Spain, in Italy only anonymous gamete donation is legal. It is as if babies born as a result of assisted reproduction must not be linked to any individuals other than their parents. For an outsider, it can be difficult to predict both what pushes national and local cultural buttons, and the internal logic of resulting laws.

Iran was undoubtedly the biggest surprise of my online research – a Mecca, in theory, for everything IVF-related, including commercial surrogacy, thanks to the adaptability of Shi'ite doctrine (which also permits temporary marriage that can enable prostitution). Khamenei's game-changing 1999 fatwa permitted infertile men and women to temporarily 'marry' an egg or sperm donor, or surrogate, to make the procedure religiously and legally acceptable (just as a man can temporarily marry a sex worker).[22] The fatwa specified that 'both the egg donor and the infertile mother must abide by the religious codes regarding parenting', and the legal implications of any babies born as a result of egg or sperm donation are complicated; for example, a married woman cannot use donated sperm unless she temporarily divorces her own husband in order to marry the sperm donor.[23] Shi'ite scholars disagree among themselves, but in most cases they agree that donor-conceived babies are to be considered adopted and not the legal inheritors of their parents' assets – not exactly customer-friendly.

Most of the Iranian clinics list their prices in American dollars and offer all-inclusive packages, including airport pick-ups and sightseeing tours, like the Northern Cypriot clinics. Their webpages are translated into English and Arabic. Sunni countries cannot match the flexibility of Iran's assisted reproductive opportunities, and some of the clinics in Tehran attract clients from the Gulf, according to an Iranian patient coordinator I met in a Northern Cypriot clinic. I wondered what it would be like to get into hot water while attempting to transfer embryos into Iran, or attempting to take a surrogate-born baby out of Iran. I had discovered it was difficult enough much closer to home.

FECKIN' EEJITS

At the Future Fertility Show in Dublin, one event stood out for its sense of urgency. Like a council of war, a panel of experts had convened to discuss the dramatic implications of new legislation in Ireland, which for the first time made altruistic surrogacy legal, while explicitly outlawing commercial surrogacy – including arrangements entered into abroad. At some point soon, Irish couples and single parents-to-be would have to find, somewhere in the world, an increasingly in-demand altruistic surrogate to carry their child.

The audience was packed and attentive. Sam Everingham, the Australian surrogacy advisor who extricates intended parents from crisis situations all over the world, was moderating the panel. The other speakers – a high-profile Irish fertility lawyer, a former surrogate, and a fertility counsellor – all agreed that the new laws were a mess; no one knew when they would be implemented, for a start.

'We were better off before the new legislation,' the lawyer had told me bluntly, before the talk. 'Before, you could go and pursue surrogacy wherever you wanted with whomever you wanted.' On stage, she advised anyone in the audience considering commercial surrogacy abroad to 'get on with it as quickly as possible'.

All arrangements would now have to be pre-approved and strictly non-commercial, with proven medical reasons for pursuing surrogacy. All intended parents would have to undergo counselling (this seemed to be widely welcomed by industry professionals). Only non-anonymous egg and sperm donors would be allowed, with the donor's contact details entered into any agreement. An anonymous donor in Northern Cyprus or Georgia, the biggest low-cost destinations for surrogacy, would no longer cut it. Ironically, surrogacy was about to get more expensive in some respects, despite the laws being designed to promote only 'altruistic' programmes. In practice, this would be questionable anyway – a lawyer in Northern Cyprus told me that, since surrogacy payments are always referred to as compensation rather than payment in legal terms, arrangements can be described as non-commercial even in places where they are obviously not.

Industry insiders had welcomed one development of the new laws in particular: intended parents would finally be recognised on the birth certificates of surrogate-born children. In most other respects, the new laws had caused alarm and confusion, particularly in the European and Northern Cypriot markets. None of the people I talked to had a definitive answer for why the Irish make up such a significant portion of that market, relative to the country's size; some speculated that it was a result of expensive and difficult-to-access IVF at home, coupled with a cultural, Catholic expectation to have children, a lack of available altruistic surrogates and a desire to go abroad to avoid the scrutiny of a relatively small home community.

PLACENTA

I'd finally met Sam Everingham in person the previous evening in Dublin, his towering, jet-lagged frame squashed into the corner of a tiny Thai restaurant where he was dining with equally exhausted colleagues. The next morning, he was brighter. We had coffee near the fertility-show venue, and he told me more about his extraordinary job parachuting into crisis situations – helping surrogates get over the borders of war-torn countries, working with lawyers to extricate babies from uncooperative authorities or providing emotional support to distraught parents. He decried the lack of screening or support offered to most people who pursue surrogacy – 'everyone suffers' – and told me one particularly harrowing story about a British couple who had abandoned their baby, born prematurely to a Ukrainian surrogate at the start of the Russian invasion in 2022, after the husband realised his wife didn't want it. Eventually, working pro bono, a team of lawyers and a volunteer from Sam's organisation, Growing Families, had rescued the baby and put it up for adoption in the UK.

We discussed recent judgments from the High Court in London, usually delivered in private but published in these instances because they had been considered to be in the public interest – a warning to others. Two of them related to surrogacies in Northern Cyprus; as I later discovered in person, a surprising number of surrogacy arrangements there pass relatively smoothly, but those that do not often find their way into the press.

The applicant of the first High Court judgment was a single, anonymised man (X), who had 'naively', in the words of the judge, signed a contract with 'FullSuccess Centre'

(I believe this was the former name of one of the agencies I'd been in contact with to source donor eggs, headquartered in Israel) and a local clinic.[24] X, like many intended parents in his situation, was actively advised by FullSuccess not to take independent advice. His embryo had been transferred to a Kyrgyz surrogate with whom no one seemed able to communicate properly – a common problem with cross-border surrogacy. He had paid €31,143 to the agency, which the judge noted as a worryingly small amount of money. The surrogate had subsequently claimed she was not paid, which the agency denied, saying she had mistranslated or misunderstood the 'compensation' payments given to her – the judge, slightly to my concern, had accepted this explanation (it is very difficult to know how common mispayments are because agencies like FullSuccess do not allow their clients to have direct contact with the surrogates).

At the last minute, X was told the surrogate would give birth not in Cyprus, but in Moldova, where surrogacy is illegal. X was told he had no choice: he had to 'look and behave' like the surrogate's husband, and was instructed to pay an extra €6,000. The High Court granted his request for a parental order, judging it to be in the child's best interests, while chastising him for his 'reckless disregard of the cross jurisdiction implications, overseen by two commercial organisations, [which] causes the court enormous concern'.

Of the roughly 400 parental orders processed by the High Court in London per year, around 75 per cent are from either the UK or the US. I had realised by now that the High Court very rarely refuses to grant parental orders for babies born from either domestic or overseas surrogacies – including obviously unethical overseas arrangements – because it is almost always in the children's best interests to remain with their intended parents (especially when there is no trace of the surrogate). According to Cara Nuttall, the British surrogacy lawyer I interviewed, and who represented X in the High Court, this policy has become known among some intended parents, who 'appear to feel less incentivised to do their due diligence'. At a London surrogacy conference I attended, Nuttall spoke by video link, saying that she suspected some of her clients are not solely naive but have a 'wilful blindness to red flags' – a sentiment echoed by Mrs Justice Theis in another recent High Court judgment: '[the intended parents] took risks to pursue their own wish to have a child, rather than confront the harsh reality of what they are doing' – again, that 'baby lust' described to me by a surrogacy consultant. Nuttall speculated that it might take the High Court starting to refuse parental order requests to change this.

Nuttall also pointed out that X had met representatives of the FullSuccess surrogacy agency at a well-established fertility show, and so had assumed that they were 'a legitimate ethical outfit' – this made me reflect that the organisers of fertility shows carry a huge responsibility to vet their exhibitors, despite the financial hit that must entail. The London Fertility Show, for example, is one of the biggest weekend events in Europe – alongside big sponsors, more than seventy exhibitors come each year, with each IVF clinic or egg bank paying at least £7,185 for a minimum-size stand.[25] On top of that, the show 'regularly' attracts 2,000 visitors, according to its organisers, paying between £20 and £25 per ticket. I went to the 2025 show; several exhibitors told me that it was noticeably less busy than previous years, in common with several other shows that year – visitors seem increasingly less likely to come to face-to-face events, and if the trend continues, exhibitors and sponsors will be less likely to rebook. Excluding any potential exhibitor does not make good business sense.

Yet this is something that Laura Biggs, the London Fertility Show's organiser, was forced to do. After we met and spoke informally at the show, she emailed me with an on-record comment: 'This year, we were made aware of a clinic with a high court judgment against them. After considering the information, we took the decision to ask them to withdraw.' I knew exactly which 'clinic' she was referring to (they are not, in fact, a clinic but a surrogacy agency). To my surprise, a couple of weeks before the show, I received a marketing email from their team offering me a one-on-one consultation on the date of the show. Looking carefully at the details, I saw that the venue they proposed was a hotel in central London – they were resourcefully wooing ticket holders in town for the show, despite being barred themselves.

Advertising surrogacy is illegal in the UK, so the agency in question should not, by law, have been exhibiting in the first place. I noticed at the show that some of the international agencies, which I knew for a fact arrange surrogacies, were presenting themselves merely as IVF clinics. One nurse representing a new London clinic told me, off-record, that her clinic has working relationships with both British and Mexican surrogacy agents. Interestingly, at the Dublin fair there was no such subterfuge – the new Irish legislation banning advertising had not yet come into effect.

I also discovered that the High Court can authorise payments made to a surrogate retrospectively, because there is no need in current English law to have a pre-birth agreement in place before the surrogacy takes place. The court takes into consideration whether the payments constitute 'reasonable expenses', and whether, according to a landmark 2014 case, 'the sum is so low that it may unfairly exploit the surrogate mother, or so high that it may place undue pressure on her with the risk, in either scenario, that it may overbear her free will'.[26] But all of this is usually, in the end, irrelevant because what the court deems 'of paramount importance' is the child's welfare. Because it is almost never deemed appropriate to refuse an order that will allow the child to remain with its intended parents, payments are, in practice, always retrospectively authorised. This is also why altruistic surrogacy in the UK – and elsewhere – can stray into commercial territory in terms of the fluidity of 'reasonable expenses' paid to the surrogate, although how often that happens is unclear – one lawyer told me that most of her clients are 'on a shoestring budget', but other, wealthier intended parents can afford to pay undisclosed expenses to their surrogates that are not strictly related to their pregnancies.

The other, even more sensational case Sam Everingham and I discussed involved a lesbian couple in their early seventies and late sixties, who had paid an agency that claimed to be based in southern Cyprus £120,000 for two babies.[27] The judge called this 'a very significant sum of money', which it was not, really, for a bill that included two parallel surrogacy programmes involving donor sperm, donor eggs and two surrogates. The agency was, of course, actually based in Northern Cyprus. The surrogates had undergone C-sections on the same day, so that the babies could be considered twins.

Then the big mistake: the agency sent one of the intended mothers to the Civil Registry Office in Northern Cyprus where she had signed documents in Turkish that – unbeknown to her, according to the judgment – registered her as the implausibly elderly biological mother of both babies. (When I interviewed a lawyer in Northern Cyprus about this, he claimed there was no way the woman would not have known what she was signing. When I asked him why the staff at the Registry Office had believed an elderly woman could have recently given birth, he said, 'The staff don't even check the details, they're so busy.')

Unsurprisingly, the Home Office refused to accept this alleged relationship, and failed to grant a parental order, which relies on a genetic relationship with the child. The couple spent four years in Cyprus, trying to get back to the UK. Eventually, they were granted an adoption order. The judge chastised them for being far too old to have embarked on the whole endeavour: 'The only sensible decision that the applicants made, as I observed during the hearing, was to commission the birth of two children so that, at least, these two full siblings will have each other as they grow up.'

When I had discussed the case, off-record, with a prominent Irish lawyer at the Future Fertility Show, her opinion on the couple was more succinct. 'They were feckin' eejits!' She told me her clients generally don't have trouble getting their babies out of Cyprus because the surrogate does not get paid her lump sum until after the birth. The surrogates often are resistant to signing papers relinquishing any rights to the baby (which usually happens several weeks later) without extra payment, but 'in the end they always do', and are usually paid a small bonus for doing so. A Turkish Cypriot surrogacy agent I met at the Future Fertility Show described the surrogates he had dealings with as 'cheeky – sometimes they won't sign before they get the money'. It seemed to me that in such a wildly unregulated and risky market, with no one to protect my interests, I would probably do the same.

As Sam and I left the café and started walking to the Royal Dublin Society, where the fertility show was about to start, he pointed out something that had not occurred to me: 'Those High Court judgments are just the tip of the iceberg. So many people don't come forward because they're ashamed of how badly it has gone wrong. They don't even apply for parental orders.'

I reflected that the members of the Irish public about to pour through the doors of the Future Fertility Show were relatively affluent and well informed, or soon would be. They were trying to make the best decision within their financial means, navigating a constantly evolving global market, but they did not know how fraught the whole picture was in reality. Sam and I talked again about the Mediterranean Fertility Institute (MFI) in Crete, which in August 2023 had been busted by Greek police, who had uncovered a human-trafficking ring involving egg donors and surrogates, alongside cases of gross medical misconduct and fertility fraud. In order to save money on IVF procedures, doctors had directly impregnated surrogates with the sperm of fathers who had paid to create embryos with their partners, resulting in babies that the surrogates – and parents – were unaware were biologically the surrogates' own. Police had been forced to keep newborn babies under surveillance while DNA tests were carried out to determine if they matched the intended parents.

The MFI scandal was so shocking that I had assumed that surrogacy programmes in Greece with non-resident surrogates would be a thing of the past – surely local authorities would be clamping down on this market? My conversations with low-cost international agencies proved otherwise.

'SHE WILL BE READY TOMORROW'

When I had been posing as a woman who wanted to buy donor eggs in Northern Cyprus, I also asked the agency reps about surrogacy options. The Ukrainian rep, Oksana, who had told me very bluntly that blonde, blue-eyed donors are more expensive, was also forthcoming about the surrogates available at her agency. In common with other agencies operating in Northern Cyprus, women employed by this agency generally come from Kazakhstan, Uzbekistan and Kyrgyzstan, and less often from Georgia, Ukraine or Thailand. Another rep had sent me some surrogate profiles to browse. I was taken aback to see full names and dates of birth listed alongside photos; one file even included a scan of a passport page, showing me the woman's Uzbek ID number.

Oksana quoted me €32,000 to €75,000 for a surrogacy programme with her agency (a reasonable quote based on her competitors), depending on how many rounds of IVF and how many embryo transfers I wanted to pay for upfront, and whether I would be using my own eggs or donated eggs. Oksana was keen to explain the merits of the higher price bracket: 'Seventy-five thousand euros is for guaranteed child in two years. If no child, we give you back money. If you pay all money at once, we discount 10 per cent.'

A rival agency offered the same terms for €88,000, while some agencies offered me a basic surrogacy programme including two embryo transfers (i.e. no 'guaranteed child') for a mere €27,700 (though I discovered that extremely cheap programmes like this often entail 'extra' charges as the surrogacy progresses, which the parents are effectively forced to pay). I tried to calculate, to my own distaste, how the agency priced in multiple transfer attempts with multiple surrogates. A surrogate who did not get pregnant after a couple of initial embryo transfers with one set of clients would presumably be offered to other clients to save the agency a wasted return journey – I wondered how long she was kept on the island, thousands of miles from home, until she was successfully impregnated.

Oksana explained that as soon as I signed the contract, they would try to match me with a suitable candidate, offering me two or three to choose from. (She suggested a relatively modest time frame of two months to source the right candidate. Rival rep Maks, who claimed that his agency's pool of girls were exceptionally reliable, 'without drugs or alcohol', promised me that 'she will be ready tomorrow'.)

My eventual choice would be flown over to Cyprus. When her period started, they would start hormonal stimulation for the embryo transfer, and once a pregnancy was confirmed, the woman (or 'girl' as Oksana called her) would be sent home, armed with hormone medication that mimicked those produced during a natural pregnancy. At around twenty-eight weeks pregnant, she would be flown back to Cyprus to prepare for the birth – or to another country like Czechia, Portugal, Greece, Georgia or Moldova, each priced individually.

At this point I had to interject. Portugal? I pointed out that commercial surrogacy is not legal there, and arguably neither is altruistic. Oksana was completely unfazed by my objection.

'We are the medical part of programme in Cyprus. Childbirth only will be in Portugal – surrogate gives birth in private hospital, near Faro. When childbirth certificate will be ready, after you can apply the embassy. Portugal is €14,000 on top of programme.'

I had doubts as to how easy it would be for a heavily pregnant woman from a Central Asian country to be granted a Schengen visa, and I wondered about the 'childbirth certificate', not to mention the complications I would encounter at the British Embassy, but I didn't press the point – I wanted to know about the other options. How much extra would Georgia cost?

'Georgia costs only €6,500 more, same with Moldova. For you it will be better Georgia; from Georgia the baby can go anywhere without passport.' (I knew this was not true.)

PLACENTA

At one point in our conversation, Oksana clearly became confused by the intensity of my questioning and the level of detail I wanted – how much contact would I have with the woman carrying my baby? How would I know how the pregnancy was going? Would I see medical reports, and could I trust the level of care provided in her home country? Could I talk to the surrogate, with a translator? Could I meet her?

Oksana assumed I thought the surrogate was also the egg donor; otherwise, her tone suggested, why on earth would I want to meet her?

'It doesn't matter what she looks like because she just carries the child,' she explained patiently. 'Main thing is that she is healthy. We can organise video call with her if you like; your coordinator will arrange.'

I kept asking questions. Sensing scepticism or fear, perhaps, or suspecting that I was after a cheaper deal, Oksana sought to reassure me further: 'If you like, you can arrange yourself the surrogate giving birth in your home country. You arrange her visas and flights, the birth. She will live in your house – you save money on accommodation.'

This blew my mind – the idea that I could or would arrange for a woman carrying my child in Central Asia to fly to the UK on some kind of spurious visa, stay in my house and give birth in an NHS hospital down the road. How many people chose this option to theoretically save money or preserve the illusion of control? How could the agency ensure the surrogate was treated well in a client's home? What happened if I was unable to arrange her visa in time for the birth – what would happen to the surrogate and the baby, registered as mother and child in Kyrgyzstan?

Quite often, agents gave me a hard sell, and in doing so revealed how precarious the surrogate's position was. Maks assured me that the surrogate would not get paid beyond basic expenses until she gave birth and then signed away her rights to the baby, which I had already discovered was standard. He was trying to reassure me that the surrogate would not make off with both my money and my baby, but all I could think about was how the surrogate was essentially in a hostage situation, so far removed from the position enjoyed by American surrogates, paid regularly from an escrow account.

Maks sent me a €63,000, seven-step payment plan in which I would have to pay the agency the two final instalments, a collective €23,000, after the surrogate became pregnant. The penultimate payment of €8,000 would be due at the twelfth week of pregnancy, and the final €15,000 payment 'within a week of delivery'. How would the agency handle the parents not paying these? Presumably with a termination or adoption, though the sunk cost by the time of birth might make a late default unlikely, to see it through a distasteful business lens.

In London, speaking off-record as a journalist to several agents operating in Northern Cyprus and Georgia, I did not come across any stories of parents failing to pay the full amount, but one agent told me about some clients of his who changed their mind about wanting the baby, giving it up for adoption in Tbilisi soon after the birth.

PLACENTA

'That nearly broke me,' he said. I believed him – he didn't need to tell me that story – but most of my interactions with international agents did not fill me with trust.

Back in my role as a potential customer, I was strongly advised by the original Israeli agency I contacted to pursue a programme in Greece (where surrogacy for gay parents was outlawed in 2025), because I would be offered a surrogate who would stay in Greece throughout her pregnancy – 'the whole pregnancy is monitored there'. The surrogate would be 'not Greek but from borders of Greece – maybe Bulgaria'. Apparently, this would be better in terms of ensuring ongoing communication and speeding up the parental order application I would make to the High Court in London, because the surrogate could not just disappear back to her home country.

As I spoke to the Israeli agency rep, all I could think of was the Mediterranean Fertility Institute scandal, and a hospital ward full of babies under police protection as their DNA tests came in. A few months after our conversation, a new law in Greece made surrogacy available only to its citizens and residents. I wondered what would have happened if I had been halfway through a surrogacy with a Bulgarian surrogate on Greek soil, and how much support I would have received from the agency.

The final rep, the uber professional Helen, claimed to have the 'largest intake of surrogates in Cyprus', including local surrogates who would agree to remain in Cyprus throughout the pregnancy, all with a variety of experience. When I asked whether those with more experience were more expensive, she said not.

'There are benefits on both sides. Experienced surrogates know what to expect, but a routine sets in. If you want enthusiasm, that might be something that is more pronounced in a new surrogate. We can find you a surrogate who doesn't mind a caesarean section, who can speak a bit of English . . . But then it takes longer to find the right candidate – let's say three months total.'

Then, an unexpected claim: 'Surrogates have the highest compensation here in Cyprus versus other countries.'

Really?

Helen was adamant, and I realised she meant this as a proportion of the overall amount paid by the intended parents for the surrogacy programme (I subsequently found out that it is actually Georgia where the surrogate compensation is the highest proportion of the overall amount – about 50 per cent). In effect, Helen was calling out the greediness of the middlemen in more affluent, 'respectable' countries.

'In Canada and the US, the IVF clinics take more than double. Health insurance is absolutely insane. Here it is high, but not insane. Each surrogate [at our agency] receives €25,000 minimum. But it depends on how many dependants she has, whether she will move back and forth. Part of our eligibility programme is financial stability. We don't take on surrogates who need a life-changing amount of money. But I don't think it's the normal way in Cyprus to be honest.'

I took her last comment to be an indirect dig at her competitors. I needed a more objective view – someone in the local market but not an agent wanting my custom. With some relief, I set up an in-person interview in Northern Cyprus, using my real persona, with a local surrogacy lawyer.

PLACENTA

PARACHUTING INTO LABOUR WARDS

The morning after I checked in to my hotel in northern Lefkoşa, an elderly woman made me an omelette, alongside a plate of olives, cucumber and white cheese for breakfast – a nostalgic meal. She asked me what I was doing in Cyprus, and I tried my best to explain, searching the recesses of my memory for the Turkish word for 'surrogate'. When I finally remembered, her astonishment was profound. 'Turkish women do that?' No, I told her. Generally, the women come from Central Asia or Georgia. She looked at me with obvious distaste. 'They give their babies away?' Not really, I explained – the baby is not biologically theirs.

'Yes,' she insisted, grasping the folds of her belly with wrinkled hands. 'I am a mother. If I carry a baby inside me, it has my blood. It is made with my blood. Is it not?' She looked at me with a kind of anguish. I'd never seen this kind of reaction until now – a reminder of the passionate convictions of the culture of my motherland, and of the older generations in particular. As I left the hotel and walked a hundred metres down the road to my meeting with the surrogacy lawyer, I reflected that this woman had no idea of the flourishing business on her doorstep.

Hasan, an overworked, friendly man in his forties, greets me in the offices of the firm he opened twenty years ago, fresh out of his Bar exams. As I arrive, a gay Irish couple are leaving and Hasan introduces us. One of them tells me excitedly that they are expecting twin boys and a girl, from two different surrogates, all due in early June. Now, they are off to the hospital to attend a scan. I wish them luck, and notice a bottle of Jameson Irish Whiskey, which has (presumably) been left as a gift on Hasan's bookshelf, as the couple haul their suitcases down the stairs.

Hasan practises various types of law – he says criminal law is his favourite – but more surrogacy cases keep coming in. Our initial conversation over video call had started in typical Cypriot fashion: he asked me where my mother was born, her father's name, which year she left the island – all clues to help him place me and my kin in the very small world that is Lefkoşa society. Hasan also had an extra incentive to grill me: he is suspicious of journalists.

He was polite but did not hide his caution, telling me that he gets a lot of 'fake journalists' asking him for interviews. When he grants them, he ends up reading homophobic articles featuring his words, railing against the surrogacy industry.

'Then it scares people about surrogacy in Cyprus,' he explained. 'I don't want my clients to be afraid.'

In person, Hasan is more relaxed – we go for a quick lunch at a scruffy but popular canteen near his office, ordering köfte, fried potatoes and stuffed courgettes. I mention that no one seems to be able to tell me exactly what the law is regarding surrogacy in Northern Cyprus. He nods and sighs, pausing a moment before he tackles the köfte that has just been laid in front of him. 'When I check it, there is not any article or any code or law which is against surrogacy.'

Though it is not illegal, there are confusing and seemingly contradictory laws within ministry departments: the Ministry of Health grants permits for female patients officially diagnosed with infertility to use a surrogate, and in practice single men and gay couples can use a surrogate because they cannot have a child without one, but the Ministry of Interior insists that the surrogate is stated as the mother on the birth certificate (this is the case in many countries where surrogacy is legal, including the UK).[28] If she is married, her husband is stated as the father, which is why surrogates working in Northern Cyprus have to be single or divorced. The intended mother or second father are not recognised on the birth certificate, and for some nationalities that is an insurmountable problem.

British couples are lucky: they are able to apply for an emergency travel document for their child directly from His Majesty's Passport Office, which usually takes a few weeks to come through. The surrogate, as the legal mother, signs papers granting powers of attorney that allow the parents to leave the borders of Northern Cyprus with their baby. Back in the UK, parents can apply for a post-birth parental order from the High Court to recognise both the intended parents.

The managing director of one of the IVF clinics I visited in my quest for egg donors had expressed frustration with the inconsistency of Northern Cypriot surrogacy law versus what is allowed in practice: 'If they allow it, they should allow it properly,' he said. I wondered about the vagueness of the laws, guessing that Turkish Cypriot citizens – like the lady at my hotel – would dislike more explicitly permissive legislation. This way, people in the industry have to deal with cumbersome paperwork and delays, but the market functions.

Apparently, 80 to 90 per cent of Hasan's clients are British, alongside a handful of Irish clients. He gets many new cases through word-of-mouth recommendations, and even more from agencies. When I ask him about one notorious agency, he tuts and shakes his forefinger emphatically, as though warning me off. They used to be business partners, he said, but no longer – ever since he realised they were trying to recruit married women as surrogates, who were then required to get divorced – or pretend to be divorced – before they could embark on any embryo transfers.

Occasionally, he represents surrogates at the request of the Irish court, who insist that foreign surrogates also have legal representation. I asked him if he could tell me why the surrogates generally come from Central Asia – is it simply because of its relative poverty?

'Northern Cyprus is not a very well-recognised country,' came the careful reply. 'But we take workers from places like Turkmenistan and Kyrgyzstan, so they know us.'

The minimum monthly wage in Kyrgyzstan is around 2,863 Kyrgyzstani soms, or €30; an average yearly salary is 472,096 soms, or €5,000. So the average payment to a surrogate in Northern Cyprus of around €20,000 to €25,000 is a vast sum – particularly for a single mother. I have travelled around Kyrgyzstan, with a male gay friend to whom I had to pretend to be married, and can imagine the stigma faced by single mothers in the conservative Muslim country. At the same time, these women receive little to no child support from the state and have relatively few options to earn a decent salary. Surrogacy, while socially taboo, has actually been legal in Kyrgyzstan since 2015, but, given its unfamiliarity as a tourist destination, and lack of English speakers, the market is much less busy than in Northern Cyprus.[29] The earning potential is also far less (the same goes for Kazakhstan, where surrogacy was legalised in 2011).[30]

Over Turkish coffee, Hasan broke down the customary payment schedule for a surrogate in Northern Cyprus for me, which I later read in a recently signed contract (where the money was specified to be paid in US dollars rather than euros, a more commonly used currency in Northern Cyprus): 'Every month they get around €500 as pocket money. The agency provides food and accommodation – which is expensive, if the agency looks after them well. Air conditioning, fresh fruit and vegetables, meat. Then, a few days after the birth, when they sign the necessary paperwork [to register the child and grant power of attorney to the parents], they get around €20,000 – they get their full amount. But around four months later, the surrogate has to sign the papers for the parental order. So usually the parents pay them another €1,000 or €2,000 or so more.'

I asked him which visas do the surrogates come in on – do they have to pretend to be tourists?

'No!' Hasan looked affronted by the question. 'They come on medical visas. The most important issue for Northern Cyprus is health tourism. It is not secret that the surrogates are doing an embryo transfer.'

The transparency of this part of the process surprised me somewhat: surrogates are issued with an invitation from the IVF centre, which gets them their medical visa, which can then be renewed if the transfer doesn't work, or extended for as long as needed – the previous limit was thirty days, but it has now been extended to ninety, which I took as a possible sign that the authorities are making things smoother for the industry. When the surrogates need to return from their home country for the birth, they are issued with another invitation from the IVF clinic.

By this point, Hasan was running late for his next meeting, in the coastal town of Famagusta an hour away, and invited me to join him on the drive so we could keep talking. It turned out to be a valuable, adrenaline-fuelled insight into his job – our conversation was interrupted by calls from clients and agency reps, and I brazenly listened in. He drove with a local's familiarity with the roads, braking with expert precision in front of strategically placed speed cameras on the motorway. We switched between English and Turkish, my brain creaking through the gears as it processed a language I rarely speak these days. Unsurprisingly, Hasan spoke with more emotion and nuance in his mother tongue – I listened as attentively as I could to his unfiltered views on the industry.

He was soon interrupted by a Ukrainian surrogate coordinator who called, speaking in English – her contact card came up on the car's display screen, and I recognised the agency as one I'd spoken to. She complained that the landlord of one of their rented apartments was threatening to kick his tenant out, because they had moved in a new surrogate who was not the one who had signed the lease. Hasan was impressively calm in the face of this seeming emergency. 'No problem,' he said. 'He just wants more money. At the end of the month, you move out. You didn't pay anything in advance? Good. We will find another apartment.'

Hasan hung up and, slipping back into Turkish, vented his frustration at the various emergencies that made his job so stressful. He was particularly annoyed by the 'ignorance' of police who sometimes stop parents with their newborn babies at the border checkpoints as they try to cross from Northern Cyprus to the south, at the Lefkoşa crossings. Despite the parents carrying papers signed by the surrogate, which grant them power of attorney, the police are suspicious because the mother named on the child's recently issued birth certificate is not present. In their defence, I thought privately, it must look like child trafficking.

Later that day, I passed the checkpoints myself from northern to southern Lefkoşa and had an unofficial meeting with someone working at the British High Commission, who confirmed that consular staff do periodically receive emergency calls from British citizens caught at the border with their babies.

'It happens, yes. We talk to the police, try to educate them about the protocol, and usually it is resolved. But cases have been dropping in the last couple of years.'

I wonder if this is because the police are becoming more au fait with the situation and less prone to interfering, or whether there has actually been a drop in cases full stop – it is impossible to track numbers, at least officially. While Hasan says he is busier than ever, I have also heard that agencies are exiting Cyprus because bad press has been affecting demand, as well as because of the infighting among the agencies that remain. I pick up from Hasan that there is some fairly aggressive competition going on; he himself is barred from working with the competitors of his current agency clients.

Hasan sends me a local contract between a surrogate and intended parents, which is a mere seven pages, compared to the forty-to-fifty-page contracts from the US I've been reading. In spirit, they are identical, except the payment schedule. The brevity and directness of the Northern Cypriot version compared to the US version is almost refreshing – it gets to the point. In place of long paragraphs of legal jargon emphasising that the surrogate has no rights to the baby she has carried, the Northern Cypriot contract has a clause simply stating: 'The Surrogate mother accepts and declares that she doesn't want the baby and leaves it to the Intended Parents.'

I arrange another meeting with the businessman Latif, who recently started an IVF clinic-cum-surrogacy agency and is navigating his way through the politics of the local market. We pop into his clinic – which looks professional, if relatively empty – and Latif describes his problems with competitors, wondering aloud how one of the Israeli surrogacy agencies that sent me egg donor files are so successful despite having no physical presence on the island and operating only as a commissioning agency. 'They are like Coca-Cola, they are everywhere. They don't even need to advertise any more.'

While there are plenty of fertility patients and a high turnover of treatments in Northern Cyprus, I realised that all the providers are jostling for a bigger piece of the pie. There is a pronounced island mentality. Sometimes alliances between clinics and agencies shift, secretly, and staff are regularly poached. I wonder how this culture affects the surrogates who put their trust in them, and tell Latif I'd like his help in meeting some surrogates – my efforts so far have been unsuccessful.

'Why do you want to meet a surrogate?' he asks, clearly surprised.

I say I need to know more about the women at the heart of this industry: their backgrounds, financial situations and families, their attitudes to what they are doing, to what extent they can be open about what they are doing in their home country, and – crucially – how they are treated by the agencies here, and whether they have experienced any coercion or abuse. I am aware of the language barrier, but I have a female Russian-speaking friend on standby to help translate. Latif considers this for a minute.

'I will ask Natalya to meet us for a coffee,' he says eventually. 'She is Georgian, she speaks Turkish, she is a good lady.'

I learn that this is Natalya's third surrogacy at Latif's clinic. She is waiting to undergo an embryo transfer there, staying in an apartment rented for her on the outskirts of Lefkoşa; Latif sends me the location of a supermarket café near to it. I jot down some questions, thinking about how to word them as sensitively as possible, and hoping that I'll get a chance to talk to Natalya in Turkish alone. As our rendez-vous approaches, Latif admits that he is 'still trying to persuade her'.

I drive to the supermarket, park and sit in the café with an olive pastry and a tea. Twenty minutes pass. Eventually Latif arrives alone, flustered, embarrassed.

'I could not persuade her, Alev, I'm really sorry.'

He sits next to me and shows me their text exchange on his phone – she is apologetic, using formal Turkish to explain that she does not feel comfortable about meeting a stranger. 'Don't take it the wrong way please,' she writes. I feel bad about putting her in this position, and wonder about her reluctance, which might well be fear – it's like trying to meet someone in a witness protection scheme. I imagine her typing on her phone in an apartment not far from here, finding the right words in a foreign language, trying not to offend Latif. More than ever I want to talk to her, just the two of us, without her male boss present. I want her to know that someone is interested in her story, wants to understand her motivations and problems, or whatever she wants to tell me about. She just wants to be left alone.

Latif tries one more time for me, with a much more audacious plan. One of his other surrogates, an Uzbek woman, is in early labour at the university hospital, where I applied to be an egg donor. Once she has given birth, he will need to go and pick up the documents from the hospital that will allow the legal team to prepare the application for an emergency travel document. The single father, Richard, is also at the hospital awaiting his baby's arrival.

'OK, how about this,' proposes Latif. 'You will go and get the documents for me, you will meet the surrogate, see the baby. I will text you when she has given birth. Do you want to do this?'

I realise I am torn – this feels horribly invasive. Of course I am curious to meet her, to see how she is treated by the hospital staff, to watch her interactions with the baby and with Richard. But what a violation of her privacy, to turn up without her consent. I imagined the scene, this poor Uzbek woman trying to recover from the ordeal of labour, when a total stranger arrives, awkwardly trying to communicate in pidgin English and Turkish. Who was I to put her through that?

To do this ethically I would have to spend weeks if not months in Northern Cyprus, taking it slowly, making friends with these women and earning their trust instead of parachuting into labour wards. Meanwhile, I was desperately missing my own children, and they were missing me – on our last video call, my daughter had cried, asking for 'mummy cuddles'. It was too much for me; I told Latif I was going home, and bought a ticket for a flight that evening. Immediately, I felt calmer. On the plane, I thought about the surrogates missing their own children, maybe watching them cry over a video call as I had done, and not being able to jump on the next flight home. I was full of regret. I felt I had let down the surrogates I was writing about by failing to give voice to their stories, and at the same time it worried me how difficult that had proved to be.

Even without the testimony of these women, what I had learned about surrogacy in Cyprus highlighted for me the scope if not the hard evidence for exploitation. I was more torn than ever about the ethics of the industry as a whole. It would be easy (and simple) to come to the conclusion that surrogacy is an unacceptably risky and unethical practice full stop, but at the same time I could not disregard the surrogates I had interviewed in the US, for whom the word 'exploitation' just did not apply, however distasteful I found some aspects of the market.

In the UK and Canada, I came across instances of altruistic surrogacy that were even more striking than the commercial arrangements I had looked into – women who wanted to give family members or complete strangers the gift of life, without any financial reward. In some ways, they were the hardest cases to get my head around.

ALTRUISTIC SURROGACY

In 2015, my friends Kath and Ben had just got married when Kath was diagnosed with cervical cancer. Kath froze her eggs before undergoing chemotherapy, which nuked her reproductive organs and meant she could not carry the embryos created in the clinic with her frozen eggs and Ben's sperm. Ben's sister offered to carry a child for the couple (the embryo split, resulting in identical twin girls). Her offer, as Kath saw it, was both natural and extraordinarily generous, but it brought Kath complex emotions: alongside the joy, a sense of guilt, inadequacy and initial estrangement as a mother.

One detail stood out for me as Kath told me this story: she had been open to adopting, but Ben wanted his own genetic children – in my anecdotal experience, this is more common among men than women. The relationship between decreasing rates of adoption and the increase in global IVF treatments is, I discovered, difficult to determine – it is not as self-explanatory as I first assumed. The global challenges of the Covid-19 pandemic, for example, contributed to a fall in overseas adoption, as did the invasion of Ukraine (previously a popular and cheap country for adoptive parents, as well as for people seeking fertility treatments); despite the orphans created by the war, children under five were unavailable to foreign adoptive parents. There has also been a decrease in the number of babies put up for adoption globally, distinct from a lack of appetite to adopt. Gay couples in the UK form an increasing proportion of adoptive parents, but they are also increasingly becoming biological parents via donors and surrogates. One surrogacy agent I spoke to told me that some of his clients had tried for years to adopt before eventually giving up and pursuing surrogacy.

I can just about imagine carrying a child for a family member, but I cannot – to my shame – comprehend the generosity of carrying a baby for a total stranger, unpaid. This was the experience of a Canadian surrogate, Linda, who carried the child of Andre and Lewis, an old friend of mine from Istanbul. The couple arranged for their embryos, stored in war-torn Ukraine, to be transferred to Canada, one of the countries in which only altruistic surrogacy is allowed. Linda 'matched' with them on an agency website; she had acted as a surrogate twice before, and nearly died once, haemorrhaging after an emergency C-section. A year after her traumatic birth, she underwent the embryo transfer and gave birth to Lewis and Andre's daughter Maria in December 2022 (she told me she prefers to say that Lewis and Andre 'got their baby' rather than that she gave birth to her – 'the baby was never mine to give'. I found it interesting that even the phrase 'give birth' was anathema to Linda, probably the most hardcore altruist surrogate I encountered).

Lewis posted a photo on X of himself and Andre with Maria at Amsterdam airport on their journey home from

Calgary to Lisbon, calling her 'our beautiful daughter, the cutest hand luggage'. The tweet went viral, with 7.6 million views and, amid the congratulations, many comments accusing him of child trafficking, 'de-mothering' the baby and treating her as a commodity. Several news sites picked up the story. 'It was a shitstorm,' said Lewis.

I met Lewis and Maria in Lisbon in August 2023. I knew, rationally, that she would be a completely normal baby, but she was such a miracle of science, created in countries thousands of miles apart in the midst of war and plague, that I had felt a powerful curiosity beforehand. She was, of course, completely normal and adorable; my then-two-year-old daughter could not stop hugging her. I had also been curious to observe the bond between Maria and Lewis, which, unsurprisingly perhaps, turned out to be closer than most fathers with their nine-month-old babies. He was her primary carer, and over lunch Lewis and I had all the boring yet vital conversations – about weaning, sleep deprivation, nurseries – I usually have with fellow mothers.

Maria's surrogate, Linda, an open, smiley woman in her mid-thirties, with two children of her own, talked to me from her rural home in British Columbia for over two hours on Zoom. We talked about why she became a surrogate, her family's resistance to it – particularly her mother and sister, with whom she still does not speak about it – and how she wants to carry another child for Lewis and Andre (she said she would feel jealous if they asked another surrogate). She told me she would feel 'dirty' doing it for money, despite financially struggling sometimes to raise her own children. It is worth noting that Canada is the strictest of the altruistic models; the surrogate's expenses are paid according to itemised receipts, unlike the vague and un-itemised 'compensation' paid in lump sums in the UK (where, in practice, payment can also be undeclared between parents and surrogates in the less formal arrangements).

By the end of my interview with Linda, I was, if anything, even more astonished by the generosity of carrying someone else's baby – I was still struggling to comprehend it, and wondered what that said about me. Linda told me she was not 'addicted' to surrogacy or pregnancy itself, as some other surrogates describe themselves, but talked of a life-affirming pride at helping others become parents – she does it all, she told me, for 'that look of joy on their faces' when they first see their baby.

What she was conveying seemed to be a powerful rush of the impure or self-congratulating altruism I felt when I gave my breast milk to my friend – that was the closest I could come to fully empathising with her motivation. Others had depended on her to create life, and she had literally delivered – in a much more giving, sacrificial and maternal way than the fertility doctors affected by a God complex. But perhaps it was a female version of this; I remember feeling like a fertile goddess when I was pregnant.

The hunger and appreciation for gratitude that Linda described was something several surrogates had individually expressed to me – the enormity of the gratitude was something of incredible value, that 'no one can take away', as Shelby put it. My interview with Linda opened my eyes to the difficulties of what cannot be defined or enforced by a legal contract: the emotional relationship between a known surrogate and intended parents. A significant part of the appeal of surrogacy for Linda, like many other altruistic surrogates, is becoming involved in (but not responsible for) the future of the baby she has carried, and feeling embraced by an extended family. Linda wants contact, she wants updates and photos and phone calls, to be called 'aunty' – an intimacy that can only grow organically, but which an agency does its best to nurture. It does not always succeed. Her first surrogate experience, when she carried twins, left her feeling 'used'.

'There were a lot of promises, but then, when the twins were born, as soon as they went home communication just died. I didn't feel good. I felt I was just used. But it didn't take away from what I did. I message the twins' mum on Mother's Day and on the twins' birthday every year. Last year she didn't reply, and that was tough.'

Privately, I wondered how it would feel to receive a text from the woman who carried your babies on Mother's Day. Would it feel like a power play – a reminder of a competing claim to motherhood, an invitation to question one's own status? I could understand feeling initially grateful but increasingly threatened by a surrogate who insisted on being actively involved in the family in a unilateral way. Equally, I could understand Linda feeling hurt and rejected by the non-replies to her texts. I wanted to ask her why she keeps texting, but it felt intrusive. I have no idea what it feels like to give birth to a child that is not yours, and then to be rejected by the mother. A special kind of lonely heartache, rational and irrational at the same time.

PLACENTA

This kind of rejection was also experienced by Jemma, a thirty-nine-year-old altruistic surrogate from Birmingham, chatty and opinionated – a slightly eccentric and very likeable woman, who loved clubbing before she had her own three children and felt a profound ostracism from her social circle when she became a mother. She has carried three surrogate children, and her initial impulse came from the fact that 'I just wanted to be pregnant and not have the baby'.

She told me – without shame – that it becomes 'very addictive' – and she is keen to carry again for one of her previous intended parents.

'I love giving birth,' she told me over the phone. 'If I had my way, I would have nobody at my birth. I'd just go outside, find a nice bush somewhere. That high that you get when you give birth – nothing else beats it. Honestly. You can just bottle up that moment, and you know that your job is done. You don't have those sleepless nights afterwards.'

I could certainly understand the appeal of not having the sleepless nights, but I realised I had not experienced giving birth (either time) as a high, exactly – I felt joy, but my main emotion was relief that my baby had made it out alive and that I could stop pushing. I envied the high.

Jemma explained the concept of incubating someone else's child to me using an analogy I had encountered a few times previously.

'Imagine one of your friends saying to you, "Would you mind babysitting my child for a couple of hours?" You say, "Sure." You take care of that child, you're responsible for nothing bad happening to them, but you don't love them because they're not yours.

'It's the total opposite of "giving your baby away", because emotionally you're not responsible for that baby any more.'

Again, like most of the surrogates I interviewed, the main bond Jemma seemed to cherish was with the parents – almost as though the carrying of a baby was primarily an opportunity to build the most intense and intimate of friendships.

'Every kick, every flutter, every craving, we go back to the parents and talk about it with them. When that journey is done and the baby is here, you do feel a loss of purpose, but the dynamic shifts a bit, and you watch people you care about become parents. You get all the good parts – parenting is the most difficult part.'

Again, like Stephenie, Jemma recognises the toll of her choices on her family.

'Your partner suffers, and your children suffer during that time – they lose their mum and their partner – but nine months is a really short time in terms of changing someone else's life like that.'

Not for the first time, I reflected that I am simply not cut out to make this kind of sacrifice, both on my own behalf and on my family's behalf. I am particularly not prepared to conceive with a total stranger and carry the resulting baby, as Jemma had been when, using a syringe, she impregnated herself with the sperm of one half of a gay couple. She tells me the pregnancy felt exactly the same, emotionally, as the other two surrogate babies she carried, but that she felt more responsibilities after the birth because she is conscious of the extra need to nurture the relationship for the sake of her children, the baby's half-siblings. She notes that the little girl, now a toddler, looks like her and like her children. 'It's not weird!' she insists, sensing my unspoken question.

Like Linda, she had a traumatic experience of being 'ghosted' by the parents of J, a baby boy she carried, just nine months after she gave birth to him: 'You have to grieve for people who are not dead.'

I found her description of her children's disappointment and bewilderment moving. Nevertheless, every year on J's birthday, Jemma, her partner and their children sit down together and watch footage of her birthing him (a rather surreal scene to imagine). She says her children receive support from other children who have lost their surrogate siblings at Surrogacy UK, the UK's main agency for matching surrogates and intended parents (the latter pay a joining fee of £800 and £1,800 for membership, though they are only allowed to join when the ratio of prospective intended parents to surrogates is low enough).[31] Jemma herself is a mentor there, 'hand-holding' the new surrogates, of which she says there are more than ever before – but never enough to meet demand.

I was interested that Jemma's opposition to paid surrogacy was not just for purely ideological reasons.

'It just gives me the ick. It's too transactional for me – once you're paid, they kind of own you. They can tell you what not to do, what to eat, where to give birth. I'd feel like an employee. Whereas me, I'm the boss – I can do what I want because it's my body.'

I thought back to Ali preferring a commercial arrangement to her friend's offer to carry her twins – the desire, in essence, to control the process. She wanted to be a paying customer with her rights enshrined in a fifty-page contract. I could see both her perspective and the perspective of a surrogate like Stephenie or Shelby or Taylor, who all told me no woman should do it for free. For Jemma, on the other hand, the absence of a transaction was a form of freedom.

'We choose who we want to help and we do it for the friendship, and for the love of pregnancy and birth. I get why the commercial surrogates would want to do it, but I'd do it over and over and over again and not want to be paid.'

At several points during my interviews, I'd sensed that money was not the only currency at play: the gratitude that Linda had spoken of was another one. All the surrogates I interviewed, altruistic or not, valued the lifelong gratitude they received from the parents extremely highly. Viewed objectively, in cold terms, it was a kind of debt owed to them, and a far more powerful one than money. By paying a surrogate, perhaps it is possible to feel you no longer owe anything to her.

I had read of this feeling – explicitly expressed – in the transcript of a 2025 High Court case; the intended parents had described why the anonymous nature of surrogacy in Nigeria appealed to them.

'We didn't want unnecessary involvement and attachment; we just want to sign the contract without owing anybody obligation. We understand someone [doing] this is really giving us something special – we don't want to carry this for the rest of our lives. Identifying the person will make us think we owe them gratitude for the rest of our life.'[32]

Brilliant Beginnings, another surrogacy agency in the UK, advises intended parents that a 'healthy' budget for a single surrogacy journey is £20,000 to 80,000.[33] This includes costs like IVF bills, the surrogate's expenses (which do not have to be capped by law) and agency fees. While surrogacy agencies in the UK must be non-profit, it costs intended parents thousands of pounds to register and retain membership of their services. Some agencies offer 'concierge' services to personally match intended parents to surrogates (Brilliant Beginnings' prices start at £26,400 without legal costs). I realised that these costs, coupled with the expenses paid to the surrogate, could easily exceed the prices I was quoted for a commercial contract in Northern Cyprus. The difference is that there are many more surrogates available there, with negligible waiting time to be 'matched', and at the upper end of the budget there is the 'guaranteed child' option, which might involve several surrogates and multiple embryo-transfer attempts. For those in a hurry, or who want to have more theoretical control over the process, it's easy to see why Northern Cyprus is so popular.

There will never be enough altruistic surrogates available worldwide to meet increasing demand, which is why – as I had realised by this point – it is so important to look at the reality of commercial surrogacy and which model works best. Luckily for me, I now had access to the kinds of events that would help me dig deeper into this question.

* * *

CASH COW

In Friends House in London, an imposing, neo-Georgian building housing the central offices of the British Quakers, I sat like an imposter in a conference room reserved for 'industry professionals only' at 9 a.m. on a Saturday. This was a closed ninety-minute session focused on international surrogacy and its recent legal challenges; later, the conference would open up to ticket holders wanting advice about where to find a surrogate, and to fertility companies paying to exhibit and market their services. The later schedule was less interesting to me: I was here for the inside intel.

I already knew some of the experts on stage; I'd interviewed them over the phone or read about them online, but they wouldn't recognise me. It was an impressive line-up – first up was a superstar of the industry: British lawyer Natalie Gamble, who was the first solicitor to build a fertility law practice in the UK. She has pioneered surrogacy law in the UK, including the introduction of same-sex parents on a birth certificate, and while she still works advising intended parents, she is best known as an advocate for global regulation on surrogacy.

I had interviewed Natalie remotely already; we talked about the Hague Conference's Working Group on Parentage/Surrogacy Project, now paused indefinitely – she thought it would be 'very challenging' for member states to reach an agreement on international surrogacy regulation, despite the 'noble' goals of the project. In general, she painted a bleak picture of any kind of international cooperation, and said she was concerned that the anti-surrogacy lobby is getting stronger worldwide. This interested me as a layperson not privy to the inner workings of surrogacy-related policy and activism – these lobby groups are not obvious from the outside.

Some of the other speakers appeared via video link, sometimes to comic effect; an Argentinian lawyer, speaking from a windswept outdoor location in the dead of night in Buenos Aires, was refreshingly blunt about the state of the industry in her country: 'Do not come to Argentina. It is a bad idea, it is very crazy.'

She explained that in October 2024, Argentinian authorities decided that the surrogate mother 'will always be the mother for all time' and cannot be removed from the birth certificate.[34] 'We have a lot of criminal investigations into human trafficking; they want to compare surrogacy to human trafficking.' (Not necessarily without basis – shortly before the judicial decision, Argentinian prosecutors had accused a 'criminal enterprise' in Buenos Aires of targeting and enlisting vulnerable women on social media to act as surrogates for foreign couples.[35]) 'A lot of agencies are under investigation, and all clinics are obliged to report all the surrogacy cases.'

I could sense unease among those listening in the room; in most of the countries represented here, such a development was not unthinkable – the legal status of surrogacy is fragile almost everywhere except the US.

Santiago Martinez, a Colombian lawyer from Bogotá, made the case that his country's judicial decisions provide a template for others: multiple embryo transfers are in most cases not allowed, surrogacy is open to both gay couples and single parents, and surrogates must not be 'vulnerable'. (Previously,

Venezuelan refugee women had been drawn into surrogacy by financial desperation, much as prosecutors had alleged was the case for surrogates in Argentina, where, until relatively recently, more than 50 per cent of people lived in poverty.[36]) Colombian surrogates typically receive $15,000 per surrogacy – far less than the travelling surrogates in Northern Cyprus receive, but the overall cost of the surrogacy programme for the parents (around $60,000 to $70,000) is similar.[37]

I found Santiago after his talk, next to his stand, which displayed traditional Colombian sweets and leaflets on his legal services. Talking to him – a quietly spoken young man, obviously passionate about his work – I discovered a niche market I had no idea existed: 60 to 70 per cent of his clients are Chinese, and almost exclusively single gay men or gay couples. In China, surrogacy is strictly prohibited and IVF is restricted, but the birth rate is problematically low, so surrogacy overseas is indirectly encouraged. According to Santiago, who is fluent in Mandarin and, I suspect, has probably cornered this particular market, the Chinese embassy in Bogotá is all too happy to assist in processing emergency travel documents for Chinese babies born to Colombian surrogates as quickly as possible.

'It's kind of a paradox,' said Santiago, amused. His clients source their eggs from donors with Chinese ancestry in Thailand, Taiwan or Vietnam, or, if they are open to non-Asian phenotypes, in Ukraine or Colombia itself (though not, interestingly, from Cyprus). Interest from China is increasing – Santiago told me that he has represented forty-five Chinese clients pursuing surrogacy in Bogotá in the past year alone.

PLACENTA

One thing was universally agreed on at the conference: there is an increasingly blurred line between altruistic and commercial surrogacy, which is fundamentally hypocritical. Natalie Gamble favours the US system, which I had also been coming round to – for all its faults, it seemed the safest, fairest model I had seen, and the huge expenses involved are partly down to the costs of the safeguards in place (as well as the ridiculous nature of health insurance). Natalie believes if higher compensation were available to surrogates in the UK, there would be a significant growth in domestic surrogates, reducing the pressure on intended parents to go overseas for transnational arrangements.

'I hear every day from parents who say they wish they could do surrogacy in the UK, but they just can't find a surrogate,' she told me.

It seems obvious that more women would sign up to be surrogates if they could earn money by doing so, but I also think that if cheaper options exist for consumers – meaning intended parents – they will find them. Market forces drive surrogacy, like anything else; some overseas destinations will always be cheaper than the UK. Surrogates will continue to cross borders for work if they can. Many women in places like Central Asia become surrogates because they are incentivised by the money that they can only earn abroad, legally or otherwise.

Relatively few surrogates worldwide will ever be truly 'financially stable', as laws dictate in the US. Reflecting on some of my initial discomfort with surrogacy, and what I had learned of the exploitation involved in some parts of the market, I realised that I still have a fundamental problem with banning it — not just because, practically, bans can make the situation worse. I dislike the idea of governments acting as the moral arbiters of any woman's decisions about her body. I am also somewhat uncomfortable with arbitrary 'caps' on payments to surrogates when the profit made from industry middlemen is not capped.

Yes, the dangers of high financial incentives are real. Travelling surrogates and their families face much more risk than domestic surrogates, while their financial reward can be proportionally much higher. At the same time, I have been struck again and again that a surrogate changes lives when she carries a stranger's baby, risking her own life in the process; can we blame her for wanting to earn a 'life-changing' amount of money for doing so?

Milling around the surrogacy fair after the conference finished, I looked at the stands decked with goodie bags and marketing paraphernalia and marvelled at the silliness of it all: branded chewing gum, sanitiser spray, key rings, 3-foot laminated cartoon sperms designed as ceiling decorations. It seemed so at odds with the enormity of creating life, and with the darker side of the industry. It didn't seem funny to me any more.

The event was winding down now; agency and clinic reps were starting to dismantle their stands, pressing their gamete-y merchandise on passing ticket holders as they left. Helping myself at the refreshment stand, I bumped into the CEO of the embryo courier company I had first encountered in Dublin — a Brit also in need of a cup of tea.

We established our mutual connections, and discussed how fundamentally messed up the industry is at a global level – how hard it is to know which organisations are operating ethically, and how challenging it would be to set and implement ethical standards internationally. The CEO sipped his tea thoughtfully.

'If only you could have a Fairtrade stamp on surrogacy,' he mused, inspired – perhaps – by the Fairtrade label dangling off his teabag.

Impractical and offensive – what better proof of the commodification of women? – but the best suggestion I'd heard all day.

EPILOGUE: BABY

In the 1997 sci-fi film *Gattaca*, no one is reckless enough to procreate naturally, and only embryos that possess the best possible traits of both parents are allowed to develop in the lab. I thought about *Gattaca* a lot while writing this book, and about the eugenicist leanings of some 'pronatalists' in the US today, who believe we must boost population rates with as much clinical efficiency as possible, embryo by perfect embryo.

I also thought about the artificial wombs that grow babies in *The Matrix* and in Aldous Huxley's *Brave New World*. In our world, artificial wombs designed to save premature babies are on the brink of clinical trials.[1] Meanwhile, the rejuvenation of human eggs is one of the latest technologies to attract venture capital investment, and synthetic embryos have already been created using stem cells, without sperm or eggs. In future, not only will women be able to conceive and gestate their babies later and later, but they may not have to at all.

Ectogenesis – the growing of babies outside a human womb – may eventually make our fertility industries redundant, but I doubt it. What I have learned so far is that, despite the sometimes prohibitive cost and heartache involved, people have a deep biological urge not just to pass down their genes, but to create and birth their own babies. Pregnancy and childbirth are in many ways magical, but they are also dangerous and painful experiences that, in a totally rational world, no one in their right mind would choose to go through. Yet we do – and there will always be industries ready to 'take advantage' of that desire, as the Californian fertility lawyer so astutely put it.

This apparent madness is something that the feminist Sophie Lewis addresses in her radical book *Full Surrogacy Now*, in which she calls pregnancy an 'extreme sport'.[2] She advocates for the abolition of family as we know it, to be replaced by a multigender feminist comradeship, a 'plural womb'. In her vision, 'mother' will not be a natural category reserved for women who bear children, but a chosen one; children will be brought up by an extended network of 'family' rather than a nuclear, biological one.

Although I am sympathetic to some of Lewis's criticisms of traditional family structure, I think many women who choose to get pregnant do so precisely because of the biological bond they anticipate creating with their child. I have asked many of my female friends, both mothers and those who hope to become mothers, whether they would rather carry a baby created from someone else's egg, or have another woman carry their genetic baby. Some, like my friend who found pregnancy a horrendous experience from start to finish, thinks that surrogacy sounds 'perfect'. But Gillian, who has seventeen frozen eggs waiting for her in Madrid and New York, told me that if she fails to become pregnant with her own eggs, she

EPILOGUE: BABY

would rather carry someone else's than have her own carried by someone else.

'I really want to go through pregnancy. I want to bear at least one kid.'

Writing this book has made me ponder questions that did not even enter my mind when I decided I wanted a child and first tried to get pregnant. What makes a mother? What is the most important bond? Would I love my children any less if they were genetically unrelated to me, or if another woman had carried my genetic children and given birth to them? Do I love them simply because I am responsible for them? Because they are 'mine'?

Why do we have children?

I've considered the idiosyncrasies as well as the more predicable market forces of the fertility industry in this book. When it comes to fertility, the stakes are high; there is nothing that many people want more at a certain point in their life than a child. Yet we all, deep down, judge the parenting and reproductive choices of others – we exist on a spectrum that extends from those obsessed with prioritising hyper-optimal embryos to those who believe that further populating the Earth is unforgivably selfish.

We feel admiration, disbelief or disgust for the woman who has chosen to sell or give away her eggs, milk or placenta, and empathy or criticism for the parents who might accept that sacrifice as a gift, or who would pay for it as a service. But very few routes to motherhood are straightforward, or possible without the service or gifts of others – or, in today's world at least, without the influence of a capitalist market.

I've written this book in what feels like stolen time, during my children's naps and nursery hours. Sometimes, I tapped away on my laptop while my baby son slept and my daughter fussed over her doll and pretended to change its nappy, aping my maternal duties. Sometimes, I absorbed myself in books and screens while another woman cared for them – she is younger than me, saving up to start her own family. I trusted her to bring my son to me when he needed breastfeeding, the only thing she could not practically do for him. I temporarily outsourced my mothering duties, in exchange for money.

There is nothing new in that transaction. Motherhood is precious and miraculous and transformative; it is also something that has always been bought, sold and shared. When I scrutinise my choices as a mother, the results are sometimes discomforting. My children probably need my attention more than they needed my breast milk. I have given them both, but my attention is worth more to me – so I pay to keep a portion of it for myself.

Am I a consumer, or am I consumed?

ACKNOWLEDGEMENTS

Writing *Cash Cow* would not have been possible without the considerable time, patience and honesty of many friends and strangers, only some of whom I have been able to name. People are understandably more willing to donate a part of themselves when their anonymity is protected, and that is also true of those who have given freely to this book. Anonymously or not, they all trusted me with their deeply personal stories. I am very grateful for that trust, particularly in light of the stigmas that still linger around infertility and assisted reproduction.

    Gillian Morris is one of several remarkable women who shared with me not only the factual details of their egg-freezing and IVF journeys, but also their hopes, fears and dilemmas. Similarly, Dr Rahi Victory had much to teach me about competing theories on hormonal stimulation, but I am particularly grateful for his reflections on the responsibilities of doctors in his field. Sam Everingham has been an invaluable source of insight, contacts and advice – thank you, Sam, for your many contributions to the book. Thank you also to 'Hasan', Ali Roy, Santiago Martinez, Natalie Gamble, Cara Nuttall, Marta Staff, Karen Pollock, Victoria Mora and many others who helped me enormously in the course of my research, including academics, doctors and journalists whose work has greatly enriched mine. I hope the talented Bloomberg team who investigated the global egg market so meticulously in 2024 get all the reporting prizes going.

My editors at HarperCollins, initially Imogen Gordon Clark and then Huw Armstrong, have been brilliantly supportive from the beginning and I feel lucky to have had both of you guiding me through the publication process – a dream tag-team, aided by my excellent copyeditor, Holly Kyte.

None of this would have happened without my agent/champion Antony Topping, who believed in the crazy kernel of an idea when I was about to give up on it, and was unfazed when I turned up to our first meeting with my newborn baby. Thank you for your friendship, your sharpness, your honesty and patience in rereading various incarnations of this text. Thank you to Navine and James, who introduced us, and to other close friends who have given me support and encouragement in writing this book.

And lastly, thank you to my family – particularly to my husband, who made heroic efforts to grant me space to write, and to my children, who may not have given me much space but who give me endless love and inspiration. You are everything.

NOTES

INTRODUCTION

1. Jean Mackenzie, 'Why South Korean women aren't having babies', BBC, 28 February 2024.
   www.bbc.co.uk/news/world-asia-68402139
2. 'Fertility Services Market Size to Reach $70.27 billion by 2030', Grand View Research, June 2024.
   www.grandviewresearch.com/press-release/global-fertility-services-market
3. 'Surrogacy Market Size', Global Market Insights, April 2025.
   www.gminsights.com/industry-analysis/surrogacy-market

MILK

1. Mika Pantzar et al., 'Configuring domestic technologies: the normalisation of freezers in Finland, Norway and the UK', Consumption, Everyday Life & Sustainability Summer School 1999, Lancaster University.
   www.lancaster.ac.uk/fass/projects/esf/freezers
2. Deepa Pandey, 'Breast Pump Market Size, Share, and Trends 2025 to 2034', Precedence Research, October 2025.
   www.precedenceresearch.com/breast-pump-market

3. Elvie Pump Double – Ultra Quiet, Wearable Electric Breast Pump, Boots. www.boots.com/elvie-pump-double-ultra-quiet-wearable-electric-breast-pump-10262311
4. 'Medolac Laboratories Prepares for Trial Against Prolacta Bioscience', Business Wire, 30 June 2020. www.businesswire.com/news/home/20200630005969/en/Medolac-Laboratories-Prepares-for-Trial-Against-Prolacta-Bioscience
5. Catharina Svanborg et al., 'HAMLET kills tumor cells by an apoptosis-like mechanism – cellular, molecular, and therapeutic aspects', *Advances in Cancer Research* (2003), 88, 1–29. https://doi.org/10.1016/S0065-230X(03)88302-1
6. 'Breast milk's benefits are not limited to babies', *The Economist*, 11 September 2024. www.economist.com/science-and-technology/2024/09/11/breast-milks-benefits-are-not-limited-to-babies
7. Erin C. Davis et al., 'Gut microbiome and breast-feeding: Implications for early immune development', *Journal of Allergy and Clinical Immunology* (September 2022), 150: 3, 523–34. https://doi.org/10.1016/j.jaci.2022.07.014
8. Margie Orford, 'Milk, Pity and Power', Aeon, 17 March 2023. https://aeon.co/essays/on-roman-charity-or-a-womans-filial-debt-to-the-patriarchy
9. Saad S. Al-Shehri et al., 'Breastmilk-Saliva Interactions Boost Innate Immunity by Regulating the Oral Microbiome in Early Infancy', *PLOS One* (1 September 2015), 10: 9. https://doi.org/10.1371/journal.pone.0135047

NOTES

10. Silvia Federici, *Wages Against Housework* (Power of Women Collective; Falling Wall Press, 1975).
https://warwick.ac.uk/fac/arts/english/currentstudents/postgraduate/masters/modules/femlit/04-federici.pdf

11. Emma Pizarro, '"They say it is love, we say it is unwaged work." Wages for Housework', London School of Economics blog post, 24 July 2024.
https://blogs.lse.ac.uk/lsehistory/2024/07/24/they-say-it-is-love-we-say-it-is-unwaged-work-wages-for-housework/

12. *Milk Report*, Conway and Young.
www.conwayandyoung.com/milk-report-publication-(2)

13. 'Egyptian pharaoh Tutankhamun's wet nurse might have been his sister', *Guardian*, 21 December 2015.
www.theguardian.com/culture/2015/dec/21/egyptian-pharaoh-tutankhamuns-wet-nurse-might-have-been-his-sister

14. F.R.C.P., 'Baby-Farming and Wet-Nursing', *British Medical Journal* (27 May 1871), 1: 543, 570–1.
www.jstor.org/stable/25229668

15. Yvonne M. Ward, 'The womanly garb of Queen Victoria's early motherhood, 1840–42', *Women's History Review* (1999), 8:2, 277–94.
https://doi.org/10.1080/09612029900200211

16. Jacqueline H. Wolf, '"Mercenary Hirelings" or "A Great Blessing"?: Doctors' and Mothers' Conflicted Perceptions of Wet Nurses and the Ramifications for Infant Feeding in Chicago, 1871–1961', *Journal of Social History* (1999), 33: 1, 97–120.
www.jstor.org/stable/3789462

17. Joan Sherwood, *Infection of the Innocents: Wet Nurses, Infants, and Syphilis in France, 1780–1900* (McGill-Queen's University Press, 2010).
www.jstor.org/stable/j.ctt811ss
18. Jacqueline H. Wolf, '"Mercenary Hirelings" or "A Great Blessing"?: Doctors' and Mothers' Conflicted Perceptions of Wet Nurses and the Ramifications for Infant Feeding in Chicago, 1871–1961', *Journal of Social History* (1999), 33: 1, 97–120.
www.jstor.org/stable/3789462
19. Mary Anne Baines, *The practice of hiring wet nurses (especially those from the 'fallen') considered, as it affects public health and public morals: a paper contributed to the Public Health Department of the National Association for the Promotion of Social Science, at the Bradford meeting, October, 1859* (John Churchill: 1859).
https://wellcomecollection.org/works/d7rmtkfr/items?canvas=6
20. William E. Wallace, 'Michelangelo's Wet Nurse', *Arion: A Journal of Humanities and the Classics* (2009), 17: 2, 51–55.
www.jstor.org/stable/40646044
21. Julius H. Hess, Chapter VI, 'Wet-Nursing' in *Premature and Congenitally Diseased Infants* (1922).
https://neonatology.net/classics/hess1922/hess.6.html
22. Thomas D. Conlan, 'Thicker than Blood: The Social and Political Significance of Wet Nurses in Japan, 950–1330', *Harvard Journal of Asiatic Studies* (2005), 65: 1, 159–205.
www.jstor.org/stable/25066766
23. Jacqueline H. Wolf, '"Mercenary Hirelings" or "A Great Blessing"?: Doctors' and Mothers' Conflicted Perceptions of Wet

Nurses and the Ramifications for Infant Feeding in Chicago, 1871–1961', *Journal of Social History* (1999), 33: 1, 97–120.
www.jstor.org/stable/3789462
24. Routh C.H.F. Routh, 'Child-Murder and Wet-Nursing', *British Medical Journal* (1861), 1: 128.
https://doi.org/10.1136/bmj.1.5.128-a
25. Menachem Klein, *Lives in Common: Arabs and Jews in Jerusalem, Jaffa and Hebron* (Hurst: 2014).
www.hurstpublishers.com/book/lives-in-common/
26. Indira Lopez-Bassols et al., 'Three Continents, Two Fathers, One Donor: A Non-Puerperal Relactation Case Study', *Journal of Human Lactation* (April 2021), 37: 4.
https://doi.org/10.1177/0890334421999327
27. Torstein Helleve, 'High standards for human milk banks in Norway', Partner.ScienceNorway, 11 January 2020.
https://partner.sciencenorway.no/health-health-services-medical-procedureshigh-standards-for-human-milk-banks-in-norway/1617690
28. Eva Kontopodi et al., '"Donor milk banking: Improving the future". A survey on the operation of the European donor human milk banks', *PLoS One* (19 August 2021), 16: 8.
https://doi.org/10.1371/journal.pone.0256435
29. Map, European Milk Bank Association.
https://europeanmilkbanking.com/map/
30. Andrew J. Schuman, 'A concise history of infant formula (twists and turns included)', Contemporary Pediatrics, 1 February 2003.
www.contemporarypediatrics.com/view/concise-history-infant-formula-twists-and-turns-included

31. Michael Obladen, 'Pap, gruel, and panada: early approaches to artificial infant feeding', *Neonatology* (26 February 2014), 105: 4, 267–74.
https://doi.org/10.1159/000357935
32. Sharon L. Unger and Deborah L. O'Connor, 'Review of current best practices for human milk banking', *Maternal & Child Nutrition* (16 May 2024), 20: 54.
https://doi.org/10.1111/mcn.13657
33. Siddika Songül Yalcin et al., 'Breastfeeding status and determinants of current breastfeeding of Syrian refugee children in Turkey', *International Breastfeeding Journal* (2023), 18: 10.
https://doi.org/10.1186/s13006-022-00538-w
34. Official Statistics: Breastfeeding at 6 to 8 weeks, 2023 to 2024 statistical commentary, Office for Health Improvement & Disparities, 5 November 2024.
https://www.gov.uk/government/statistics/breastfeeding-at-6-to-8-weeks-after-birth-annual-data-april-2023-to-march-2024/breastfeeding-at-6-to-8-weeks-2023-to-2024-statistical-commentary
35. 'Türkiye bans sale of breast milk amid rising health concerns', *Hurriyet Daily News*, 29 May 2025.
www.hurriyetdailynews.com/turkiye-bans-sale-of-breast-milk-amid-rising-health-concerns-209695
36. Ceren Varer Akpinar et al., 'Attitudes towards human milk banking among native Turkish and refugee women residing in a rural region of Turkey: a mixed-methods approach', *International Breastfeeding Journal* (27 October 2022), 17: 74.
https://doi.org/10.1186/s13006-022-00516-2
37. Ibid.

NOTES

38. Cassia Roth, 'Black Nurse, White Milk: Breastfeeding, Slavery, and Abolition in 19th-Century Brazil', *Journal of Human Lactation* (November 2018), 34: 4, 804–9. https://doi.org/10.1177/0890334418794670

39. 'Learning from Brazil's success with milk banks', *Michigan News*, University of Michigan, 12 December 2014. https://news.umich.edu/learning-from-brazil-s-success-with-milk-banks/

40. Brazil, Law No 11265 on Marketing of Infant Foods, translated from Portuguese by J-P. Allain, 3 January 2006. www.ibfan.org/wp-content/uploads/2023/05/Brazil-2006-English-Code-Regulations-Lei-No-11265.pdf

41. 'Brazilian Courts Protect Vulnerable Children and Youth in Decision Against Nestlé Brazil', Global Health Advocacy, 13 July 2022. www.advocacyincubator.org/news/2022-07-13-brazilian-courts-protect-vulnerable-children-and-youth-in-decision-against-nestle-brazil

42. Cesar Gomes Victora and Fernando Celso Barros, 'Infant mortality due to perinatal causes in Brazil: trends, regional patterns and possible interventions', *Sao Paulo Medical Journal* (4 January 2001), 119: 1, 33–42. https://doi.org/10.1590/s1516-31802001000100009

43. Hannah Partos, 'Why are women more willing donors than men?' Wellcome Collection, 12 June 2019. https://wellcomecollection.org/stories/why-are-women-more-willing-donors-than-men-

44. Who can give blood, NHS Blood and Transplant. www.blood.co.uk/who-can-give-blood/

45. 'Effects of Oxytocin on Socio-Cognitive Processes: New Insights from Spatio-Temporal EEG Analyses', German Digital Trials Register.
https://drks.de/search/en/trial/DRKS00017150
46. A. Carver et al., 'What motivates men to donate blood? A systematic review of the evidence', *Vox Sanguinis* (April 2018), 113: 3, 205–19.
https://doi.org/10.1111/vox.12625
47. https://philanthropy.indianapolis.iu.edu/doc/institutes/wpi-gatefold1.pdf
48. Carlo Petrini, 'Is my blood mine? Some comments on the Convention on Human Rights and Biomedicine', *Blood Transfusion* (July 2013), 11: 3, 321–3.
https://doi.org/10.2450/2012.0103-12
49. 'Regulation (EU) 2024/1938 of the European Parliament and of the Council of 13 June 2024 on standards of quality and safety for substances of human origin intended for human application and repealing Directives 2002/98/EC and 2004/23/EC', *Official Journal of the European Union*, EN, L series, 17 July 2024.
https://eur-lex.europa.eu/legal-content/EN/TXT/PDF/?uri=CELEX:32024R1938
50. 'Revision of the EU legislation on blood, tissue and cells', European Parliamentary Research Service, September 2022.
www.europarl.europa.eu/RegData/etudes/BRIE/2022/699492/EPRS_BRI(2022)699492_EN.pdf
51. 'The plasma trade is becoming ever-more hypocritical', *The Economist*, 29 August 2024.
www.economist.com/finance-and-economics/2024/08/29/the-plasma-trade-is-becoming-ever-more-hypocritical

NOTES

52. 'People should be paid for plasma', *The Economist*, 29 August 2024.
www.economist.com/leaders/2024/08/29/people-should-be-paid-for-blood-plasma

53. Kathleen McLaughlin, 'Blood for money: my journey in the industry buying poor Americans' plasma', *Guardian*, 23 March 2023.
www.theguardian.com/us-news/2023/mar/23/selling-blood-plasma-donations-us-health

54. Kathleen McLaughlin, *Blood Money: The Story of Life, Death, and Profit Inside America's Blood Industry* (Simon & Schuster: 2023).
www.simonandschuster.com/books/Blood-Money/Kathleen-McLaughlin/9781797155395

55. 'Notification of a recall of a small number of human breast milk products', Food Standards Agency, 6 January 2023.
www.food.gov.uk/news-alerts/news/notification-of-a-recall-of-a-small-number-of-human-breast-milk-products

56. Prolacta Bioscience Overview, PitchBook.
https://pitchbook.com/profiles/company/53328-16#faqs

57. Sushma Subramanian, 'She Pioneered the Sale of Breast Milk, Then Lost Everything', *Washington Post*, 13 May 2022.
www.washingtonpost.com/magazine/2022/05/13/price-of-selling-breast-milk/

58. Sarah Boseley, 'Sale of Cambodian breast milk to mothers in US criticised by UN', *Guardian*, 22 March 2017.
www.theguardian.com/world/2017/mar/22/unicef-condemns-sale-cambodian-breast-milk-us-mothers-firm-ambrosia-labs

59. 'Cambodia bans export of breast milk by US company', CBS News, 28 March 2017.
www.cbsnews.com/news/cambodia-bans-export-of-breast-milk-by-u-s-company/
60. Khmer Times, 'Cambodia outlaws trade in human breast milk', *Bangkok Post*, 29 March 2017.
www.bangkokpost.com/world/1223279/cambodia-outlaws-trade-in-human-breast-milk
61. 'India's Top Food Safety Body Bans Sale of Human Milk and Products', Foodtech Insider, 30 May 2024.
https://foodtechinsider.com/indias-top-food-safety-body-bans-sale-of-human-milk-and-products/
62. NorthernStar Mothers Milk Bank.
www.northernstarmilkbank.ca/
63. Julie F. Tate, 'Feeding Practices of Mothers in the Gobi Desert of Mongolia', (2011), *Electronic Theses and Dissertations*, Paper 1228.
https://dc.etsu.edu/etd/1228
64. Emily Steel, 'Financial worth of data comes in at under a penny a piece', *Financial Times*, 12 June 2013.
www.ft.com/content/3cb056c6-d343-11e2-b3ff-00144feab7de
65. Caroline Picard, 'Baby-related expenses now cost parents $20,384 in the first year alone', Babycenter, 19 February 2025.
www.babycenter.com/family/money/first-year-baby-related-expenses_41002904
66. Warning Letter: Owlet Baby Care, Inc., U.S. Food & Drug Administration, 5 October 2021.
www.fda.gov/inspections-compliance-enforcement-and-criminal-investigations/warning-letters/owlet-baby-care-inc-616354-10052021

NOTES

EGGS

1. National Centre for Women's Health, Saint Paul VI Institute. https://saintpaulvi.com/national-center-for-womens-health/
2. The Medical & Surgical Practice of NaProTechnology, Saint Paul VI Institute. https://saintpaulvi.com/product/npt/
3. Kayla Epstein, 'Alabama IVF ruling: what does it mean for fertility patients?' BBC, 22 February 2024. https://www.bbc.co.uk/news/world-us-canada-68366337
4. Travel Insurance Cyprus, AXA. www.axatravelinsurance.com/destination/asia/cyprus
5. 'IVF Over 50 in North Cyprus – What You Must Know', Fertility Clinics Abroad. www.fertilityclinicsabroad.com/ivf-clinics-abroad/ivf-over-50-in-north-cyprus-what-you-must-know/
6. 'Donor anonymity and the regulation of egg donation', Ova Blogs, London Women's Clinic, 26 January 2020. www.londonwomensclinic.com/ova/articles/donor-anonymity-and-the-regulation-of-egg-donation/
7. 'Anonymous gamete donation banned from fertility clinics under new law', *Law Society Gazette*, 5 May 2020. www.lawsociety.ie/gazette/top-stories/2020/05-may/anonymous-gamete-donation-banned-from-fertility-clinics-under-new-law/
8. Mike Butcher, 'Gaia, a platform to finance IVF treatments, closes $20M Series A led by Atomico', TechCrunch, 14 February 2022. https://techcrunch.com/2022/02/14/gaia-a-platform-to-finance-ivf-treatments-closes-20m-series-a-led-by-atomico/

9. Gaia.
   www.gaiafamily.com
10. 'What is ICSI? Understanding IVF vs ICSI', Access Fertility, 22 February 2022.
    www.accessfertility.com/blog/what-is-icsi-understanding-ivf-vs-icsi/
11. Traveling Donors.
    https://travelingdonors.com/#
12. The Ethics Committee of the American Society for Reproductive Medicine, 'Financial Compensation for of Oocyte Donors: An Ethics Committee Opinion', *Fertility and Sterility* (August 2021), 116: 2, 319–325.
    https://doi.org/10.1016/j.fertnstert.2021.03.040
13. Jacqueline Mroz, 'The Case of the Serial Sperm Donor', *New York Times*, 1 February 2021.
    www.nytimes.com/2021/02/01/health/sperm-donor-fertility-meijer.html
14. Lab supervision, PUAH.
    www.puahfertility.org/service/lab-supervision
15. Natalie Obiko Pearson et al., 'The Egg: A story of extraction, exploitation and opportunity', *Bloomberg Businessweek*, 12 December 2024.
    www.bloomberg.com/graphics/2024-fertility-egg-trade/?embedded-checkout=true
16. Egg Donor Compensation, Giving Tree Surrogacy.
    www.givingtreesurrogacy.com/donors/egg-donor-compensation
17. Kimberly D. Krawiec, 'Egg-Donor Price Fixing and Kamakahi v. American Society for Reproductive Medicine', *AMA Journal of Ethics*, January 2014.

NOTES

https://journalofethics.ama-assn.org/article/egg-donor-price-fixing-and-kamakahi-v-american-society-reproductive-medicine/2014-01

18. 'Egg Donor Compensation: How Much to Expect in 2025', Reproductive Medicine Associates of Michigan, 15 February 2025.
www.rmami.com/how-much-money-can-you-earn-as-an-egg-donor/

19. S. Schleissing et al., 'Ethical Issues Currently Being Discussed in Relation to Reproductive Medicine and the Laws Governing Reproductive Medicine', *Geburtshilfe und Frauenheilkunde* (May 2014), 74: 5, 436–440.
https://doi.org/10.1055/s-0034-1368393

20. Egg donation: Remuneration, Ovumia.
https://ovumia.fi/en/donating-eggs/egg-donation-remuneration/

21. Dr Joanne Delange, 'Shortage of sperm donors despite men willing to donate', PET, 27 June 2022.
www.progress.org.uk/shortage-of-sperm-donors-despite-men-willing-to-donate/

22. SIRHA: Assisted Human Reproduction Information System.
https://sirha.mscbs.es/sirha/login.do

23. Egg Donation, Elite IVF.
www.elite-ivf.com/how-to-become-a-parent/egg-donation/

24. Christina Farr, 'Apple, Facebook will pay for female employees to freeze their eggs', Reuters, 14 October 2014.
www.reuters.com/article/technology/apple-facebook-will-pay-for-female-employees-to-freeze-their-eggs-idUSKCN0I32KP/

25. Marcia C. Inhorn, *Motherhood on Ice: The Mating Gap and Why Women Freeze Their Eggs* (NYU Press: 2023).
https://nyupress.org/9781479813049/motherhood-on-ice/
26. 'Women's tennis: players to get protected WTA ranking after time away to freeze eggs', Sky Sports, 11 June 2025.
www.skysports.com/tennis/news/12110/13382103/womens-tennis-players-to-get-protected-wta-ranking-after-time-away-to-freeze-eggs
27. 'Own your future today by starting with a Fertility Assessment', Kindbody.
https://kindbody.com/wp-content/uploads/2021/10/Tesla_FertilityAssessment_OnePager.pdf
28. Anna Collinson, Maryam Ahmed and Bella McShane, 'Egg freezing patients "misled" by clinics', BBC News, 13 March 2024.
www.bbc.co.uk/news/uk-68505321
29. Amazon Infertility Journey: IUI/IVF, Facebook.
www.facebook.com/groups/202008127571846/
30. Ryan Deer, 'Kindbody Raises $100M, Reaches $1.8B Valuation', Fitt/Insider, 7 March 2023.
https://insider.fitt.co/kindbody-raises-100m-reaches-1-8b-valuation/
31. Jackie Davalos and Sarah Frier, 'Fertility Startup Kindbody Considers Sale While Seeking Funding', Bloomberg, 6 December 2024.
www.bloomberg.com/news/articles/2024-12-06/fertility-startup-kindbody-considers-sale-while-seeking-funding
32. 'Big Baby', *Prognosis: Misconception*, Bloomberg Podcasts, 6 August 2024.

NOTES

www.youtube.com/watch?v=DwD8nw8tnKk

33. Doc Louallen et al., 'Inside IVF mix-ups that left women carrying embryos that weren't theirs', ABC News, 7 March 2025.
https://abcnews.go.com/Health/inside-ivf-mix-ups-left-women-carrying-embryos/story?id=119429927

34. 'Overview of HFEA public consultation on law reform 2023', Human Fertilisation & Embryology Authority, November 2023.
www.hfea.gov.uk/about-us/modernising-the-regulation-of-fertility-treatment-and-research-involving-human-embryos/overview-of-hfea-public-consultation-on-law-reform-2023

35. Precedence Research, 'U.S. Fertility Market Size to Achieve USD 8.69 Billion by 2033', Yahoo! Finance, 6 September 2024.
https://finance.yahoo.com/news/u-fertility-market-size-achieve-150000734.html

36. 'Fact Sheet: President Donald J. Trump Expands Access to In Vitro Fertilization (IVF)', The White House, 18 February 2025.
www.whitehouse.gov/fact-sheets/2025/02/fact-sheet-president-donald-j-trump-expands-access-to-in-vitro-fertilization-ivf/

37. Dr Antony Starza-Allen, 'High Court rejects fertility clinic challenge to HFEA website', PET, 24 April 2017.
www.progress.org.uk/high-court-rejects-fertility-clinic-challenge-to-hfea-website/

38. Fair IVF, Avenues.
https://avenues.life/fairivf/

39. Sara Lafuente-Funes et al., 'Egg donation in the age of vitrification: A study of egg providers' perceptions and experiences in the UK, Belgium and Spain', *Sociology of Health & Illness* (28 November 2022), 45: 2, 259–78. https://doi.org/10.1111/1467-9566.13590
40. Blair Sowry, 'China considers allowing single women to access IVF', PET, 15 May 2023. www.progress.org.uk/china-considers-allowing-single-women-to-access-ivf/
41. 'Yale Agrees to Pay $308K to Resolve Allegations of Violations of Controlled Substances Act', United States Attorney's Offices, 4 October 2022. www.justice.gov/usao-ct/pr/yale-agrees-pay-308k-resolve-allegations-violations-controlled-substances-act
42. Lanlan Zhang et al., 'Gender Biases in Estimation of Others' Pain', *Journal of Pain* (September 2021), 22: 9, 1048–59. www.jpain.org/article/S1526-5900(21)00035-3/fulltext
43. 'The cost of hormonal medication in assisted reproduction treatments', Invitra. www.invitra.com/en/the-cost-of-hormonal-medication-in-assisted-reproduction-treatments
44. Agencia Española de Medicamentos y Productos Sanitarios. https://cima.aemps.es/cima/publico/detalle.html?nregistro=62431
45. Jacqueline Mroz, 'When an Ancestry Search Reveals Fertility Fraud', *New York Times*, 28 February 2022. www.nytimes.com/2022/02/28/health/fertility-doctors-fraud-rochester.html

NOTES

46. Amy Dockser Marcus, 'A Sperm Donor Chases a Role in the Lives of the 96 Children He Fathered', *Wall Street Journal*, 27 August 2023.
www.wsj.com/lifestyle/relationships/sperm-donor-family-children-146617c8

47. 'Surrogacy scandals: Allegations of human trafficking, and illegal adoptions leave Australian families devastated', *Neos Kosmos*, 25 August 2023.
https://neoskosmos.com/en/2023/08/25/news/australia/surrogacy-scandal-human-trafficking-illegal-adoptions-and-heartbroken-aussie-families/

48. Natalie Obiko Pearson et al., 'The Egg: A story of extraction, exploitation and opportunity', *Bloomberg Businessweek*, 12 December 2024.
www.bloomberg.com/graphics/2024-fertility-egg-trade/

49. Richard Marosi, 'Fugitive Fertility Doctor on the Run Again?' *Los Angeles Times*, 10 February 2001.
www.latimes.com/archives/la-xpm-2001-feb-10-me-23591-story.html

50. Suzanne Goldenberg, 'Doctors accused of stealing human eggs', *Guardian*, 18 May 2000.
www.theguardian.com/world/2000/may/19/suzannegoldenberg

PLACENTA

1. Alexandra Herweck et al., 'International gestational surrogacy in the United States, 2014–2020', *Fertility and Sterility* (April, 2024), 121: 4, 622–30.
https://pubmed.ncbi.nlm.nih.gov/38176517/

2. Surrogacy Pay and Compensation for Surrogates, Growing Generations.
www.growinggenerations.com/surrogacy/for-surrogates/pay
3. California Income Tax Calculator 2024–2025, *Forbes*.
www.forbes.com/advisor/income-tax-calculator/california/?deductions=0&filing=married&income=70000&ira=0&k401=0
4. Recommendations for Practices Using Gestational Carriers: A Committee Opinion, American Society for Reproductive Medicine, 2022.
www.asrm.org/practice-guidance/practice-committee-documents/recommendations-for-practices-using-gestational-carriers-a-committee-opinion-2022/
5. Ben Shemang, 'Why Nigeria's "baby factories" continue to thrive', DW, 18 March 2024.
www.dw.com/en/why-nigerias-baby-factories-remain-a-grim-reality/a-68595335
6. Our Fees, Lifelink fertility Clinic.
https://lifelinkfertility.com/Our-Fees.html
7. H (anonymous surrogacy) judgment, [2025] EWHC 220 (fam), 6 February 2025.
www.judiciary.uk/wp-content/uploads/2025/02/Re-H-Anonymous-surrogacy-judgment.pdf
8. Sally Williams, 'An English couple, a Ukrainian surrogate and a baby: the extraordinary story of how war united two unlikely families', *Guardian*, 9 December 2023.
www.theguardian.com/lifeandstyle/2023/dec/09/an-english-couple-a-ukrainian-surrogate-and-a-baby-the-extraordinary-story-of-how-war-united-two-unlikely-families

NOTES

9. Surrogacy, Law Commission.
   https://lawcom.gov.uk/project/surrogacy/
10. Dog breeding licensing: statutory guidance for local authorities, Department for Environment, Food & Rural Affairs, Gov.UK. www.gov.uk/government/publications/animal-activities-licensing-guidance-for-local-authorities/dog-breeding-licensing-statutory-guidance-for-local-authorities
11. 'Gestational carriers face higher health risks during pregnancy compared to IVF and natural conceptions, new study shows', EurekAlert!, 7 July 2024.
    www.eurekalert.org/news-releases/1050185
12. Matter of Baby M, Supreme Court of New Jersey, 109 N.J. 396 (1988), Justia U.S. Law.
    https://law.justia.com/cases/new-jersey/supreme-court/1988/109-n-j-396-1.html
13. 'High Court rules baby should stay with surrogate after "Facebook" surrogacy arrangement ends in bitter dispute', NGA Law, 3 July 2016.
    www.ngalaw.co.uk/high-court-rules-baby-should-stay-with-surrogate-after-facebook-surrogacy-arrangement-ends-in-bitter-dispute/
14. Hannah Roberts, 'Meloni's surrogacy ban hits immediate backlash in Italy', Politico, 17 October 2024.
    www.politico.eu/article/giorgia-meloni-ban-surrogacy-big-backlash-italy/
15. Julia Banim, 'I had a baby at 68 with my dead son's sperm – and I might not be finished yet', *Mirror*, 15 April 2025.
    www.mirror.co.uk/lifestyle/family/i-gave-birth-68-dead-35056461

16. Arnau Nonell i Rodríguez, 'Unblocking the implementation of altruistic surrogacy in Portugal: inclusive legal reform proposals through a comparative analysis', *International Journal of Law, Policy and the Family* (2025), 39: 1. https://doi.org/10.1093/lawfam/ebaf003
17. Surrogacy Pay and Compensation for Surrogates, Growing Generations. www.growinggenerations.com/surrogacy/for-surrogates/pay
18. Emi Nietfeld, 'The baby died. Whose fault is it?', Wired.com, 3 September 2025. www.wired.com/story/the-baby-died-whose-fault-is-it-surrogate-pregnancy/
19. 'Birthstory', Radiolab Podcast, YouTube, 4 February 2023. www.youtube.com/watch?v=FCphZZsF4jg
20. Oksana Grytsenko, 'The stranded babies of Kyiv and the women who give birth for money', *Guardian*, 15 June 2020. www.theguardian.com/world/2020/jun/15/the-stranded-babies-of-kyiv-and-the-women-who-give-birth-for-money
21. Kate Stafford, 'Special Connection: "One day they'll understand" says Rosanna Davison as she shares adorable snaps with surrogate's family', *Irish Sun*, 17 December 2024. www.thesun.ie/tvandshowbiz/14378733/rosanna-davison-surrogacy-ukrainian-family-kids/
22. Azadeh Moaveni, 'The Islamic Republic of Baby-Making', *Foreign Policy*, 17 January 2014. https://foreignpolicy.com/2014/01/17/the-islamic-republic-of-baby-making/
23. Aida Ghajar, 'Sperm Banks and the Iranian Market', Iranwire, 14 April 2016.

NOTES

https://iranwire.com/en/society/61754/

24. X v. W & Anor judgment, [2025] EWFC 25, 14 February 2025.
www.bailii.org/ew/cases/EWFC/HCJ/2025/25.html

25. Exhibit With Us, Fertility Show.
www.fertilityshow.co.uk/exhibit-with-us-2026

26. WT (A Child) judgment, [2014] EWHC 1303 (Fam), 4 March 2014.
www.bailii.org/ew/cases/EWHC/Fam/2014/1303.html

27. Z (Unlawful Foreign Surrogacy: Adoption) judgment, [2025] EWHC 339 (fam), 19 February 2025.
www.judiciary.uk/wp-content/uploads/2025/02/Re-Z-Unlawful-Foreign-Surrogacy-.pdf

28. Surrogacy in Cyprus, Dünya IVF Clinic.
www.dunyaivf.com/en/surrogacy/

29. Intended Parents, International Surrogacy Consulting.
https://internationalsurrogacyconsulting.life/intended-parents/

30. On marriage (matrimony) and family, Adilet.
https://adilet.zan.kz/rus/docs/K1100000518

31. Join as an Intended Parent, Surrogacy UK.
https://surrogacyuk.org/join-as-an-intended-parent/

32. H (anonymous surrogacy) judgment, [2025] EWHC 220 (fam), 6 February 2025.
www.judiciary.uk/wp-content/uploads/2025/02/Re-H-Anonymous-surrogacy-judgment.pdf

33. What is a realistic budget for costs and expenses for a UK surrogacy journey? Brilliant Beginnings.
https://brilliantbeginnings.co.uk/what-is-a-realistic-budget-for-costs-and-expenses-for-a-uk-surrogacy-journey/

34. Dr Paula Siverino Bavio, 'The chaotic landscape of surrogacy in Argentina', PET, 28 April 2025.
www.progress.org.uk/the-chaotic-landscape-of-surrogacy-in-argentina/
35. Harriet Barber, 'Surrogacy ring accused of exploiting vulnerable women in Argentina', *Guardian*, 22 October 2024.
www.theguardian.com/world/2024/oct/22/surrogacy-ring-argentina
36. Robert Plummer, 'Argentina records sharp rise in poverty', BBC, 27 September 2024.
www.bbc.co.uk/news/articles/ceqn751x19no
37. Surrogacy in Colombia, The Surrogacy Insider.
www.thesurrogacyinsider.com/surrogacy-in-colombia

EPILOGUE: BABY

1. Dr Elizabeth Chloe Romanis, 'Ethical considerations for clinical trials of artificial placentas', PET, 9 October 2023.
www.progress.org.uk/ethical-considerations-for-clinical-trials-of-artificial-placentas/
2. Sophie Lewis, *Full Surrogacy Now: Feminism Against Family* (Verso: 2019).
www.versobooks.com/en-gb/products/711-full-surrogacy-now